News for Everyman

News for Everyman

Radio and Foreign Affairs in Thirties America

David Holbrook Culbert

GREENWOOD PRESS
WESTPORT, CONNECTICUT ● LONDON, ENGLAND

Library of Congress Cataloging in Publication Data

Culbert, David Holbrook.
  News for everyman.

  Bibliography: p.
  Includes index.
  1. Radio journalism—United States—History.
  2. Journalists—United States. 3. Foreign news.
  I. Title.
  PN4888.R33C8   384.54′0973   75-23862
  ISBN 0-8371-8260-3

Library of Congress Catalog Card Number: 75-23862
ISBN: 0-8371-8260-3

First published in 1976

Greenwood Press, a division of Williamhouse-Regency Inc.
51 Riverside Avenue, Westport, Connecticut 06880

Printed in the United States of America

For
Robert E. Neil

Contents

He Drove Himself Terribly
He Never Worked on a Newspaper
Musician of the Spoken Word
"Merely a Recording Tape"
"This is London"

Acknowledgments

I wish to thank the staffs of the following institutions for their help in locating records and for permission to use certain manuscript materials: the Broadcast Pioneers Library; the Herbert Hoover Library; the Hoover Institution on War, Revolution, and Peace; the Houghton Library of Harvard University; the Manuscript Division of the Chicago Circle Campus Library of the University of Illinois; the Manuscript Division and Recorded Sound Section of the Music Division of the Library of Congress; the National Archives and Records Service; the Public Record Office in London; the Special Collections Division of the New York Public Library; the Northwestern University Library; the Manuscript Division of Princeton University Library; the Franklin D. Roosevelt Library; the Manuscript Division of Syracuse University Library; the Washington National Records Center; the Manuscript Division of the State Historical Society of Wisconsin; and the Manuscript Division of Yale University Library.

Professor Marvin R. Bensman provided copies of several taped broadcasts in his Radio Archive at Memphis State University; Mr. Michael Biel of the University of Missouri offered technical assistance and let me hear his personal copy of one broadcast. Professor Philip K. Hastings of The Roper Public Opinion Research Center at Williams College sent selected examples of public opinion questionnaires from the 1930s. Mr. Joseph P. Hehn sent copies of recorded news broadcasts in his private collection. Professor Milo Ryan, now retired as director of the Milo Ryan Phonoarchive at the University of Washington, taped a quantity of broadcasts in his Phonoarchive for me. The Speech Department of Northwestern University provided a substantial number of blank reels of tape to facilitate the purchase of these recordings.

The New York City staffs of the Columbia Broadcasting System and

xii   *News for Everyman*

the National Broadcasting Company were extremely helpful. The CBS Library and Program Information Department proved especially useful. Mr. Harold Queen, NBC's Director of Corporate Information, after an initial reluctance to permit use of company records, went out of his way to be kind. He let me visit the following offices: Central Records; the NBC Warehouse; Program Analysis; Program Reference Library; and Research Department. He even arranged for me to spend ten hours observing the preparation of NBC's one remaining analytical radio news program.

I am particularly indebted to those who have read the entire manuscript, in one or more of its versions, and made numerous helpful suggestions: Professor James B. Chapin of Rutgers University; Professor William J. Cooper, Jr., of Louisiana State University; Professor George M. Fredrickson of Northwestern University; Professor Anne C. Loveland of Louisiana State University; Professor Martin J. Maloney of Northwestern University; Professor Burl Noggle of Louisiana State University; Professor Gaddis Smith of Yale University; and Professor Allan M. Winkler of Yale University. I am also grateful to Professor Marvin R. Bensman of Memphis State University; Professor John Morton Blum of Yale University; Professor Bernard C. Cohen of the University of Wisconsin; the late Herman Kahn of Yale University; and Professor T. Harry Williams of Louisiana State University for reading a number of chapters of an earlier version of this book and commenting so fully. Priscilla T. Jackson suggested numerous stylistic improvements. Professor Barry F. Machado of Washington and Lee University called my attention to several valuable manuscript sources. Helene K. Ward carefully typed several drafts. The editors of *The Historian, The Journal of Popular Culture,* and *The Pennsylvania Magazine of History and Biography* kindly granted permission to use materials that I have previously published. A faculty summer grant from the Graduate Research Council of Louisiana State University helped make the completion of this book possible.

My greatest debt is to Professor Richard W. Leopold of Northwestern University. He and the person to whom this book is dedicated have been major influences on me.

February 1975

DAVID HOLBROOK CULBERT

List of Abbreviations

BP-1969—Broadcast Pioneers History Project, *Fifth Progress Report* (New York, July, 1969), listing contents of Broadcast Pioneers Library, 1771 N St. N.W., Washington, D.C.

Burlingame MSS—Roger Burlingame MSS, Manuscript Division, Syracuse University Library, Syracuse, New York

Carr MSS—Wilbur J. Carr MSS, Manuscript Division, Library of Congress, Washington, D.C.

Castle MSS—William R. Castle MSS, Herbert Hoover Library, West Branch, Iowa

CBS Library—Columbia Broadcasting System Library, 524 W. 57th St., New York, New York

CBS Program Information—Columbia Broadcasting System, Program Information, 51 W. 52d St., New York, New York

Comm OF, HHL—Official File, Secretary of Commerce, Herbert Hoover Library, West Branch, Iowa

Davies MSS—Joseph E. Davies MSS, Manuscript Division, Library of Congress, Washington, D.C.

Davis MSS—Elmer Davis MSS, Manuscript Division, Library of Congress, Washington, D.C.

Davis MSS, NYPL—Elmer Davis MSS, Special Collections, New York Public Library, New York, New York

FCC, WNRC-Suitland—Station Files, Federal Communications Commission, Washington National Records Center, Suitland, Maryland

FD-NBC—National Broadcasting Company, Program Reference Library, unmarked file drawer, Room 279, Rockefeller Center, New York, New York

FO—Correspondence of the Foreign Office, Public Record Office, Portugal St., London

Frankfurter MSS—Felix Frankfurter MSS, Manuscript Division, Library of Congress, Washington, D.C.

Hopkins MSS— Harry L. Hopkins MSS, Franklin D. Roosevelt Library, Hyde Park, New York

Hornbeck MSS—Stanley K. Hornbeck MSS, Manuscript Division, Hoover Institution on War, Revolution, and Peace, Stanford, California

Hull MSS—Cordell Hull MSS, Manuscript Division, Library of Congress, Washington, D.C.

Kaltenborn MSS—H. V. Kaltenborn MSS, State Historical Society of Wisconsin, Madison, Wisconsin

Kaltenborn MSS, NYPL—H. V. Kaltenborn MSS, Special Collections, New York Public Library, New York, New York

Kent MSS—Fred I. Kent MSS, Manuscript Division, Princeton University Library, Princeton, New Jersey

Lewis MSS—Fulton Lewis, Jr., MSS, Manuscript Division, Syracuse University Library, Syracuse, New York

Lohr MSS—Lenox R. Lohr MSS, Manuscript Division, Chicago Circle Campus of the University of Illinois, Chicago, Illinois

Moffat Diary—Jay Pierrepont Moffat Diary, Houghton Library, Harvard University, Cambridge, Massachusetts

NBC-*Talks*—Mimeographed lectures to National Broadcasting Company employees, 1939-1941, copies in Program Reference Library, unmarked file drawer, Room 279, Rockefeller Center, New York, New York

NBC Warehouse—National Broadcasting Company Warehouse, 136 W. 52d St., New York, New York

OF,FDRL—Official File, Franklin D. Roosevelt Library, Hyde Park, New York

Personal Letters—Elliott Roosevelt and Joseph P. Lash, eds., *F.D.R.: His Personal Letters, 1928-1945,* 2 vols. (New York, 1950)

Phonoarchive—Milo Ryan Phonoarchive, University of Washington, Seattle, Washington

PPI, HHL—Post-Presidential Individual File, Herbert Hoover Library, West Branch, Iowa

PPF, FDRL—President's Personal File, Franklin D. Roosevelt Library, Hyde Park, New York

PSF, HHL—President's Secretary's File, Herbert Hoover Library, West Branch, Iowa

PSF, FDRL—President's Secretary's File, Franklin D. Roosevelt Library, Hyde Park, New York

Radio Archive-Memphis—Radio Archive, Dr. Marvin R. Bensman, Department of Speech & Drama, Memphis State University, Memphis, Tennessee

"A Reporter Remembers!"—"Edward R. Murrow: A Reporter Remembers, Vol. I, The War Years," 33 1/3 rpm commercial recording Columbia 02L-332

RG 44—Office of Government Reports, Record Group 44, Archives Branch, Washington National Records Center, Suitland, Maryland

RG 59—Department of State Files, Record Group 59, National Archives, Washington, D.C.

RG 122—Federal Trade Commission, Record Group 122, National Archives, Washington, D.C.

RG 173—Federal Communications Commission, Radio Division, Record Group 173, National Archives, Washington, D.C.

RG 208—Office of War Information, Record Group 208, Archives Branch, Washington National Records Center, Suitland, Maryland

RPORC—The Roper Public Opinion Research Center, Williams College, Williamstown, Massachusetts

RSS-LC—Recorded Sound Section, Music Division, Library of Congress, Washington, D.C.

Secret Diary—Harold L. Ickes, *The Secret Diary of Harold L. Ickes,* 3 vols. (New York, 1953-1954)

Sevareid MSS—Eric Sevareid MSS, Manuscript Division, Library of Congress, Washington, D.C.

Stimson MSS—Henry L. Stimson MSS, Manuscript Division, Yale University Library, New Haven, Connecticut

Swing MSS—Raymond Gram Swing MSS, Manuscript Division, Library of Congress, Washington, D.C.

News for Everyman

Introduction:
Social History and Foreign Affairs

The greatest shortcoming of historians, Felix Frankfurter once observed, is their failure to describe the "things that aren't written down because everybody takes them for granted."[1] Surely radio news has fit this category far too long. For in the 1930s everyone listened to the radio. "The Romance of Helen Trent" brought dark strangers into the lives of women of thirty-five "and even more." "America's Town Meeting of the Air" carried debate of current issues to serious listeners. Arturo Toscanini conducted the "NBC Symphony of the Air" in the homes of rich and poor; critics spoke optimistically of culture for all. Americans almost forgot the Depression, the empty bank book, the overdue rent as they turned in an endless variety of "free" programs designed to entertain and, occasionally, uplift.

In time most Americans listened to foreign news also—leaders as well as followers, urbanites and farmers, active politicians and lonely invalids. They heard overseas events interpreted by a new kind of communicator—the news commentator. These men—pundits, preachers, critics, special pleaders, as well as reporters—broadcast their way into positions of immense national fame. They became the new voices of authority, the new delineators of meaning. Listeners believed them to be educated, intelligent, privy to the secrets of the great. Commentators often sounded impartial, and somehow wise beyond other men. Their familiar voices—their unmistakably individual delivery—crackled into parlors, restaurants, and automobiles across the land. Radio made each listener feel personally concerned about foreign affairs.

This book discusses the broadcasts and the careers of six prominent newscasters of widely varying political persuasions: Boake Carter, H. V.

3

Kaltenborn, Raymond Gram Swing, Elmer Davis, Fulton Lewis, Jr., and Edward R. Murrow.[2] These oracles, heard but never seen, interpreted the world to America, in the process saying something about America's obligations toward the rest of the world and America's image of itself. Radio is central to an understanding of the United States during the decade of the Depression. But national self-awareness of the sort suggested by representatives of the electronic medium has also had consequences that have persisted long after most people forgot the individual voices of those who spoke. In this sense this book represents a first effort toward a more scholarly understanding of the roots of our age, the age of radio and television, the age of the aural and visual image.

The overseas events of the late 1930s created a new role for radio. Following the Munich crisis of September 1938, the newspaper extra became obsolete. Radio emerged as the major source for foreign news. The sounds and images of foreign events suddenly gained dramatic appeal for the listener, who could now hear the participants involved in far off crises. No matter if Hitler's tirades were incomprehensible; radio provided a running translation. More than ever before, the average person seemed to become genuinely fascinated by what took place overseas. The overwhelming amount of news—reported in bulletins almost as an event occurred—also made for widespread uncertainty and confusion. Hence the rise of the serious news commentator—desired by the bewildered listener who could hear the sounds of distant places but could not always understand what it all meant. Commentators tried to offer analysis. Their newscasts provide a diary of the day's events— particularly valuable since the keeping of formal diaries has largely disappeared.

Aside from experience in journalism and a flair for publicity, there were no specific requirements for becoming a commentator. Those who did so came from widely differing backgrounds. Davis was a Rhodes Scholar; Carter, a British immigrant who never attended college. Swing, an intensely moral man, joined his wife in committees of protest, such as one for Spanish intellectuals seeking asylum in America. Kaltenborn, Lewis, and Carter unashamedly used such promotional techniques as broadcasting aboard a ship on its way to Havana, or setting up a microphone in the middle of a Spanish battle in progress so that listeners could hear bullets whizzing overhead. Lewis and Carter read their own advertising copy and tried to make even the sponsor's product seem newsworthy. Such devices help explain how radio news made itself attractive to the average person.

Much has been written about the impact of newspapers, books, and articles on American foreign policy before Pearl Harbor.[3] But the tyranny of custom, to say nothing of the easy availability of newspapers as opposed to broadcasts, has led to a curious phenomenon. Radio, although a major independent news source after 1938, has been assessed solely in terms of newspaper accounts. This book provides the first detailed description, based on the broadcasts themselves—in both recorded and written form—of radio's role in reporting foreign affairs during the 1930s. It examines six intermediaries between current events and the average person's understanding of what happened in the rest of the world.

This book has two purposes and thus properly focuses on two related problems: it describes the development of radio news commentary in the 1930s and discusses the relation between radio's coverage of foreign affairs and the making of foreign policy. To guard against misunderstanding I have decided to list the major points I am trying to make in this book at the outset:

1. Radio news created mass interest in foreign affairs beginning with the Munich crisis of September 1938. As a result radio emerged as the principal medium for combatting isolationism in America.[4]

2. Radio news was not objective in spite of government and network regulations requiring strict impartiality. Every commentator allowed his personal convictions to creep into his reporting of the news. Before August 1938, Boake Carter was a major force in keeping alive isolationist sentiment in the United States. No matter what happened in Europe or the Far East, Carter had a simple response: America had no business trying to take care of the rest of the world when there was so much to do at home. After August 1938, with the removal of Carter from CBS, none of the most popular commentators opposed the foreign policy objectives of Franklin D. Roosevelt. It proved impossible to discuss what was happening to Great Britain after 1939 without letting one's intonation or analysis betray what America's foreign policy should be. If some newspapers continued to attack the President, the same was not true for the major medium that provided information about the rest of the world for the average person.

3. The world situation created an interest in surprisingly serious commentary. The millions who listened to Raymond Gram Swing or

Elmer Davis got more immediate information, plus analysis about European affairs, than the reader who put twice as much time into reading a newspaper. For a time serious journalism captured a mass audience. After 1945 this audience largely disappeared, not because commentators prepared their analyses less carefully, but because most persons considered world events somehow less dramatic and immediate.

4. Before 1941 radio news devoted almost no space to news about the Far East. Listeners actually heard events as they happened in Europe; for the Far East they got little more than occasional brief summaries. As a result, the average person had much less emotional commitment to what happened in the Far East.

5. Radio commentators played a major role in creating a climate of opinion favorable to an interventionist foreign policy though they did not directly make foreign policy.[5] Roosevelt, with the lesson of Woodrow Wilson firmly in mind, was determined his foreign policy would find general acceptance. Radio commentators, willing after May 1940 to support any major proposal advanced by the President, greatly aided Roosevelt's campaign to create a popular majority favorable to full-scale intervention in Europe.

This book attempts a group portrait of six very individual personalities. The organization of this volume is determined by each news analyst's period of greatest national prominence. For Boake Carter the emphasis is on his activities between 1935 and August 1938; after that date he was banned from CBS and NBC. Although Kaltenborn broadcast the first news commentary in 1922, he did not become a household name until September 1938. Accordingly, I have described at length his coverage of the Munich crisis and what this meant for public acceptance of radio as a foreign news source. Davis, Swing, Lewis, and Murrow were not widely known as news analysts until after war began in Europe in September 1939.

The confines of a five- or fifteen-minute period, plus the obligation to present the day's major news, left little time for sustained analysis. Kaltenborn, Lewis, and Carter frequently offered hasty and unthinking remarks about foreign affairs. I felt it would be more helpful to demonstrate their broadcasting techniques and general attitudes than repeatedly to point out wild guesses and misinformation. Speaking nightly from London, Murrow described Britain at war. He did not attempt comprehensive world coverage, for he was a foreign correspondent in

London. In discussing English bravery, however, he used radio as a documentary medium more successfully than any other commentator before Pearl Harbor. Swing and Davis prepared their broadcasts carefully. I have therefore discussed their assessments of certain events more fully.

The most-discussed topic in American foreign policy between September 1939 and December 1941 concerned what the United States response should be toward German aggression. All six commentators dealt with this topic again and again. For this major issue I have reviewed each man's assessment and provided examples of what was said.

Because of network and Federal Communications Commission rulings concerning objectivity, before December 1941 no broadcaster stated explicitly that the United States should declare war on Hitler. With the exception of Murrow, it is not possible to give a precise date when those who favored increased American involvement overseas first spoke on the air about the necessity of full hostilities. But Murrow, Swing, Davis, and Kaltenborn welcomed deteriorating relations with Japan and Germany. To express their feelings they used such euphemisms as America's need to become a "fighting ally" or "full belligerent." After May 1940 they accepted the possibility of using armed force to stop Nazi aggression. Those who supported Roosevelt were willing to risk full hostilities because of American naval forces escorting merchant-ship convoys or a shoot-on-sight policy in the Atlantic. Two others, Carter and Lewis, vigorously opposed what they termed steps toward war, although their impact after 1939 was smaller since they broadcast over weaker station affiliates and at less popular hours.

Between May 1940 and December 1941 most commentators supported American intervention abroad. They believed fervently in the President and placed the initiative for making foreign policy in Roosevelt's hands. After Hitler invaded the Low Countries on May 10, 1940, and France fell a month later, commentators of such differing political beliefs as Davis, Swing, Kaltenborn, and Murrow accepted virtually any proposal that the President favored in foreign policy. And to these four, those who opposed Roosevelt became not political opponents, but villains.

How much did these commentators actually affect the making of foreign policy? Did Roosevelt or other administration leaders take specific courses of action because of what a radio commentator said in a broadcast? Did news commentators contribute in an informal way to the governing process? Like everyone else who has tried to gauge the influence of the mass media on governmental decision-making in foreign policy, I have been unable to prove any direct connection. After reviewing the literature of public opinion theory, both by political scientists and by social psychologists, I became convinced that there is no way of showing the exact effect of what a journalist says or writes on those in authority.[6]

Yet to deny any direct connection—since there is no way to demonstrate it—is not to say that radio commentators had no impact on American attitudes toward foreign affairs. All six had millions of listeners who after 1938 tuned in overseas news before they read it in newspapers. Swing, Davis, Murrow, and Kaltenborn greatly influenced public thinking about the issue of war or peace after September 1939. The President found it useful to have unofficial spokesmen who commanded such large audiences urging the same policies he favored. What these commentators said helped significantly to define the issues of the so-called Great Debate in American foreign policy between 1939 and 1941. The removal of Boake Carter from regular broadcasting in 1938 because of his opposition to anything Roosevelt proposed concerning foreign affairs suggests that the administration found radio a medium where irrational criticism could be more damaging than similar remarks in printed form. My attempt to assess the friendships each man cultivated through personal visits and correspondence with those in positions of power shows that the radio commentator tried to increase his impact through the traditional methods employed by all journalists. In sum, what all six said on the air mattered to the country at large. They spoke at a time when public attention increasingly turned from domestic to foreign events.

The news analysts spoke over the three national networks, NBC, CBS, and MBS. All considered themselves experts on foreign affairs, although in some cases such self-assurance seems to have been the product of a heated imagination. I purposely selected two commentators who bitterly attacked Roosevelt—Carter and Lewis—as well as those who became staunch administration supporters. For each man there is, first, a biographical sketch focusing on his career in radio; then a description of his voice, diction, and manner on the air; an analysis of broadcasts that gained particular note; a summary of his attitudes toward the question of war or peace, 1939-1941; and finally, an attempt to assess his impact.

I have not tried to discuss everyone who covered news on radio. I did not include Lowell Thomas, the most successful commentator of the decade and the one who probably attracted the greatest number of listeners, because he did not write his own copy, he did not analyze the news, and he omitted almost all political comment. In a 1969 oral history interview he described his approach:

MR. HENLE: But you never did parade your politics as newsman.
MR. THOMAS: No. In fact, I avoided this to the point where my radio sponsors . . . seemed uncertain as to what my politics were.[7]

Years before he explained that "talks should be sprinkled with nonsense, with here and there a thrill, perhaps a sob. My talks are planned as entertainment, not education."[8]

Thomas had a kinship with an early news program, "The March of Time," in which actors impersonated the voices of persons in the news. He might well be included in another study of radio news in the 1930s—one focusing on the connection between news and entertainment.[9]

This book does not present the views of six newscasters on every substantive issue in American foreign policy between 1935, or even 1939, and 1941. For instance, the diplomatic historian will not find what each news analyst said about the Atlantic Charter or the repeal of the arms embargo in September 1939. For some commentators not every broadcast has survived; on almost no occasion were all six on the air the same day. Those interested in what these men said about most of the major foreign events during the six years before Pearl Harbor can consult the last three hundred pages of my doctoral dissertation, where such statements are arranged topically.[10]

I believe that a book about radio commentators must be based on actual tapes or original transcriptions of newscasts. Fortunately, for each commentator recorded broadcasts have survived.[11] But I have not hesitated to use other material as well. All but Murrow were experienced newspaper journalists before they began their careers in radio; all continued to publish even after they became prominent in the newer medium. The impact of Elmer Davis, in particular, came through both his written and his spoken work. Listening to numerous recorded broadcasts for each commentator has enabled me to suggest what each sounded like on the air, as well as to indicate how news commentary related to surrounding commercial copy and to programs that preceded or followed.

Radio's evanescence has posed special problems in uncovering information. The networks and most commentators long ago destroyed recordings and printed copies of broadcasts made before Pearl Harbor. Fortunately, Swing and Kaltenborn saved almost all of their commentaries. The Milo Ryan Phonoarchive at the University of Washington contains hundreds of prewar recorded broadcasts by Davis and Murrow. Lewis kept a few mimeographed copies of newscasts made before Pearl Harbor. The Radio Archive at Memphis State University has several of his in recorded form; so does a private collector in Allentown, Pennsylvania. Others are printed in the appendix of the *Congressional Record.*

Boake Carter presented greater difficulties. He left few records save a daily newspaper column. Happily, CBS Program Information in New York has brief summaries of every Carter broadcast from September 1933 to May 1935. Over one hundred complete typed transcripts of his commentaries turned up at the National Archives in Washington. They form part of a massive, though heretofore unused collection that the Federal Trade Commission assembled for an investigation of radio health commercials in 1936-1937.

Information about the development of foreign affairs broadcasting is based in large part on records CBS and NBC have at their headquarters in New York. Unpublished letters and diaries of many administration leaders and one NBC president have been searched for comments concerning the various commentators, the major networks, and radio in general. There is some valuable material concerning American commentators in the Public Record Office in London.

All six men dramatized the news to make it appealing. They recognized that listeners identified with the quirky vocal mannerisms of the unseen speaker. Thus style helps explain how these men attracted such large audiences. All were characters who loved public acclaim. Accordingly, I have emphasized the personalities of the six and their techniques for self-publicity; I have focused both on how they reported foreign news and on what they said. In the process I have tried to recreate the aural impact of the 1930s for a generation born too late to have known the golden age of radio news.

I have also tried to suggest something about how radio news demonstrates popular culture's impact on American life and thought. One student of the subject has termed "the most important single function of popular culture . . . the dissemination of common values, symbols and attitudes in such a manner as to create a sociocultural 'consensus.' '' [12] It seems to me that radio commentators in their discussion of foreign affairs, particularly after 1939, fulfilled precisely this function. Radio helped create a consensus in two ways: first, by making foreign policy of concern to a majority of Americans; second, by urging a consensus as to what sort of foreign policy this country should have. What I have to say in the following pages is a detailed explanation of how these two processes developed. The issue of war or peace made a debate over foreign policy a sociocultural problem. Unfortunately, this is just what traditional accounts by diplomatic historians ignore.

In general, as Professor William Stott argues so persuasively, radio news served as a particularly successful type of documentary expression. "Radio was such an effective documentary medium, a central medium of the 1930s," he writes,

> because it inextricably joined . . . two methods of persuasion, direct and vicarious. The listener witnessed firsthand, yet through another's eyes. The relation of listener and speaker was paradoxical, and like all paradoxes instable and unresolvable. The listener never could get from the speaker just the information he wanted as he wanted it, because to believe entirely he needed it firsthand. The speaker never could give the information he wanted as he wanted to. Always an insuperable limitation remained. . . . "These things must be experienced to be understood." The speaker really couldn't take the listener there via radio. And yet, paradoxically, not being able to, he could. Radio's limitation became its strength. For as the speaker acknowledged his limits, the listener grew less observant of them. . . . All that the speaker left unspoken—found unspeakable—testified to the reality of his experience. [13]

This is of course part of what Felix Frankfurter was talking about. At a more basic level, when discussing public opinion and foreign policy in the 1930s we must think in terms of radio, not newspapers. The images and examples must come from an electronic medium or we do great violence to the past.

NOTES

1. Harlan B. Phillips, *Felix Frankfurter Reminiscences* (New York, 1960), p. 57.

2. This book does not present a comprehensive history of radio. Those unfamiliar with the development of the industry can turn to Erik Barnouw, *A History of Broadcasting in the United States: A Tower in Babel; The Golden Web;* and *The Image Empire,* 3 vols. (New York, 1966-1970); in briefer form, see Sydney W. Head, *Broadcasting in America,* 2d ed. (Boston, 1971), in particular, pp. 103-84.

3. For instance, Dorothy Borg and Shumpei Okamoto, eds., *Pearl Harbor as History: Japanese-American Relations, 1931-1941* (New York, 1973); Borg, *The United States and the Far Eastern Crisis of 1933-1938: From the Manchurian Incident Through the Initial Stage of the Undeclared Sino-Japanese War* (Cambridge, Mass., 1964), pp. 88, 388; William L. Langer and S. Everett Gleason, *The Challenge to Isolation 1937-1940* (New York, 1952), pp. 11-21, 428, 770-71; and *The Undeclared War 1940-1941* (New York, 1953), pp. 170, 258-59, 271-73; Robert E. Sherwood, *Roosevelt and Hopkins: An Intimate History* (New York, 1948), pp. 165-67, 129, 131.

4. Isolationism is not easily defined because so-called isolationists held so many different ideas about what the term meant. In general an isolationist felt that America should act unilaterally; that there should be no permanent alliances with other countries; that America could stay out of the European war; and that America should enjoy equal trading rights with the rest of the world. For the varieties of isolationist thought, see Manfred Jonas, *Isolationism in America 1935-1941* (Ithaca, 1966).

5. Interventionism is not easily defined either—also because so many differed as to what the term meant. An interventionist believed that America should do all it could to aid the opponents of fascism in Europe though few publicly advocated the sending of any army overseas before December 1941. Such a person felt a major struggle with fascism was inevitable and that America could not remain aloof from the affairs of the rest of the world. For varieties of interventionist thought, see Mark L. Chadwin, *The Hawks of World War II* (Chapel Hill, N.C., 1968).

6. For a recent summary of this problem, see Bernard C. Cohen, *The Public's Impact on Foreign Policy* (Boston, 1973), pp. 1-42. See also V. O. Key, *Public Opinion and American Democracy* (New York, 1961), pp. 535-36; Ernest R. May, "An American Tradition in Foreign Policy: The Role of Public Opinion," in William H. Nelson, ed., *Theory and Practice in American Politics* (Chicago, 1964), pp. 101-23; Lee Benson, "An Approach to the Scientific Study of Past Public Opinion," *Public Opinion Quarterly* 31 (Winter 1967): 522-67; Bernard Berelson and Morris Janowitz, eds., *Public Opinion and Communication,* 2d ed.

(New York, 1966), p. 5; James B. Reston, "The Press, the President, and Foreign Policy," *Foreign Affairs* 44 (July 1966): 562-69; and "Theories of Public Opinion," in David Holbrook Culbert, "Tantalus' Dilemma: Public Opinion, Six Radio Commentators, and Foreign Affairs, 1935-1941" (Ph.D. dissertation, Northwestern University, 1970), pp. 12-27, 643-47.

7. Lowell Thomas Oral History Interview, October 7, 1969, Herbert Hoover Library, West Branch, Iowa [hereafter HHL].

8. Quoted in Robert West, *The Rape of Radio* (New York, 1941), p. 333.

9. This is the perspective of Raymond Fielding in his *The American Newsreel, 1911-1967* (Norman, Okla., 1972); see also the angry denial from Bertram Kalisch, managing editor of Pathé News during the 1930s, who claims that newsreels provided much more than entertainment; letter in the *New York Times Book Review,* September 10, 1972, p. 20.

10. See Culbert, "Tantalus' Dilemma," pp. 277-628.

11. I have discussed the problems of using recorded broadcasts as historical sources in more detail in "Radio Broadcasts and Related Records as Historical Sources: News Commentary in the 1930s," a paper presented at the 1972 National Archives Conference on the Use of Audiovisual Archives as Original Source Materials, University of Delaware, to be published by the Ohio University Press; and in "Radio and the Historian: Recorded News Broadcasts as Historical Sources," a paper read at the 1973 Saint Louis meeting of the Society of American Archivists. See also Milo Ryan, "Here are the Materials—Where are the Scholars?" *Association for Recorded Sound Collections Journal,* Vol. 2, Spring/Summer 1970, unpaged, copy in Broadcast Pioneers Library, 1771 N St., N.W., Washington, D.C.

12. Garth S. Jowett, "Popular Culture and the Concept of Consensus," *Popular Culture Methods,* n.d. [Spring 1973], p. 19; see also Louis Wirth, "Consensus and Mass Communication," *America Sociological Review* 13 (February 1948): 1-15.

13. William Stott, *Documentary Expression and Thirties America* (New York, 1973) pp. 90-91; see also his entire chapter, "The Central Media," pp. 75-91.

1 | "Air News Pays Off Big" The Development of News Broadcasting

Industry executives knew it was impossible. News could not be sold. Radio provided entertainment, not instruction. The few commentators on the air seldom attracted sponsors. Appearing at unpopular hours, a program's exact time might change from week to week. The news division for a major network consisted of one or two employees. Considered a cultural attraction, news was a sop to quiet the critics of radio's frequent vulgarity.

But a major transformation of the news department's position in broadcasting occurred during the 1930s. Why it happened is obvious. Quite simply, after the Munich crisis in September 1938 events abroad seemed so ominous that listeners began depending on radio as a major source of news. How it happened is less well-known.

That radio was not pervasive in American life until after the Great Crash is reflected in the two sociological studies of Middletown (Muncie, Indiana) by Robert S. and Helen Merrell Lynd. The 1929 study, *Middletown,* contained only three brief references to radio. The Lynds claimed that "the place of the radio in relation to Middletown's other leisure habits is not wholly clear." *Middletown in Transition,* published in 1936, told a different story:

> If a comparable time count were available, it would probably be found that the area of leisure where change in time spent has been greatest since 1925 is listening to the radio. The earlier study of *Middletown* has been increasingly criticized in the last two or three years for "the small amount of attention paid to the radio."[1]

14

A few statistics illustrate this enormous change. In 1924, Americans owned 3 million radio sets; in 1936, 33 million; in 1940, 50 million. In 1929 the total annual gross network revenues for CBS and NBC totaled $19 million. Six years later NBC reported revenues of $31.4 and CBS $17.6 million. By 1940, CBS sales had increased dramatically to $41 million, NBC to $51.6 million. The same year the Mutual Broadcasting System, founded in 1934, reported nearly $5 million in gross revenues. Within eleven years network gross sales had increased from $19 million to nearly $100 million. And this in the midst of the worst depression in the nation's history and despite the refusal, even in 1940, of thirty of the nation's leading advertisers—including General Motors—to buy time on the new medium.[2]

CURIOSITIES AND SPECIAL EVENTS

On May 25, 1932, Columbia's European representative arranged for Americans to hear thirty minutes of an English nightingale singing in a Surrey wood. Radio editors in the United States voted this the most interesting program of the year. A CBS executive quite seriously declared this transmission to be the "greatest thing his company had ever done for Anglo-American relations."[3] As CBS president William S. Paley publicly admitted the year before, "international broadcasts . . . have retained the character of novelty broadcasts in the minds of most people."[4] In 1932 the object of overseas radio news was only to broadcast curiosities.

During the summer of 1933, in England, H. V. Kaltenborn covered the ill-fated Monetary and Economic Conference. He tried a man-on-the-street interview. "Do your beauty parlour customers talk about the London Economic Conference?" was a typical question.[5] That this program actually could be heard in the United States seemed, to most listeners, its most interesting aspect. Never before had such an interview originated abroad.

At home, radio offered only four national news commentators. NBC's Lowell Thomas already had a sponsor and spoke five nights a week. Boake Carter, on CBS, broadcast with equal frequency, sponsored by Philco radio. Edwin C. Hill sometimes had a sponsor, but shifted times and even networks. Kaltenborn was heard only occasionally, always as a

sustaining (unsponsored) feature. Perhaps the most popular news program was "The March of Time." More reenactment than reporting, and
with no attempt at analysis, its actors impersonated the voices of important public figures:

> Listeners began to make the acquaintance of such colorful impersona-
> tions as a fruity Huey Long, played by Jack Smart; a vainglorious
> Mussolini, played by Ted de Corsia; and (later) a quaint Eleanor
> Roosevelt, played by Jeanette Nolan, and a faintly superior FDR, by
> Bill Adams.[6]

The soon-to-be-ubiquitous soap opera and broadcast journalism had a
great deal in common in 1933.

Even such inconsequential news programs, however, caused conster-
nation among many newspaper publishers. In the midst of the depression,
they saw the new medium increasing its advertising revenues at a phenomenal rate, while their own income declined sharply. The result was the
Press-Radio War of 1933-1935. The powerful American Newspaper
Publishers' Association (ANPA) decided to prevent as much radio news
as possible, allegedly fearing that otherwise the newspaper would
become an anachronism. In particular, Edward H. Harris, publisher of
the insignificant *Richmond* (Indiana) *Palladium Item,* but chairman of
ANPA's National Radio Committee, worked zealously to put an end to
all radio news.

Publicly Harris cloaked in altruistic language his alarm over declining
revenues. He claimed that the Federal Communications Commission's
right to license radio stations made the new medium fundamentally
different from its competitor: "A licensed agency can never be free in the
gathering and the dissemination of news. This must be the function of an
unlicensed agency if the value of news is to be maintained."[7] This
somehow meant that radio should broadcast no news.

In April 1933 members of the Associated Press voted to stop selling
their wire service to any radio stations. In response, CBS set up its own
news agency. Moving quickly in response to this newest threat, the
ANPA's National Radio Committee ordered CBS and NBC to meet with
the press wire services at the Hotel Biltmore, in New York City, on
December 10-11, 1933. The networks agreed to a humiliating ten-point
program. News could not be sold commercially. There would be only

two five-minute summaries daily, and late enough in the morning and evening so as not to interfere with newspaper sales. The ANPA would provide the bulletins—which urged listeners to purchase a newspaper for details. Radio commentators could not present headlines. They would confine themselves to "generalizations and background of general news situations." In return, the newspapers promised to continue publishing daily radio schedules.

Such a draconian measure proved impossible to enforce. First, CBS and NBC made an artificial distinction between news commentators and broadcasters who read news bulletins. Advertisers continued to sponsor the former. Second, network news directors successfully used foreign wire services and long-distance telephone calls to piece together news programs without relying on the Associated Press. Third, stations unaffiliated with the major networks, particularly the small Don Lee chain in New England, began gathering their own news as though the Biltmore Agreement had never existed. In 1935 Hearst's International News Service, soon followed by the United Press, began selling news to the networks. The efforts of the ANPA amounted to little more than delaying the use of news bulletins on the major networks for a year. Still, the Associated Press refused to sell its wire service to CBS and NBC until 1940, a testament to how strongly some in the newspaper profession felt about their competitor.[8]

During the 1930s few network broadcasts originated overseas. This was partly due to poor shortwave transmission. A voice from London or Paris frequently faded out in the middle of a program. Therefore NBC and CBS had very few men in Europe. Overseas representatives spent most of their time arranging the transmission of concerts.

NBC enjoyed exlusive foreign rights in Austria and Germany. Many Europeans believed that NBC was the state network in America. Max Jordan, the German who directed NBC's European operations, did nothing to dissuade foreigners from their misconception. Thus when Chancellor Engelbert Dollfuss was assassinated in Vienna during July 1934, Jordan alone received authorization from the Austrian government to broadcast directly to America. It was not until three full days later that CBS finally gained permission to give a summary of events from Vienna.[9]

In these years newspaper reporters frequently covered crises in distant places for the major networks. Floyd Gibbons became quite popular for a time. He promoted the image of the dashing foreign correspondent by wearing a large black patch over one eye. He personally provided much of radio's coverage of the Ethiopian War, and did so with breathless enthusiasm. Not everyone enjoyed his dramatic approach to the news, however. One unimpressed reviewer called him "trigger-tongued Floyd Gibbons, the *Chicago Tribune's* gift to journalistic exhibitionism." When Gibbons died in 1939, *Variety* admitted that his "rapid-fire style of announcing" had become "passé after a time."[10] But until 1936 many listeners associated the reporting of foreign battles with his pell-mell delivery.

At home, presidential campaigns opened new opportunities for radio coverage. In 1932 and 1936 both major networks sent representatives to the national conventions. On election night each used a large staff to analyze the returns from individual states and to predict how the electoral vote might finally turn out.[11]

Serious discussion of foreign affairs proved surprisingly popular during the decade. NBC sponsored "America's Town Meeting of the Air," broadcast directly from New York's Town Hall. A live audience asked questions after each formal lecture. Across the country, study groups listened faithfully. A publicity photograph taken in 1937 shows a group of earnest-looking men standing in front of an enormous floor-length radio set. The caption reads: "A Y.M.C.A. Town Meeting discussion group taking notes for their own after-the-broadcast forum."[12] This program and a similar "Chicago Round Table" under the auspices of the University of Chicago persuaded some listeners that radio could clarify the complexities of international relations.

For everyone, however, serious and frivolous alike, the abdication of Edward VIII in December 1936 proved to be high drama. Censors prohibited English newspapers and radio (the BBC) from discussing the affair. British listeners, therefore, were reduced to learning from the United States. During a ten-day period, all three American networks sent about eight fifteen-minute broadcasts daily from London to the United States. American listeners agonized with their favorite, Edward, through this classic love story of kings and commoners. For the first time radio listeners in large numbers paid close attention to a foreign crisis as it happened.[13]

Network executives, however, failed to realize at once radio's potential for broadcasting foreign events. As late as 1938 Columbia's

European representative could still say that "none but the most urgent or important news would displace temporarily a program designed to entertain."[14] The news directors at NBC and CBS considered their primary function "special events," and spent most of their time devising publicity stunts. NBC's Abel A. Schechter dreamed up a contest to determine which mouse could sing the best. Another broadcast involved two turkeys discussing whether November 23 or 30 was the better day for Thanksgiving. Schechter admitted his purpose:

> I remember picking up one midwestern newspaper—it was a Sunday radio section—and it had an eight-column streamer across the radio page saying—"Singing Mice on Air Today." And then a little two-column head with "Lily Pons Makes Debut"—so you see who's more important. . . . [People will] be listening to NBC instead of another station. If we can get them to do it, we will have accomplished our purpose to a degree.[15]

The threat of war in Europe soon made passé Schechter's juvenile approach to the news. But Schechter stayed on, and NBC fell behind CBS in both quantity and quality of serious commentary. The older network had little more than bland Lowell Thomas until April 1940. That month H. V. Kaltenborn, by then a household name, moved to NBC. During the Munich crisis in September 1938 he had made eighty-five broadcasts in eighteen days. Radio executives learned for the first time that news commentary might be salable. In April 1939, Lenox Lohr, president of NBC, wrote David Sarnoff, alarmed at the network's loss of listeners to CBS. Lohr believed that NBC's lack of news broadcasts explained the decline, citing Columbia's greater coverage of foreign affairs, in particular the astonishing drawing power of star commentator H. V. Kaltenborn.[16] His move to NBC was a public admission by the network that news commentators had come of age.

The change did not come overnight. War began in Poland in September 1939, and still Raymond Gram Swing could complain that his sustaining commentary remained "an orphan in the network family." As late as August 1940 one of his newscasts was unceremoniously canceled in favor of a baseball game.[17] And sponsors felt unhappy about the news programs they bought. "Up to the present time," wrote the director of the advertising agency handling H. V. Kaltenborn's newscasts in May 1939,

we believe that these programs have been very largely altruistic and that
something must be done to derive greater commercial advantage from
them.
I do not mean by this that we are in favor of any "hammer and tongs"
sales messages. . . . However, we feel that the appeal must be sharpened if satisfactory accumulative effects are to be derived. . . .[18]

"Air News Pays Off Big: Newscasters in Star Coin Class," read
Variety's giant page-one headline on October 25, 1939. NBC's Abel
Schechter remained unimpressed. Two weeks later he responded to a
query about selling war broadcasts with: "What sponsor would want to
sponsor death?"[19]

Advertisers also felt reluctant about buying news programs because
overseas radio reception sometimes became hopelessly distorted. In
April 1939, Kaltenborn, in New York, was translating one of Hitler's
speeches. European transmission suddenly ceased. Finally, in desperation, CBS introduced an organist playing "Jeannie with the Light Brown
Hair." As late as October 1940 *Variety* reported that "reception from the
Far East is still pretty much of an in-and-out affair."[20] This helps explain
why the major networks seldom covered Chinese and Japanaese affairs in
detail before Pearl Harbor. Even in July 1941 one of Swing's commentaries from London could not be heard in the United States. An announcer
used an unfortunate adjective in explaining the problem: "Due to atmos-
pheric conditions unfavorable to transoceanic telephonic reception, we
find it impossible to continue with Mr. Swing's broadcast from London
which has been so unintelligible."[21]

In spite of such occasional technical difficulties, by 1940 Americans
could listen to an enormous amount of news each day. A large part of
Mutual's evening fare consisted solely of newscasters. For instance,
Fulton Lewis, Jr., immediately followed Swing several nights each
week. In September 1940 an NBC announcer in New York told his 6:15
A.M. listeners just what news programs his station would offer for the rest
of the day, a not atypical schedule for the news-hungry east coast:

Throughout the day WJZ will continue its wide coverage of the world's
news with the following broadcasts. At 7:55 this morning there will be
another complete news summary; followed at 8:00 AM by on the scene
accounts by NBC war reporters in Berlin and London. Then—a report
from Washington. News summaries during the day are scheduled for

8:55 AM, 12:55 PM, 1:45 PM, 4:55 PM, 6:00 PM, and 6:25 PM. At 9:30 this evening you are invited to listen to the comments of John B. Kennedy. More news on WJZ will be heard at 11:00 PM and at 12:00 midnight. Late bulletins from the Associated Press go on the air at 12:57 and 1:57 tomorrow morning.[22]

HOOPERATINGS: HOW MANY LISTENED

From the beginning, radio tried to measure the number of listeners for a given program. At first they relied solely on mail from listeners. For instance, in 1929 the president of NBC, hoping to prove to the President of the United States that a particular program enjoyed a large audience, could only say that "Cheerio received 51,129 letters in March, which is the largest number of letters relating to one program received in any one month."[23] Counting the number of letters from each town supposedly determined a station's popularity within a given region. Although the networks talked bravely of scientific accuracy, advertisers remained skeptical—and with cause.

In January 1929 the Radio Commission of the Association of National Advertisers funded the Cooperative Analysis of Broadcasting. By February of the following year, the CAB offered subscribers regular audience surveys. CAB analyses, or Crossley ratings, were based on telephone calls in thirty-one cities. CAB reports told nothing of rural areas, or homes without telephones. At first the recall technique was used. Respondents tried to remember having listened to a list of radio programs broadcast the previous day.[24]

A group of magazines originated the other principal rating service, C. E. Hooper, Inc., in 1934. They believed that a truly scientific study would prove the inflated character of CAB ratings. To their surprise, Hooper's surveys showed even larger listening audiences than the CAB's. The magazine publishers soon gave up, but Hooper established himself as the CAB's competitor. Selling market research to advertisers posed no problem for him. "Few scholars or technically trained people really know anything," he asserted, "that cannot be explained in words of two syllables when the one who knows is not too infernally lazy to learn the rudiments of conversation."[25]

Hooper used the coincidental method. When telephoned, the

respondent was asked whether he had been listening to the radio, and if so, to identify the program, station, sponsor, etc. Though not very accurate, Hooperatings soon "became the principal yardstick of the industry."[26] The A. C. Nielsen audimeter—a device placed inside a radio to record when and what was played—did not go into operation until 1942.

Neither rating service could be termed scientifically accurate. Hooper himself admitted that an hour-long radio program consistently received a higher rating than any fifteen-minute broadcast. If a program vied with two popular shows at the same hour, its rating might be but a quarter of what it would be without strong competition. An evening show meant two or three times as many listeners as the same broadcast during the day. A regular program generally received a much higher rating than one heard only rarely.[27] As a result, networks also continued to use fan mail as an index of popularity.

Though sponsors talked publicly of shortcomings in audience ratings, in private they paid careful attention to downward trends reported by any rating method. H. V. Kaltenborn, who preserved the business correspondence between the Leo Burnett Company (his sponsor's advertising agency) and himself, can be used as an example of a news commentator's problems with ratings. In October 1940, Leo Burnett arranged for Hooper to survey Kaltenborn's popularity in a number of cities. The findings showed a drop in the size of his audience. "All the other commentators gained in rating," declared an agency representative in February 1941, "but you dropped from 16.2 to 13.0 in a month's time. Quite a substantial loss as these surveys go." After another decline, an agency executive wrote: "I know you will be as concerned as I am on hearing that your latest Hooperating has dropped to 8.4." He wondered if Kaltenborn had been "hastier and less careful" in his preparation.[28]

In December 1941, Kaltenborn's rating suddenly shot up to an incredible twenty-five. "Want to congratulate you," wired a Leo Burnett representative, "and express my sincere admiration of the marvelous reporting and analysis job you have been doing. . . ." Kaltenborn replied to "My dear Burke Herrick" the next day: "Thanks for your all-too-generous telegram. I haven't been on often enough to do an outstanding job this time."[29]

Two months later, the agency introduced yet another theory about the significance of Hooperatings:

> Another interesting thing is how your rating and Lowell Thomas'
> jockeyed back and forth. . . . As a result of variations of this kind . . .
> most of us in the radio business have come to view the rating services as
> somewhat questionable in their absolute accuracy.[30]

Apparently Kaltenborn could not win.

NEWS ON THE AIR: WHAT THEY HEARD

Any discussion of radio journalism must include a comparison with newspaper journalism. In the first place, radio commentators had much more difficulty gaining access to public officials than newspapermen. H. V. Kaltenborn raised just this problem in a 1931 letter to one of Herbert Hoover's secretaries. He explained that he was "broadcasting a news analysis" over CBS. He continued: "Does this entitle me to participate in the White House press conferences on those occasions when I am in Washington? Has the status of the radio editor been defined in this connection?"[31] Kaltenborn received permission.

Others, even years later, were less fortunate. Eric Sevareid, writing of his experience in France during 1939 and 1940, complained that neither the French press authorities nor the American embassy regarded radio journalists as "legitimate." He also commented bitterly about the attitude of Washington newspaper correspondents toward him in 1941. He claimed that at White House press conferences he might be greeted with a jeering: " 'Make way for the com-men-ta-*tor!* Make way for the ideology boy who sees all, knows all, and don't say nuthin'!' "[32] Edward R. Murrow broadcast a story concerning the notorious Norwegian fifth columnist, Major Vidkun Quisling, which had appeared in the *London Daily Express*. The newspaper reported that all Quisling's activities had brought him was a job as radio news commentator. "The *Express* implies," Murrow noted wryly, "that Quisling as a radio commentator has indeed reached a low station in life."[33] Radio newsmen, particularly the younger ones, were often discouraged by official indifference or active hostility from newspaper reporters. For certain, no broadcaster ever seemed as indispensable as a renowned member of another medium: "A *New York Times* reporter once asked Under Secretary of State Sumner Welles, 'Do you know anything we don't know today?' To which Welles replied, 'Of course not, where do you think we get our information?' ''[34]

But sponsors cared. They cared about numbers, not the importance of those listening. Newspaper publishers and radio networks paid a variety of pollsters, offering a variety of questions, to determine which medium best carried the news. In 1935 three psychologists at Harvard announced that facts and abstract material were comprehended better when heard than read. In *Exact Measurements of the Spoken Word, 1902-1936,* CBS circulated these findings among prospective advertisers.[35]

The 1936 election made everyone realize radio's impact on national affairs. *Middletown in Transition* agreed with Franklin D. Roosevelt: the New Deal reached voters primarily through radio. In the weeks preceding the election, the Lynds concluded, ''radio was a more important channel of national political news to Middletown than were the local newspapers.''[36]

This can, in fact, be documented. A rash of polls questioned respondents about whether most of their news came from radio or newspapers. An unmistakable trend appeared. Although as late as August 1938 most people preferred newspapers over radio for news, by 1941 radio emerged the victor. And all levels of society seemed to favor radio news programs.[37] The world, as interpreted by the commentators, had at last caught the American consciousness.

Bernard DeVoto, touring the West in the summer of 1940, wrote a letter providing evidence of radio's pervasive and effective coverage of overseas events. Shortly after the fall of France in June, he reported his impressions to a friend, CBS commentator Elmer Davis:

> I could usually manage to tune in—usually at the disconcerting hour of 5:55 [P.M.]—and it was heartening to hear your voice in the Sangre de Cristo, the Tetons, the Wyoming badlands, along the Yellowstone, and in the barrens of North Dakota. What's more to the point, I heard you quoted and analyzed everywhere. Shoe drummers, gas station attendants, truck drivers, county farm agents—everybody was listening to you, learning from you, and applying you. And your colleagues. The radio had completely repaired the failure of the press, which appalled me. . . . In a town like Santa Fe, Pueblo, Ogden, Pocatello, Cheyenne, Great Falls, Helena, [or] Grand Forks, the war news in the local papers would average between a half and three quarters of a column. Comment on the war, apart from the syndicated columns, would be nothing at all.

Describing his trip from Casper to Muddy Gap, Wyoming, he went on:

> I drove through seventy-five miles of empty desolation . . . there was the crossroads and there was Muddy Gap—three unpainted shacks, each of them a filling station. I stopped at the first one and blew my horn. A woman came out . . . her face and hair were monuments to the Wyoming sun. She said: "Has Roosevelt declared war on 'em yet?" She said her radio had been out of order for three days. . . . Well, everywhere I went everyone had the most astonishing amount of information about the war.[38]

Innovation followed programming innovation as radio news gained public acceptance. In March 1938 CBS originated the first multiple-pickup international broadcast. While Edward R. Murrow described the end of Austrian independence in Vienna, William L. Shirer discussed its significance to Great Britain from London, and a senator in Washington was pressed into service to assess American reactions.[39] Soon NBC and CBS offered daily news roundups, including live broadcasts from countries as distant as Egypt and Finland.

With war seemingly on its way, Paul W. White, of CBS, flew to Europe in July 1939. He arranged with Edward R. Murrow, chief of European operations, that CBS news would use only American correspondents, stationed in various capitals.[40] NBC's Abel Schechter remained in New York. "Strange how many times that accursed word 'education' bobs up in connection with haywire suggestions," he remarked.[41] His European representative, Max Jordan, continued to be in charge; Schechter ignored gossip about Jordan's Nazi sympathies because of special favors the Germans had granted him.[42]

All broadcasts originating overseas had to be cleared in advance by government censors in each country.[43] In America a different sort of censorship prevailed. There were pressures, if not outright prohibitions. Roosevelt's press secretary, Steve Early, said that radio "might have to be taught manners if it were a bad child."[44] The President himself, in notes he dictated as the basis for a speech by Early before the National Association of Broadcasters, warned the networks not to let "false news" be broadcast. "The Government is watching," he added ominously, "and will continue to watch with great interest to see whether those who control radio will carry out this public duty of their own accord."[45] The President did not explain what he meant by "false news.'' The networks understood this to mean news unfavorable to the administration's point of view. In March 1939 an NBC vice-president begged his superior not to mention how easily the government could take control of the networks.[46] When war began six months later, the three major broadcasting companies agreed to avoid discussing how America should respond to Hitler. The president of NBC, Lenox Lohr, told his board of directors that this decision had been ''favorably commented upon in the press by certain White House attachés.''[47]

Even with such an agreement to remain noncontroversial, so fearful were broadcasting companies of federal regulation that the president of NBC actually declared, before the Federal Communications Commission in 1940, that freedom of speech for radio did not exist. ''I object to people saying [that there is] freedom of speech over the air,'' he stated. ''I don't think there is any such thing.''[48] Shortly after, in May 1941, the FCC, in the Mayflower decision, held that ''the broadcaster cannot be an advocate.''

The ruling seemed a direct threat to every commentator. In practical terms, however, it proved impossible to analyze the news without offering opinion or implicitly advocating a position. Edward R. Murrow claimed that he could do this, but a close reading of his broadcasts before 1941 reveals his partisanship on many important issues. The threat of censorship led to results that neither the FCC nor the White House really intended. For instance:

> MAN: Does NBC have a policy not to broadcast labor strikes?
> SCHECHTER: [Director of News and Special Events at NBC] No, there's no such policy. We always have had a policy to cut down and minimize strike threats. . . Our policy has been not to use that on the air until it actually happens, because just the very idea of saying something will happen is apt to cripple the industry and the business, and the commerce of an entire town.[49]

Nor was Schechter alone in his attitude toward controversial subjects. William S. Paley, president of CBS, admitted trying to force Elmer Davis to cut back on the sharpness and number of opinions in his broadcasts. Kaltenborn stated that CBS vice-president Edward Klauber gave him the same kind of orders.[50]

Sponsors and advertising agencies also attempted to control content by means of their option to cancel a program contract every thirteen weeks.[51]

They frequently did so if they did not agree with the opinions of a news commentator. The Leo Burnett Company's correspondence with H. V. Kaltenborn contains numerous admonitions to be less opinionated. Sometimes the agency representative used the carrot: "Don't think I am criticizing, but I just want to throw in a note of caution in the interests of good showmanship." Sometimes the stick: "Most of the trouble we get in arises from misinformation you pick up on your trips."[52]

"WHICH SIDE IS SUPPOSED TO WIN THIS WAR?"

A certain muting of opinion is all that administration and sponsor pressures brought about. No type of censorship proved effective against the creativity and verbal skills of the commentators. September 1939's moderate positions became increasingly rare as the months passed. In May 1940 the *Nation*'s literary editor did, in fact, report that "Davis and Swing have achieved an objectivity that is truly remarkable. . . . When I say objectivity I mean just that."[53] The *Chicago Tribune* offered a different assessment: "Inflamed by commercial radio commentators, the east has fallen into a complete state of hysteria. . . . The mental confusion could hardly be worse if the enemy were in Long Island again."[54]

By June 1940 virtually all news commentators except Fulton Lewis, Jr., and Boake Carter were committed to increasing American aid to Britain beyond the amounts being provided by the administration. These men had a cause they believed in—and they found it increasingly difficult to keep their feelings to themselves. Listeners considered newscasts objective if they agreed with what they heard. If not, they condemned radio's war hysteria.

And with good reason. Enormous changes in allowable sorts of opinion about the war occurred between September 1939 and September 1940. Then networks forbade that an air raid alert be heard in a news report, terming it "unneutral." One year later Edward R. Murrow, in a classic broadcast, let Americans hear the wail of air raid sirens warning of another wave of German bombers over London. Eric Sevareid admits that he could not keep his voice quite steady during his last broadcast on French soil in June 1940. After the war, William L. Shirer said of the commentators: "Most, I think, lost their old fire."[55]

Variety, unofficial spokesman for the radio industry, best summarized the change in attitude between 1939 and 1941. In "Words Win Wars," a prominently displayed editorial (not a regular feature) published in June 1941, the editors proclaimed:

> There is something both ridiculous and unwholesome in the continuing spectacle of radio broadcasters and commentators being publicly "accused" of the crime of being pro-British when the official policy of the United States is frankly and completely pro-British. . . . The people's airwaves have some relationship to the people's government and the policy of the latter must, in the pinch, be the policy of the former. . . . Which side is supposed to win this war? Who doesn't want England to win? Why are we taxing ourselves until it hurts?[56]

On July 5, 1941, in a CBS broadcast, Eric Sevareid openly questioned "what weight shall be given the remarks of a minority [isolationists] whose responsibility in the decisions is only a fraction of those in power."[57] He defended his statement in a letter to his news director: "To my mind, we are already in a state of war." Drawing on his experiences in France the year before, he declared that "no one can convince me that . . . journalists cannot help contribute to the suicide of their own country."[58]

Such fervent expressions of opinion help suggest where the radio industry stood by June 1941. The medium best able to present a specific point of view about foreign policy to the entire nation openly urged Roosevelt to increase American involvement overseas. And this just one month after the FCC had solemnly decreed that "the broadcaster cannot be an advocate." By the summer of 1941, radio commentators reflected the attitude of most Americans; they certainly shaped their news analyses to agree with what they hoped to be the prevailing consensus—"Who doesn't want England to win?"

NOTES

1. Robert S. and Helen Merrell Lynd, *Middletown: A Study in Contemporary American Culture* (New York, 1929), p. 271; *Middletown in Transition: A Study in Cultural Conflicts* (New York, 1937), p. 263.

2. RCA, *The First 25 Years of RCA* (New York, 1944), n.p., copy in Giraud Chester dissertation notes, Box 213, H. V. Kaltenborn MSS, State Historical Society of Wisconsin, Madison, Wisconsin [hereafter Kaltenborn MSS]; H. M. Beville to William S. Hedges, January 12, 1965, 5, copy in 4-C, Broadcast Pioneers History Project, *Fifth Progress Report* (New York, July 1969) [hereafter BP-1969]; *Variety*, January 12, 1938, p. 30; "Data for Board Report," R.C. Witmer to Lenox Lohr, November 17, 1939, p. 2, in Board of Directors Meeting folder, November 24, 1939, NBC Box I-A, Lenox Lohr MSS, Manuscript Division, Chicago Circle Campus of the University of Illinois, Chicago, Ill. [hereafter Lohr MSS]; *Variety*, January 8, 1941, p. 90; June 12, 1940, p. 27.

3. César Saerchinger, *Hello America! Radio Adventures in Europe* (Boston, 1939), p. 272. Saerchinger was European representative for CBS until 1938. A recording of the nightingale, which became something of a joke among news commentators, is available on Frederic Mullally, "The Sounds of Time," 33 1/3 rpm record, CBS 62888, copy in Recorded Sound Section, Music Division, Library of Congress, Washington, D.C. [hereafter RSS-LC]; CBS Black Book, "Radio Programs 1932," Columbia Broadcasting System Program Information, 51 W. 52d St., New York, New York [hereafter CBS Program Information].

4. Mimeographed CBS press release, August 3, 1931, copy in Frederic W. Wile to Herbert Hoover, August 4, 1931, "CBS" folder, President' Secretary's file 1382, HHL [hereafter PSF, HHL].

5. A 78 rpm original transcription [June] 1933, Kaltenborn MSS.

6. Barnouw, *A Tower in Babel*, 1: 277 (cited above, Introduction, note 2); see also Robert R. Smith, "The Origins of Radio Network News Commentary," *Journal of Broadcasting* 9 (Spring 1965): 113-22.

7. E. H. Harris, "Radio and the Press," *Annals of the American Academy of Political and Social Science* 177 (January 1935): 166-67 [hereafter *Annals*]. The Press-Radio War has been discussed in numerous places. An adequate treatment is Giraud Chester, "The Press-Radio War: 1933-1935," *Public Opinion Quarterly* 13 (Summer 1949): 252-64.

8. Chester, "The Press-Radio War," p. 256; A[bel] A. Schechter with Edward Anthony, *I Live on Air* (New York, 1941), pp. 1-4; Paul W. White, *News on the Air* (New York, 1947), pp. 43-48.

9. Max Jordan, *Beyond All Fronts: A Bystander's Notes on This Thirty Years War* (Milwaukee, Wis., 1944), pp. 185-86.

10. T. R. Carskadon, "The Press-Radio War," *New Republic*, March 11, 1936, p. 133; *Variety*, September 27, 1939, p. 24.

11. Boake Carter, CBS broadcast, November 3, 1936, Box 184, Federal Trade Commission Records, Record Group 122, National Archives, Washington, D.C. [hereafter RG 122].

12. The photograph appears in *America's Town Meeting of the Air*, III (November 11, 1937), copy in Box 1, Raymond Gram Swing MSS, Manuscript Division, Library of Congress, Washington, D.C. [hereafter Swing MSS].

13. Raymond Gram Swing, MBS broadcasts December 2, 7, 10, 11, 1936, all in Box 3, Swing MSS; Saerchinger, *Hello America!*, pp. 236-38.

14. Saerchinger, *Hello America!*, p. 177.

15. A. A. Schechter, "The News and Special Events Division," mimeographed copy of lecture to NBC employees, November 8, 1939, p. 4, copy in unmarked file drawer, Program Reference Library, room 279, National Broadcasting Company, Rockefeller Center, New York, New York [hereafter, NBC-*Talks*].

16. Lenox R. Lohr to David Sarnoff, April 6, 1939, Sarnoff folder, NBC Box IV-A, Lohr MSS.

17. Quoted in Charles A. Siepmann, "The Shortage of News Analysts," *Nation*, January 24, 1948, p. 97; note on MBS broadcast, August 17, 1940, Box 11, Swing MSS.

18. Leo Burnett to F[rancis] H. Marling, Advertising Director, Pure Oil Company, May 13, 1939, Box 150, Kaltenborn MSS.

19. *Variety*, October 25, 1939; Schechter, "The News and Special Events Division," p. 10. CBS's reaction is suggested in H. V. Kaltenborn to Edward R. Murrow, November 24, 1939, Box 148, Kaltenborn MSS.

20. Kaltenborn's CBS broadcast, April 1, 1939, cited in Giraud Chester's dissertation notes, Box 213, Kaltenborn MSS; *Variety*, October 9, 1940, p. 1.

21. Swing MBS broadcast from London, July 21, 1941, Box 15, Swing MSS.

22. NBC-Blue, September 21, 1940, Microfilm Box 20-F, Central Records, Room 2M1W, NBC, Rockefeller Center, New York, New York.

23. M. H. Aylesworth to Herbert Hoover, "Radio" folder, PSF 75, HHL.

24. NBC, "How NBC Station Areas are Determined" (New York, March 1935), p. 5, FD-NBC; Cooperative Analysis of Broadcasting [CAB], *Ten Years of Network Program Analysis* (New York, 1939), pp. 1-3, copy in Program Reference Library, FD-NBC; "How Radio Measures its Audience: A Special Study," *Printers' Ink Monthly*, July 1939, pp. 7-8, CBS reprint, in CBS Library, 524 W. 57th St., New York, N.Y. [hereafter CBS Library].

25. Matthew N. Chappell and C[laude] E. Hooper, *Radio Audience Measurement* (New York, 1944), pp. 62, 49.

26. H. M. Beville, "Research," mimeo., May 8, 1940, p. 12, NBC-Talks, FD-NBC; Beville to Hedges, January 12, 1965, pp. 5-6, BP-1969; Llewellyn White, *The American Radio* (Chicago, 1947), p. 115.

27. C. E. Hooper, "What *is* a Radio Program Rating?", *Printers' Ink*, May 11, 1939, CBS reprint, no. 3, copy in CBS Library; Paul F. Lazarsfeld and

Patricia L. Kendall, *Radio Listening in America: The People Look at Radio—Again* (New York, 1949), p. 19.

28. Paul C. Harper to Kaltenborn, October 4, 1940; Harper to Kaltenborn, February 20, 1941; Harper to Kaltenborn, May 19, 1941, all in Box 150, Kaltenborn MSS.

29. Telegram, Burke Herrick, Director of Radio, Leo Burnett Company, to Kaltenborn, December 8, 1941; Kaltenborn to Herrick, December 9, 1941—both in Box 150, Kaltenborn MSS.

30. Herrick to Kaltenborn, February 20, 1942, Box 150, Kaltenborn MSS.

31. Kaltenborn to George Akerson, January 12, 1931, "Kaltenborn" folder, PSF 534, HHL.

32. Sevareid, *Not So Wild a Dream* (New York, 1946), pp. 196, 110-11.

33. Murrow broadcast quoted in *Variety,* July 10, 1940, p. 24.

34. Quoted in Bernard C. Cohen, *The Press and Foreign Policy* (Princeton, N.J., 1965), p. 210.

35. New York, March, 1936, pp. 24-25; copy in CBS Library, based on Hadley Cantril and Gordon W. Allport, *The Psychology of Radio* (New York, 1935).

36. Robert and Helen Lynd, *Middletown in Transition,* pp. 377-78, footnote, p. 386.

37. Some of these questions are conveniently summarized in Hadley Cantril and Mildred Strunk, *Public Opinion, 1935-1946* (Princeton, N.J., 1951), p. 524. For more information, see Paul Lazarsfeld's influential *Radio and the Printed Page: An Introduction to the Study of Radio and its Role in the Communication of Ideas* (New York, 1940), pp. xi, 211, 256-57.

38. "Benny" [Bernard DeVoto] to Davis, July 21, 1940, Box 1, Elmer Davis MSS, Manuscript Division, Library of Congress, Washington, D.C. [hereafter Davis MSS].

39. CBS, *Vienna: March, 1938* (New York, 1938), p. 27; William L. Shirer, *Berlin Diary: The Journal of a Foreign Correspondent, 1934-1941* (New York, 1941), pp. 110, 112. An excellent description of this broadcast appears in Alexander Kendrick, *Prime Time: The Life of Edward R. Murrow* (Boston, 1969), pp. 157-59.

40. CBS, "Fifteen Minutes—March 5, 1942" (New York, April, 1942), an account by an outside observer of a CBS newscast, copy in CBS Library.

41. Schechter, *I Live on Air,* p. 103.

42. *Variety,* October 26, 1938, p. 36.

43. For details on how a news broadcast was prepared, see "Behind the Scenes in the CBS Newsroom," CBS broadcast, June 1, 1941, reel 545, Milo Ryan Phonoarchive, University of Washington, Seattle, Washington [hereafter

Phonoarchive]. A brief description of this broadcast and thousands of others in the Phonoarchive appears in Washington (State) University. Phonoarchive [Milo J. Ryan], *History in Sound: A Descriptive Listing of the KIRO-CBS Collection of Broadcasts of the World War II Years and After, in the Phonoarchive of the University of Washington* (Seattle, 1963).

44. Quoted in Davis, "Broadcasting the Outbreak of War," *Harper's Magazine* 179 (November 1939): 587.

45. A note reads: "The President dictated this as a basis for Mr. Early's broadcast [speech?] before the Broadcasters' Association in Atlantic City on July 11, 1939." Box 49, President's Secretary's File, Franklin D. Roosevelt Library, Hyde Park, New York [hereafter FDRL].

46. Niles Trammell to Lenox Lohr, March 29, 1939, NBC Box III-C, Lohr MSS.

47. Report, Board of Directors Meeting, September 22, 1939, folder with identical title, NBC Box I-A, Lohr MSS; see also NBC, "Interpretation of NBC Policies as Applied to Broadcasts During the Current European War," mimeo. (New York, September 7, 1939), copy in FD-NBC; CBS, "CBS European War Coverage," mimeo. (New York, September 5, 1939), copy in NBC Box III-C, Lohr MSS.

48. Transcript of FCC hearings Docket 5060 (Mayflower), copy in Giraud Chester dissertation notes, Box 213, Kaltenborn MSS.

49. Schechter, "The News and Special Events Division," p. 11 (cited above, note 15).

50. Memorandum of conversation, Roger Burlingame with Paley at CBS, New York City, May 24, 1960, in Notebook, "Radio," 35, Box 53, Roger Burlingame MSS, Manuscript Division, Syracuse University Library, Syracuse, New York [hereafter Burlingame MSS]. Kaltenborn in *Radio Daily,* September 16, 1943, quoted in Giraud Chester, "The Radio Commentaries of H. V. Kaltenborn: A Case Study in Persuasion" (Ph.D. dissertation, University of Wisconsin, 1947), p. 529.

51. William L. Shirer, *Stranger Come Home* (Boston, 1954), pp. 69-70, contains a blunt discussion of what a thirteen-week contract can do to a commentator's freedom of expression.

52. Paul C. Harper to Kaltenborn, March 9, 1942; Harper to Kaltenborn, May 18, 1942; see also Harper to Kaltenborn, October 3, 1941—all in Box 150, Kaltenborn MSS.

53. Margaret Marshall, "Notes by the Way," *Nation,* May 4, 1940, p. 570; Paul F. Lazarsfeld and Harry Field, *The People Look at Radio* (Chapel Hill, N.C., 1946), p. 45.

54. June 8, 1940, quoted in Walter Johnson, *The Battle Against Isolation* (Chicago, 1944), p. 2.

55. Sevareid, *Not So Wild a Dream,* pp. 112, 79 (note 32, above); Shirer, *Stranger Come Home,* p. 190.

56. June 18, 1941, p. 25.

57. CBS broadcast, July 5, 1941, copy in Box D1, Eric Sevareid MSS, Manuscript Division, Library of Congress, Washington, D.C. [hereafter Sevareid MSS].

58. Typed rough draft, Sevareid to Paul White, July 11, 1941; see also White to Sevareid, July 7, Office Communication, White to Sevareid, July 15—all in Box A1, Sevareid MSS.

2 | Boake Carter:
Columbia's Voice of Doom

Westbrook Pegler, who hated almost everybody, might be considered the closest thing newspaper journalism ever had to a Boake Carter.
The broadcaster became an extraordinarily powerful and effective critic
of the New Deal before Pearl Harbor, especially between 1935 and 1938,
when few commercially sponsored news commentators were on the air.
Administration leaders frequently mentioned their extreme dislike of
him. Carter's greatest national prominence, or notoriety, occurred during
1937 and the early part of the following year. The major networks banned
him after August 1938. At the time, some of his millions of nightly
listeners insisted that Franklin D. Roosevelt had been responsible. The
news analyst spoke over the Mutual Broadcasting System from September 1939 on, but never regained his popularity. He died in 1944,
already largely forgotten. Now, over thirty years later, it is time for
another look. Historians recognize the importance of radio in understanding American society during the 1930s. For this reason, the career of such
a notorious broadcaster has particular value. And those interested in
radio's role as administration critic—for example, in the area of foreign
affairs—need to know more about this commentator's impact.

Short, with red hair and a carefully groomed moustache, Carter tried to
look commanding in publicity photographs. But above all he relished
controversy. "Meat is in argument," he once said. "If I can provide an
argument, so much the better."[1] He seemed to feel his success was
directly proportional to the number of enemies he made. There were
many. The Secretary of the Interior dubbed him "Croak" Carter. Ickes
claimed that the newscaster could "enter any intellectual goldfish-

34

swallowing contest and the result would be as impressive as his journalistic career."[2] A distinguished journalist, making no attempt to disguise his loathing, termed the broadcaster a "mercenary poseur."[3]

Early in his career, Carter claimed to have studied the techniques of Detroit's demagogic radio priest, Father Coughlin.[4] He proved an apt pupil. Listeners believed that anyone who daily accused administration leaders of shocking laxness and irresponsibility must have good reason. They loved his tough "psychological realism."[5] And Carter was clever. If a public official proved that the news analyst had distorted the truth, or manufactured a story out of the whole cloth, Carter invoked freedom of speech, or excused himself by saying that every reporter made occasional slips. He concentrated on sensitive areas where the administration could not afford to make its dealings public knowledge, knowing that government leaders would have difficulty refuting his accusations.

Carter's dire forebodings did not appeal to everyone. In 1937, the *New Yorker*'s E. B. White expressed his indifference in a bit of patronizing verse:

> I like to hear him summon us
> With all things ominous:
> Munitions makers, plotting gain,
> Asylums bulging with insane,
> Cancers that give no hint of pain,
> Insurgency in northern Spain,
> And rivers swollen with the rain.
> For Boake,
> Has spoke,
> And it's no joke.[6]

Roosevelt himself tried to affect a similar pose. In December 1937, he told his son that "if the President (or anyone else) were to undertake to answer Boake Carter, he would have no time to act as the Executive head of the Government!"[7]

THE BLOOD OF AN ENGLISHMAN

Harold Thomas Henry Carter was born on September 15/28, 1903, in

Baku, a city on the Caspian Sea in what is now the Soviet Union. Until 1924, it is difficult to establish an exact chronology, particularly because the broadcaster afterward manufactured a past to suit his own purpose. He gave his date of birth as 1898, or 1901. He declared that his Irish father had been Britain's consul in Baku. Carter's official birth certificate, on file in London, shows that Thomas Carter was "Company Secretary" for an English oil firm. In 1938 the Treasury Department made an official inquiry into the commentator's origin. An investigation of British diplomatic records revealed that no Carter had served in the foreign service in any capacity anywhere in the world since 1850.[8] It is typical of Carter that he would make himself older than he really was and give his father a fictitious diplomatic career.

Sometime after 1903, the Carter family returned to Britain. At fifteen, the son enlisted in the Royal Air Force. He served as a member of the coast patrol for eighteen months.[9] From 1918 to 1921 he attended Tonbridge, a prestigious public (i.e., private) boys' school in Kent, England. The third year he was active in rowing. His knowledge of the sport held him in good stead when he began his career as a radio broadcaster.[10]

Carter claimed to have attended Christ College, Cambridge, but there is no record of his ever having been a student there.[11] He also said that he had served as a reporter for the *London Daily Mail*. If so, it was probably during the summer of 1921. On September 25 of that year, he entered the United States for the first time, "charged to the quota for Russia."[12]

In the meantime, his father had gone to Mexico in search of oil. His mother, Edith Harwood-Yarred, and sister Eileen remained in England. After a brief stay in New York, the younger Carter joined his father. He worked as a journalist in the various parts of Central America where Thomas Carter was located. In 1923 the son visited Cuba. For a time, both were in Tulsa, Oklahoma. Then the father became a director of an oil refinery in Philadelphia. Shortly after, his son joined him. Hoping to make a fashionable impression, the young Carter reputedly arrived attired in "spats, monocle and cane."

The diminutive Englishman began as a rewrite man on the city desk of the *Philadelphia Evening Bulletin*. In April 1924, after a brief courtship, he married the assistant society editor of the same paper, Beatrice Olive Richter. The Carters gave their children exotic names: Gwladys Shealeagh Boake and Michale Boake. Within a couple of years the family moved to an old farmhouse in Torresdale, outside the city. Carter added many rooms over the years. A photograph taken in the 1930s shows him attired as a British country gentleman—high boots and riding breeches—though having trouble removing a book from the third shelf of a bookcase.

Carter painted more than one hundred portraits, termed by one reporter "high in color but not noteworthy for technique." He occasionally exhibited some of these at Philadelphia art shows. At one time he claimed to own a sixty-foot ketch and to belong to the Delaware Yacht Club. Having married a more socially prominent person (Beatrice Richter's father was editor and publisher of *Sporting Life*), Carter seemed especially pleased at being asked to present a lecture at the Philadelphia Junior League's annual party in January 1936. His audience included more than fifteen hundred guests.[13]

Carter's first radio experience came in the spring of 1930. A local Philadelphia station needed someone to broadcast a description of a rugby match. Nobody else knew anything about the game. Carter's next radio appearance demonstrated his ingenuity:

> The broadcast of the rugby game inspired WCAU to simulate a from-the-spot description of the Oxford-Cambridge boat race. Carter, in the studio, pretended he was a spectator on the bank of the Thames. He got the facts for his description from early editions of the afternoon newspapers, and was "supported" by a number of wax recordings of English crowd sounds.[14]

The following year, Boake (the program director at Philadelphia's WCAU suggested that he stop calling himself Harold Carter) became the Hearst Globe Trotter in the City of Brotherly Love. He made two five-minute news broadcasts daily, at 12:30 P.M. and 5:00 P.M., publicizing the Hearst-Metrotone newsreel and the theaters where it appeared. The Pep Boys, a chain specializing in automotive parts, soon began sponsoring him.[15] Almost immediately his broadcasts resulted in controversy. One outraged listener wrote President Herbert Hoover to describe what was going on:

> We are amazed and troubled that he has not been held accountable for his outspoken and venomous remarks. He seldom fails in either talk each day, to take a fling at the President or the administration. We think

he is an Englishman as he has quite a decided Cockney-English accent.
He laughs frequently and uproariously at his supposed jokes.[16]

The kidnapping of Charles A. Lindbergh's baby brought Carter to
national attention. WCAU's owner, Dr. Leon Levy, was the brother-in-
law of the CBS president. He enthusiastically described the new commentator to William S. Paley, also a WCAU stockholder. Paley seemed
unimpressed. Levy tried another tack. It was the height of public interest
in the kidnapping. The former dentist refused to allow CBS the use of his
station's "mobile broadcasting unit" unless Carter received a national
hookup. Levy got his way. On March 2, 1932, the newscaster began
speaking over most CBS affiliates from Trenton, New Jersey. He
"roared at the forces of crime, instead of giving a straight news-
broadcast." Columbia canceled him. Listeners deluged the network
demanding more of Carter's analyses. He quickly returned to the air.[17]

Some remained outraged by what he said. In May 1932 the Federal
Radio Commission received an official complaint concerning Carter's
newscasts as "The Globe Trotter." The commission's Philadelphia
office hired a stenographer to take down Carter's "news flashes." An
official declared that "any expense necessarily incurred in procuring the
transcript will be borne by the Commission, not to exceed twenty dollars." The commentator received no reprimand.[18]

Carter considered himself an authority on air power, based on his
experience with the Royal Air Force's coast patrol during World War I.
He persuaded Brigadier General William Mitchell to appear on his
program in October 1934. He became good friends with Congressman
John J. McSwain, chairman of the House Military Affairs Committee.[19]
During the next several years, the news analyst devoted many broadcasts
to military matters. His support of air power often meant accusing others
of preventing its development. "Trans-Atlantic commercial aviation is in
one hell of a mess!" was the way he began one 1938 article.
As to shipping, Carter claimed:

> The U.S. merchant marine has been allowed to slide into decay and rot
> and not [sic] so very far from ruin. The vessels we do have are
> ninety-seven percent ancient, hardly seaworthy old tubs. They crawl
> when it comes to speed. . . . Other nations laugh at America on this
> score. . . .[20]

The newscaster often hinted darkly of conspiracies. In discussing national defense, he exposed unnamed persons:

> And we in our small way, try to point toward a better national air defense at less cost. But likewise, never get to first base either. For what reason? . . . Because at the tops in both services, the gold braid and the brass hats like to play politics as much as any politician.[21]

The administration at first attempted to be friendly toward Carter. In November 1935, Roosevelt gladly talked privately with the newscaster after one of his press conferences.[22] When the news analyst praised Cordell Hull's trade agreement program in a broadcast, the Secretary sent a personal note of thanks:

> It is very gratifying to have some of the important facts with regard to this matter made so clear to the public as you have made them.
> Will you accept my good wishes for a happy and successful New Year. . . .[23]

As late as April 1936, Senator Joseph T. Robinson of Arkansas spoke somewhat tongue-in-cheek on the floor of Congress about "that great radio speaker to whom all delight to listen, Mr. Boake Carter," and cited one of the newscaster's recent analyses.[24]

In February of that year, the commentator conducted a number of interviews. Guests such as Postmaster General James A. Farley and FCC Commissioner George Henry Payne discussed what radio networks should do about handling public affairs. Edward L. Bernays, a highly successful "publicity specialist" then working for the newscaster's sponsor, had come up with an idea. CBS had no desire to publicize further the question of how much time the Republican party should be given or allowed to purchase in the coming campaign. They arranged for the programs to be unsponsored, and quickly terminated the series. That cabinet members would immediately accept an invitation to appear on a program with Boake Carter indicates something of the news analyst's importance in early 1936.[25]

Another publicity scheme involved the Department of State. The commentator was sponsored by Philco radio of Philadelphia. In May 1936 Hull not only wrote a letter supporting Bernays's next promotional gimmick, but ended up talking with a number of the company's Canadian salesmen in Washington. Philco chartered the *Monarch of Bermuda* and took eight hundred dealers to Cuba. Carter broadcast nightly aboard ship. On May 15 he told his listeners that "Philco, in going to Havana, Cuba, serves to carry out into actuality President Roosevelt's good neighbor policy."[26] In Havana, Jefferson Caffery, the American ambassador, spoke cordially to the radio distributors.[27] That evening the newscaster told his enormous CBS audience of the ambassador's kind words. On the air, he interviewed James Phillips, Cuban correspondent for the *New York Times*. "The Reciprocity Treaty and sugar quota granted by the United States," declared Phillips, "are directly responsible for the business improvement of the island."[28] The commentator was equally enthusiastic. Laurence Duggan, of the State Department's Latin American Division, sent a copy of the broadcast to a superior. "I should say that our effort for the Philco company was richly repaid by this interview," he added.[29]

During the summer of 1936, Carter involved himself in a battle between his sponsor and the Radio Corporation of America. The two companies had long experienced strained relations. In 1927 RCA brought forth a much-improved vacuum tube. Before then, every radio required a storage battery. The development nearly put the Philadelphia Electric Storage Battery Company (Philco) out of business. It had sold fifteen million batteries that year. In desperation, Philco turned to manufacturing radios. The company pioneered in inexpensive sets and models for automobiles. RCA demanded a small percentage of the selling price because of patents it held. In 1936 Philco sued, charging monopolistic practices. Carter infuriated RCA by defending the suit during several broadcasts. Philco ran a full-page advertisement in *Time* denying that company policies influenced its commentator.[30] Few were convinced, and RCA least of all.

U.S. NEWSHAWK MISLED BY FALSE INFORMATION

Carter's next crusade involved the Department of State. In June 1935, Lawrence Simpson, an American sailor, was arrested in Hamburg. German police charged him with treason. According to custom, the American consul was present when the prisoner was taken into custody.

The State Department official reported that for "a native-born American," Simpson demonstrated "an astounding knowledge of German." Two months later Secretary of State Cordell Hull wired Hamburg. He told the consul to request a speedy trial for the seaman.[31] One year later, the seaman remained in prison. He had never been indicted. Gifford A. Cochran, wealthy associate of the National Committee for Defense of Political Prisoners, went to Germany to see whether he could secure a trial for Simpson. On July 29, 1936, Hull spoke with the German ambassador in Washington. He questioned the Nazis' harsh treatment of the prisoner, even if he were a Communist who had conspired with seventy German nationals as charged. The Secretary sent a memorandum of his conversation to the American representative in Berlin.[32]

As late as the beginning of September, Carter remained unaware of the Simpson case. On September 6 he discussed Hull's trade agreement with Nicaragua. "Some day some historian will give him the credit that is his due," he concluded, "and it will only be just and fair." He praised the Secretary again on September 9 and 10.[33] Eight days later, the commentator finally learned of the seaman's case. That Friday he devoted much of the broadcast to the matter, taking time out from his daily prognostications concerning November prospects for Alf Landon and Roosevelt. He began:

> Well, from the remoteness of his Connecticut farm, the keen eyes of columnist Westbrook Pegler cover much ground and see many things. . . . So he brings to light the story of Lawrence Simpson, a U.S. citizen and a seaman, who has been locked up in a Nazi prison for fifteen months. . . . And columnist Pegler directs a satirical comparison between what has happened to this plain U.S. sailor Simpson, and what might have happened had the prisoner been Vincent Astor, wealthy crony of President Roosevelt. . . . And it is to be hoped that its [Pegler's column] sting may shame supercilious under secretaries of the State Department into forgetting their friends of the upper strata of the social scale long enough to bestir themselves to see that justice is done to a plain forty-dollar fo'c'sle hand of an American ship.[34]

On Monday, September 21, he eagerly returned to the same subject. The news analyst announced that the department finally had "prodded" the Nazis into arranging a trial date. The next night he referred to Hull's comments on the case. The Secretary's "anger" could be "easily understood," Carter added, "for nobody liked to be prodded with the charge of official laxity in performance of official duties."[35]

On Monday, September 28, Simpson confessed that he had in fact distributed Communist literature and sought to overthrow the German government. Hull wired Ambassador William E. Dodd, demanding he "make strongest possible representations" to the Nazis to have the remaining part of the seaman's sentence revoked, and instead deport him.[36] The Germans released their prisoner on December 20.

Carter's crusade evaporated with the sailor's public statements. The commentator had to admit his error. His apology, broadcast on September 28, the day of Simpson's trial, sounded less than gracious:

> It now seems that Mr. Hull's anger over the case of sailor Simpson . . .
> is understandable . . . the U.S. sailor over whose case considerable
> furor was aroused and over whose plight numbers of U.S. newshawks
> were apparently genuinely misled by false information, convicted
> himself before a German court for being a Communist.
> Thus, we for one promptly lose interest in the Simpson affair. . . .[37]

There are three reasons for emphasizing the fortunes of one American sailor. First, the Simpson case demonstrates Carter's willingness to condemn the State Department without checking his facts. Second, for this controversy copies of almost every one of the newscaster's daily broadcasts have survived. Third, important correspondence from officials in the Department of State, including Hull himself, points out not only how carefully members of the department listened to the news analyst's attacks, but in what high esteem they had previously held his commentaries.

On September 30, 1936, U. Alexis Grant-Smith, a retired foreign service officer, wrote a long letter to the broadcaster concerning the Simpson analyses. He sent copies to Westbrook Pegler, Cordell Hull, and Assistant Secretary of State Wilbur J. Carr, among others. Grant-Smith began:

> Your attack on Secretary Hull, made some days ago in your broadcast
> with regard to the American citizen Simpson . . . was a source of great
> disappointment to me, and, to be quite frank, it seriously shook my
> confidence in your fairness and objectivity. You obviously had made

no attempt to confirm the statements made on the subject derogatory to the Secretary of State and his subordinates before launching your attack. . . .

I am seriously disappointed, because you were one of the few commentators, either on the radio or in the press, whose judgment and fairness I had long counted upon. You can imagine, therefore, how I felt when, after your first broadcast on the Simpson subject, a masseur at a western sanitarium introduced the subject and, referring to your attack, remarked, "It's that sort of thing which makes us little fellows feel dissatisfied."[38]

Wilbur Carr responded enthusiastically:

Your letter of September 30 to Boake Carter gave me a real thrill. . . . I have always had a great deal of confidence in Boake Carter's statements over the radio but last summer I listened nightly to his broadcasts and found those in regard to the Department of Commerce very much at variance with the facts as I personally knew them and I began to lose confidence not in his honest intention but in the care with which he gathered his information.[39]

Though appreciative of Grant-Smith's effort, Hull was pessimistic: "Confidentially, I doubt if i[t] has any effect whatever upon his system and methods."[40] Actually, the Secretary's gloom was unwarranted, which suggests an essential difference between Carter's methods in 1936 and in 1938. On October 21, 1936, the broadcaster returned to a favorite subject: Hull's trade agreements and the wonders they had wrought in Nicaragua. He offered effusive praise for the Secretary's magnificent achievements, including his ability to bring "bright young boys" such as Dean Acheson "back to the administration bandwagon." Carter declared that the transformation of Nicaragua represented "a personal triumph for one of the most unselfishly patriotic gentlemen in America, bar none."[41] There is no indication that Hull heard these fine words.

The Simpson case demonstrates that the broadcaster, while stumbling onto something with the faintest bit of truth to it, used familiar stereotypes of the forgotten common man and rich, disdainful foreign service officers to manufacture an incident of considerable proportions. Hull found himself spending as much time with the American press as he did trying to free Simpson. Finally, Carter dropped the case when the seaman confessed to being a Communist. The newscaster had something of a phobia about Communists, in part because of his abiding belief in all manner of conspiracies.

A VOCAL ZOOT SUIT

A discussion of Carter's broadcast style—including vocal mannerisms—helps make clear why he enjoyed such an enormous audience. When the news analyst first went on the air, he spoke with a very proper British accent. Listeners had trouble understanding him. Carter soon changed his style. As one writer commented: "What he employs now is a sort of pseudo-accent, about as authentic as the Negro dialect of Singing Sam, the Barbasol Man. The intonation is British, but the qualities and emphases are American." "Predecessor" became "pre-duh-sessuh"; "year after year," "yeahr ahfter yeahr." Otherwise, pronunciations remained free of noticeable affectations.[42]

Carter spoke at a tremendous rate of speed. Either the listener followed every word, as Carter rushed on, or he understood nothing. The news analyst made comprehension simpler by employing myriad bromides, platitudes, stereotypes, and the flashy, gauche language—sort of a vocal zoot suit—found in "as told to" books. Nobody ever said something, he "retorted" or "shot back." Descriptions at first seemed exciting. A person whom the newscaster liked was "young, two-fisted, red-haired." Officials were not defeated. Voters would "sweep them from the seats they have warmed for the past four years."[43] Opponents were "on the outs" with the administration. Liberal professors became "as pink as a midsummer sunset" or "academic gentlemen." Government leaders in disfavor turned into "our erudites, learned savants [who] do not understand the essence of the bicycle."[44]

The Postmaster General might be described as "the bank of brilliant white lights reflecting the sheen of his shiny dome . . . the smiling affable ring-master, two job man James Aloysius Farley." The commentator talked of Senator "Bob" Wagner or "young Mr. Hopkins." He loved to refer to Roosevelt as "the Boss."[45] The barely suppressed sneer and the intimate language helped convince listeners that this was a person close to the mighty, who saw through their every pretense.

The news analyst occasionally reported alleged conversations with well-known officials in verbatim fashion. "Well, last Friday, a week ago,'' Carter would say, ''National Committee Chairman Farley said to me over the telephone, 'Monday, Boake, I'm going to come out and claim forty-six states for Roosevelt.' '' In 1940 the broadcaster repeated a discussion with Wendell L. Willkie at the Republican convention: '' 'Hells bells!' he [Wilkie] retorted. . . . 'I get your point exactly,' I answered. . . . 'Exactly,' shot back the blue-eyed, square-jawed Hoosierite.''[46]

Carter loaded his sentences with homely metaphors. On March 11, 1938, discussing Hitler's plan to force an Austro-German *Anschluss*, he belittled talk of a serious European crisis: ''It is my belief that war is nowhere near Europe, that these events are what might be called surface rashes due to fundamental readjustments. Pimples of adolescence, one might say!'' He turned to the country's economic condition after 1919:

Austria became a stomach without a mouth. For her very existence she was obliged to depend upon forced financial feeding from the British and French bankers. The beginning of the end was in sight when the Credit-Anstaldt [sic] bank collapsed several years ago and the French and British financiers were rowing with one another—say tit to you and tat to you![47]

Returning to facial blemishes, the commentator reminded his listeners: ''There'll be a lot more pimples break out in rashes here and there. But underlying the pimples. . . .'' Carter felt that the *Anschluss* would right the wrongs of the Versailles treaty. To him, the risk of war came not from Hitler but from the ''World Savers brigade.'' Without mentioning anyone in particular, he made it clear that Roosevelt was the chief offender. Other countries were ''padding along nicely and quietly.'' They did not have to send a ''continual stream of notes to their neighbors suggesting that this and that nation ought to be quarantined.''[48]

Overseas events also offered a chance to work in a commercial for Philco radios. Carter read his own advertising copy, and introduced it with absolutely no warning:

Thus when the shadows of two mailed fists etch their dark outlines across war-torn, fire-ridden Madrid today, there stretched another dark shadow across the whole of Europe.

So today too we find many a new Philco tuned to the far-flung capital cities of Europe to keep many an American home informed of these critical events of history in the making on the anvil of time. For it is indeed a simply easy thing to follow the world the Philco way now, especially when you have a Philco high efficiency aerial attached to your set.[49]

No matter how breathlessly the commentator spoke—and it was so fast that sentences were incomplete and phrases such as "a simply easy thing" occurred frequently—it proved impossible to overlook the endless clichés. Within two sentences, Carter had introduced "war-torn," "dark shadow," "whole of Europe," "far-flung . . . cities," "critical events," "history in the making," and the "anvil of time."

For a change of pace, Carter frequently turned to the afflictions of the blind. Helen Keller, "gradually like a flower opening its petals beneath the caresses of a warm sun . . . grew to love life and all that it meant to one snatched from the very depths of suffering."[50] In 1936 the newscaster berated Secretary of Labor Frances Perkins for favoring strikers in San Francisco. He suddenly switched to a lengthy story about seeing-eye dogs. The commentator described a school in New Jersey for "man's best friend." Two years later, he talked of the death of one of these animals. He ended by vowing that this was "a dog who will live forever after, for his service to mankind."[51]

Carter's popularity with the average listener is better documented than for most commentators. Only sponsored news programs received regular Crossley and Hooperatings—devices employed by advertisers to determine the size of radio audiences. The newscaster's Philco contract began in 1933. Generally, from 1934 until August 1938, he was as popular as the highest-paid news broadcaster of the decade, NBC's Lowell Thomas. In January 1934 Carter had a Crossley rating of 8.1; Lowell Thomas's was 30.7, one of the highest for any radio show. A year later, the CBS broadcaster was up to 18.9; Thomas led by only five points. In February 1936 Carter's rating sometimes went above his chief rival's.

Until 1936 the newscaster spoke five times a week over twenty-three CBS stations at 7:45 P.M., eastern standard time. In July 1937 the network increased his coverage to sixty stations. His schedule, however, was reduced to Monday, Wednesday, and Friday. When General Foods began its sponsorship in February 1938, the commentator was heard over eighty-five stations five days a week at 6:30 P.M. Thus in terms of number of affilitates, Carter's greatest national coverage came between July 1937 and August 26, 1938, when he was taken off the air.[52]

Other measuring devices demonstrate the newscaster's large following. In June 1938 the fifth annual *Radio Guide* program poll named Carter the most popular radio commentator. As late as January 1940, a *Fortune* survey showed that Boake Carter's newspaper column ran second only to Walter Winchell and Dorothy Thompson in number of readers. The same month, an American Institute of Public Opinion poll reported that even though the broadcaster had been off the air for more than a year, respondents favored him over such influential commentators as Elmer Davis or Raymond Gram Swing by a substantial margin.[53]

FORCED OFF THE AIR

A central question in any consideration of Boake Carter concerns his removal from regular broadcasting in 1938. Exactly who was responsible? In contrast to the documentation of the Simpson affair, few actual broadcasts for 1937 and 1938 have survived. The commentator began a nationally syndicated daily newspaper column on March 1, 1937, but these accounts do not deal with exactly the same things discussed on the air. In spite of this absence of material, however, it is possible to reconstruct a surprising number of Carter's broadcast statements.

The CBS news analyst took on two powerful opponents beginning in 1937, and both forced changes in the content of his talks. The first was organized labor. During the Little Steel strike of 1937 Carter attacked the CIO day after day. Labor responded by picketing the newscaster's home station in Philadelphia. The CIO voted a general boycott of Philco products. Radio sales dropped precipitously, although not necessarily solely because of union action. Since the company had pioneered in low-cost radios, it is hardly surprising that a CIO boycott seemed especially disturbing. Carter admitted that pressure on Philco could be effective:

> What we couldn't understand was the sponsor's multiple fears and piling up of problems where problems didn't exist. Company executives were always eager to drop important business to dabble with

their radio program. . . . When it proved vexatious, [they] were scared out of their wits.[54]

The commentator came to an understanding with John L. Lewis during the fall of 1937. CIO members voted to continue the boycott anyway. Philco terminated its contract with the broadcaster on February 18, 1938.[55]

In the meantime, another corporation, General Foods, decided to sponsor Carter over an increased number of stations. Colby M. Chester, chairman of the board of this corporation, actively opposed the New Deal. He served as president of the National Association of Manufacturers and had been prominent in the American Liberty League from its inception. Not surprisingly, the board chairman was no friend of organized labor. Chester, however, was not the only one involved in deciding what kind of talent the company might pay for. Some questioned whether a firm that manufactured breakfast cereals should risk sponsoring anyone so controversial.

One of these people was Joseph E. Davies, ambassador to the Soviet Union. His new wife, Marjorie Post, owned a substantial amount of stock in General Foods. As Davies later explained to Cordell Hull:

> Last winter [December 1937] we . . . expressed our concern to the officers lest a merchandising and commercial business should alienate possible customers by . . . sponsoring a broadcast that took sides on controversial questions. We were then assured that the arrangement made had expressly precluded such a possibility. . . .[56]

During much of 1937, Carter attacked the administration with increasing viciousness. In July 1937, at the height of the battle over whether to increase the number of Supreme Court justices, the newscaster, according to one listener, accused the President in a "sneeringly derisive" manner of trying to avoid paying his proper income tax. In the same broadcast, the listener continued, he made even wilder accusations:

> In commenting upon the tragic death of Senator Joseph T. Robinson, Carter directly and unequivocally charged that the Senator's fatal heart attack was due to the extreme pressure brought to bear upon him by the President. In fact, Carter unmistakably implied that the Senator's death was caused by the President. . . .

The same person decried the commentator's "attitude of an infallible omniscience . . . [and] his very obviously contemptuous vituperation." Others, equally livid, sent angry letters and telegrams to Philco.[57]

In spite of this, the President tried to accommodate the news analyst. In September Carter telephoned the White House, hoping to see "the Boss" privately. Roosevelt agreed. The Chief Executive still indicated a spirit of resigned tolerance toward the newscaster in December. "Boake Carter's statements," he told a worried acquaintance, "as a general proposition, are half of them untrue and the other half misstated. The particular ones you wrote about fall into both categories."[58]

When the commentator started flaying the Department of State, he created at first only a small stir. In October 1937 the newscaster exposed the department's alleged persecution of an American shipping line operating in South America. Assistant Secretary of State George S. Messersmith explained to a worried associate that the company had been "notoriously inefficient in operations." He noted that the Munson line generally had been unfriendly to the department, snidely adding: "This attitude has done us more honor and credit than otherwise."[59]

In November 1937 Congresswoman Virginia E. Jenckes became infuriated when Carter twitted her in a broadcast. She had spoken before a meeting of the Daughters of the American Revolution. Mrs. Jenckes urged that every cherry tree around Washington's Jefferson Memorial be cut down to show Japanese spies that the United States meant business. The news analyst suggested sarcastically that all foreign trees in America be felled. Enraged, Mrs. Jenckes began an investigation of the broadcaster's background. The congresswoman sought to have Carter declared an undesirable alien. After receiving a formal report from the Commissioner of Immigration and Naturalization, she read it into the *Congressional Record.*[60]

At the same time, the Special Intelligence Unit of the Treasury Department began its own inquiry into the newscaster's origins. Carter learned of at least one of these attempts to deport him. He told his radio audience all about the conspiracy. He explained that although born in the Soviet Union, he was no Communist agent. The broadcaster then filled out an official Unemployment Report Card and sent it to the White House. *"Who* said that I should be Deported? Beware! Libel me at your Peril," was one remark. The commentator asserted that his job was "Hatching canards 'Yellow' Revising and Editing U.S. History 1776-

1937.''[61] For Carter to have sent such an irrational outpouring to the President suggests that perhaps he believed himself genuinely threatened. Unfortunately for those opposing him, the report that the Department of State received from London indicated nothing amiss in the newscaster's background.[62]

Carter's antiadministration onslaught continued unabated. On January 25, 1938, he spoke at the District of Columbia's Washington Forum. The news analyst ''opposed America's joining any movement against non-democratic nations on the ground that it would lead us into war.''[63] His broadcast the previous evening seemed exceptionally strident in tone. On January 26 Pierrepont Moffat described the response of some:

> Mr. Hull is in a state of repressed rage with Boake Carter who is leading the attack against the Administration on foreign policy, but Mr. Hull's rage is nothing to that of Norman Davis and Stanley Hornbeck who would like, I think, to emulate the Nazis in silencing embarrassing critics. Stanley in particular thought that making use of Carter's foreign birth and upbringing would scare him off, instead Boake Carter beat them to it and announced over the radio his whole past history. Whatever one may think of him he's a clever one.[64]

Secretary of the Interior Harold Ickes reports Roosevelt told Secretary of Labor Frances Perkins ''that he would be happy if she could discover that Boake Carter . . . was not entitled to be in this country. It appears that an investigation of his record is being made.''[65]

On January 31, Moffat noted with ''amusement'' that the newscaster had termed him a ''member of the Anglophile group who is 'trying to educate the country to war.' '' The same day, members of the Committee for Concerted Peace Efforts wrote to Philco protesting Carter's ''distortion of facts [and] his aspersions on the Secretary of State.''[66] But the news analyst knew that Philco would soon have no control over him. He continued his tirades. As of February 8, 1938, he had apparently devoted every broadcast for three solid weeks to assailing the President and the Department of State.[67]

The commentator began selling Huskies, a breakfast cereal manufactured by General Foods, on February 28. He found a new area of attack in the Naval Expansion Bill of 1938. In Congress, Representative Noah M. Mason of Illinois, himself a naturalized citizen, told members that three government departments were investigating Carter. The congressman added that he himself had "dared to express doubt about the proposed Navy expansion program." He feared for free speech in America.[68] On March 14 Martin L. Sweeney, "a professional Irishman from Cleveland, Ohio," another long time opponent of Roosevelt's, introduced legislation concerning the newscaster. House Resolution 436 told of an alleged secret meeting recently held in New York City. Norman H. Davis, among others, had attended. The participants supposedly plotted to force Carter off the air and prepare the country for war. H.R. 436, which demanded exhaustive study of these matters, was quickly buried in the Committee on Rules.[69]

If investigations of Carter's entrance into the United States did not bring any results, something else did. On April 7, 1938, a reviewer noted that the news analyst had praised Cordell Hull and Roosevelt for their Latin American policy and their efforts to keep the United States out of war. Broadcasts on May 24 and 25 in large part are so pallid as seemingly to come from another person. He discussed whether night baseball actually would prove profitable. He spend much of his time describing the death of an old friend, a seeing-eye dog. The next day listeners learned about an honest carpenter in Rochester, New York, an airplane crash in Ohio, a new regulation for small boat owners in the New York City area, and some other trivia. On June 30 he discussed America's consumption of Australian wool and baseball for the blind. Someone had finally brought pressure to bear on the news analyst.[70]

One person was Frank C. Page, of the International Telephone and Telegraph Corporation. On March 18, 1938, he wrote a careful letter to Colby M. Chester of General Foods:

> Boake Carter's criticisms and unwarranted attacks on the State Department are utterly unfair and based entirely on what he picks up in gossip and in the papers. He has not contacted the State Department nor does he know the underlying facts of many of the things he talks about. I sincerely regret that General Foods is willing to sponsor irresponsible comments on this particular subject.[71]

On March 21, Page informed Cordell Hull of what he had been doing:

> Last time I saw you, you expressed considerable concern over the remarks of one of the commentators over the air. . . . I then talked to

some of my good friends in Columbia Broadcasting and they informed
me that under his new contract Carter was going to stop his commentaries on situations and merely pass out the news. It seems that this
assurance on the part of the Columbia Broadcasting [sic] was not
correct although I think it was made in good faith on their part. I talked
to them this morning and they assure me that now they have it straigh-
tened out and the comments will only contain news.[72]

Page had already sent a copy of his March 18 letter to Joseph Davies. As
soon as the ambassador received it, he wired Hull. "I cannot adequately
tell you," he added in the accompanying letter, "how shocked, grieved,
and chagrined I was by this news. I was mad clean through."[73] He
explained that because his wife had only a minority control in General
Foods, they had not been able to alter the company's decision to hire
Carter in the first place.

The same day, he also replied by telegram and letter to Frank Page.
The letter began:

What you tell me is the worst news I have had in many a day. It has
really distressed me beyond measure, for you know I have the greatest
admiration and respect for Cordell Hull. Apart from that, I am pulling
foot, horse and dragoon [sic] for what he is trying to do.

Davis continued: "I am going to find out what happened. It is a direct
breach of faith somewhere along the line."[74]

From April 1, Carter did not dare to attack the State Department on the
air. In his daily newspaper column, however, he now accused the
administration of destroying radio commentators' freedom of speech. As
Moffat had remarked, "Whatever one may think of him he's a clever
one." This time the administration was not without its guile. James
Roosevelt solemnly told members of the press that the White House, far
from attempting to throttle the newscaster, "had used its influence to
keep Carter's radio chain and sponsor from bearing down on him lest
Carter become a martyr."[75] In a private letter, Roosevelt happily returned
to his earlier attitude toward the commentator: "The President of the
United States cannot engage in a radio debate with the Boake Carters and
Father Coughlins of life!"[76]

There are two unresolved problems in connection with what happened to the newscaster in April 1938. First is the general question of freedom of speech, which the broadcaster talked about for months after in lectures all over the United States. Even in the absence of transcripts of Carter's commentaries, available information indicates that the news analyst relied almost entirely on innuendo, invective, distortion, and misinformation in his attacks. Does a newscaster have the right deliberately to misinform his audience? And who is to decide if someone is guilty of such an offense? Such are the fundamental concerns of censorship. It seems clear that Carter became irrationally extreme by January 1938. He moved so far beyond what is considered journalism's code of ethics concerning the truth that he deserved to be bridled. But his example made others afraid to criticize the administration. By 1941 all of the important radio commentators openly favored Roosevelt's foreign policy. Some, such as Raymond Gram Swing, went so far as to accept unquestioningly every word that the President said was true. Unfortunately, the Chief Executive did not enjoy a reputation for complete candor. Radio commentators stopped fulfilling their functions as independent critics.

The second consideration concerns CBS. Why did a network allegedly friendly to the New Deal seem so reluctant to censor Carter's comments? After all, the president of CBS himself owned stock in the Philadelphia station where the news analyst originated his broadcasts. What finally persuaded network officials to do what they could have done anytime after 1935 with some justice—order the newscaster to restrict himself to what had some likelihood of being true? The answer quite possibly has a great deal to do with money. Carter made enormous profits for the network in its leaner early days. CBS knew that the broadcaster's popularity stemmed from his being controversial. The commentator's personal manager was the brother-in-law of William S. Paley. This put him in an excellent position to protect his investment. In fact, Carter may have felt invulnerable because of his connections. Thus the company, fearful of government regulation by the FCC, and eager to cooperate with Roosevelt, still allowed the newscaster to remain on the air. Certainly CBS would not have banned the broadcaster from its network forever in August 1938 unless most persuasive pressure had been brought to bear. It seems clear that only Carter's irrational and unfounded attacks on the administration provided sufficient reason for the efforts of Joseph Davies, Frank Page, and others to be effective.

"A MOTH-EATEN, MOSS-COVERED WHIPPING POST"

After Carter left CBS, he had but six years to live. He did not disappear, though he was not heard in Chicago again before 1941. When he returned to the air in September 1939, a few small firms such as the First National Bank of Kalamazoo, Michigan, or the Gander Motor Company in Des Moines, Iowa, sponsored him. Carter tried sending recorded transcriptions to MBS affiliates. Each station could listen to the analyses before broadcasting them. Listeners complained of stale news.[77]

Other advertisers and schemes followed. For a few weeks, beginning in October 1940, United Airlines sponsored the commentator over a national network. In New York during May 1941, Carter appeared Monday, Wednesday, and Friday at 8:30 P.M. From September to December 1941, he spoke only on Monday. In March 1940 Carter broadcast on Saturday at 7:30 P.M. in Washington , D.C. A year later he appeared Tuesday and Thursday at the same hour. By June 1941 he was heard Monday and Wednesday at 7:30 P.M.; he presented a different program on Tuesday and Thursday at 6:30 P.M. In November 1941 he was down to twice a week at 7:30 P.M. This dizzying succession of programs, times, and days emphasizes the vast difference between the enormous CBS audience the newscaster reached five nights a week at an excellent hour in 1938, and the sporadic Mutual coverage of 1939-1941.[78]

Carter now reached most of his audience through his daily newspaper column. Many pieces were filled with hatred of the New Deal, although quite often they contained philosophical advice about such matters as America's youth, or business, or topics of equivalent immediacy. A bit of the old Carter returned to combat census enumerators in a bizarre episode during 1940. The columnist believed these persons to be subversive agents of a giant Roosevelt conspiracy, as did the congressman who had the exposé read into the *Congressional Record.* "The administration of Franklin D. Roosevelt," Carter insisted,

> replete with its staggering army of "snoops and peeps," its philosophy of materialism and its chicanery and double-dealing, which seeks to pry into the most intimate matters of every citizen's private life, is the factor which has created most of the public nausea.[79]

In the next few months even more of the old Carter form revealed itself. There were frequent diatribes against Roosevelt's attempt to gain his party's nomination for a third term. On July 19 Carter produced possibly the most bitter column of his career. He began by quoting Senator Alban Barkley's pious declaration that " 'we know, too, that in no way whatsoever has he [Roosevelt] exerted any influence in the selection of the delegates, or upon the opinion of the delegates to this convention.' " Carter went to work:

> "The voice is Jacob's voice, but the hands are the hands of Eassau.". . . It was all a matter of spontaneous combustion. The "smoke-filled rooms" of Hopkins and those "servants of the people," Mayors Kelly of Chicago, and Hague, of Jersey City. . . . As Mr. Roosevelt's field major, Harry Hopkins, once observed: "The public is too damn dumb to understand." . . . That they have debauched national morals and morale by bribery, mouthing the meanwhile that it is for "the ill-fed, ill-housed, and ill-clad" [sic]; that they can now do no more than hark back to 1932, and invoke the threadbare, moth-eaten, moss-covered whipping post of Hoover as their 1940 justification to be allowed to continue to bury their miserable snouts in the public trough. . . .[80]

After these encomiums, few would have predicted Carter's actions a few months later. Following Roosevelt's victory in November, the commentator told radio listeners he had telephoned the White House to offer congratulations and support. In a telegram to "Dear Boss," the news analyst added: "Since yesterday's decision puts you again at the tiller, I'm ready to fall to and help trim sheets when you shout: 'stand by.' " On the air, Carter quoted the President's secretary as "expressing amazement."[81]

Shortly after, a brewing company wrote Steve Early concerning the advisability of sponsoring the broadcaster, "who might be construed as having opinions not in sympathy with the administration's policy." The firm was told that the White House "would not express an opinion one way or another."[82] Piel Brothers decided that they had better not take the chance.

Others took the same attitude. The agency handling another commentator's sponsor's account wrote that H. V. Kaltenborn's antilabor broadcasts could result in a situation that might "grow to dangerous proportions as it did in the case of Boake Carter."[83] The president of the

Pure Oil Company believed that something besides attacks on the CIO explained why Carter had lost his sponsor: "Their [Kaltenborn's analyses'] influence was tremendously increased because Mr. Kaltenborn had in the past avoided the pitfalls of partisanship in a way which Boake Carter, for example, did not."[84] Only a few members of Congress, such as West Virginia's reactionary Senator Rush D. Holt, continued to claim that the British had forced the broadcaster off the air.[85]

By 1941 a new element crept into Carter's newspaper columns. On May 5 he told readers that "the war had helped to clarify much in a mind that was disordered a great deal by material things and personal suffering." Six days later, the journalist reported that he had been reading the Bible intensely, particularly "Ezekiel, Daniel and St. Paul's revelations," and had "applied the simple rules of the science of nature to each day's news."[86] Increasingly, religious comments filled his column.

On the air, at least after Pearl Harbor, Carter generally supported the war effort. On March 24, 1942, he devoted much of his newscast to the need for war bonds. "Give thanks that this is the United States and not Germany" was a typical remark. Another broadcast told of the President's need for an adjective to describe a war "for the preservation of the democracies and for the small people of the world."[87] Carter had become a patriotic booster.

In 1942, papers such as the *New York Journal American* carried a headline story, Carter's "Why I Embraced Biblical Hebrewism." He had become a mystic. Divorcing one wife, he married a second and "instituted a biblically kosher kitchen." The commentator now believed that citizens of Britain and America had descended from the ten lost tribes of Israel.[88] He claimed that Moses Guibbory, a religious zealot living in Jerusalem, had made the first correct translation of the Bible. Carter wrote to Roosevelt in March 1943, trying to interest him in his new project. That year, the first volume of *The Bible in the Hands of Its Creators,* nearly two thousand pages long, was published at five dollars a copy. The book was essentially an interpretation of the Old Testament, with Hebrew and English in parallel columns. Its mystical language made it difficult to know which passage was being reinterpreted.[89]

The news analyst continued to broadcast at noon a couple of times a week for Chef Boy-Ar-Dee in 1944. He died of a heart attack in Hollywood, California, on November 16, 1944. He had just turned forty-two.[90] Few national leaders mourned his passing. An exception was Herbert Hoover. He wired his condolences to Carter's first wife: "I was greatly shocked to learn of your husband's passing. America lost an independent and courageous mind. I lose a good friend. But your loss is far greater, and I want you to know of my deep sympathy."[91]

Carter's behavior during his last years suggests that he labored under severe mental strain from late 1940 until his death. His actions, as described by his friend David Horowitz, sound highly irrational. Carter's sister hinted of some such difficulty in a letter she wrote Hoover in December 1944: "For my own self I do not grieve. Because Boake has now found the answers to the problems that were worrying him on this earth." She added that others besides a former President of the United States mourned Carter's death:

> Yes, indeed, it is a loss to the whole country. The good folks here have written me letters from practically every state in the Union. And I feel very humble and proud when I realize how integral a part Boake was in the daily thinking lives of so many Americans. How much they relied on him to set them straight when so many people were saying first one thing and then another.[92]

In one sense Sheelah Carter was right. For many Americans, her brother simplified thinking about current events, particularly foreign affairs. Boake Carter's attitude is best described by the titles of two of his books, *Why Meddle in the Orient?* and *Why Meddle in Europe?* The former he admitted to "tearing out in four weeks"; the latter probably took about as long.[93] In his broadcasts and writings Carter repeated incessantly that any American action overseas represented not involvement but meddling. There were problems enough at home, he claimed. The United States must not join the world-savers' brigade or serve as errand boy for the London Foreign Office. Before September 1938, when most Americans felt little interest in what took place in the rest of the world, Carter seemed to show why such an attitude was logical.

Carter's approach to broadcasting depended on aggressive opposition to whatever public officials hoped to accomplish. After September 1939, millions of Americans became concerned about the implication of German and Japanese actions for the United States. Carter found it difficult to make any sort of adjustment. He knew that overseas events did not concern America; his mind lacked the ability to distinguish between conditions before and after World War II began. Instead he transferred unchanged to another medium the flashy superficial techniques of the syndicated newspaper columnist. Those radio commentators who came to prominence after Carter, with the exception of Fulton Lewis, Jr., believed that talking of foreign affairs demanded a less unthinking approach.

In appraising Carter's contribution to American foreign policy-making in the 1930s, it is important to understand the effectiveness of his tirades against involvement in the rest of the world. He discouraged greater involvement in the problems of the rest of the world on the part of the State Department, and he strengthened the mood of isolationism so popular in America through 1938. Carter alone, of all the newscasters broadcasting in the 1930s, was forced off the air for his isolationist views. Perhaps such action was extreme; surviving broadcasts suggest otherwise. Carter served as a major voice of American isolationism—the extreme, convenient kind of isolationism that insisted that the rest of the world was of no concern to America. Carter's approach never allowed for such basic distinctions as whether this country would have to abandon foreign trade to keep its isolationism intact. War in China, Ethiopia, Spain, the occupation of the Rhineland, the annexation of Austria—in each case Carter insisted that America had no stake in the outcome.

Only the fact that Carter spoke over radio and that his broadcasts disappeared from public notice explains why he has been so ignored in assessing the continuing strength of American isolationism. His popularity with the average person, his high rating in public opinion polls, his syndicated newspaper column, his many books, his national coverage over the second largest radio network at a good hour—all suggest how much the popularity of isolationism owes to Carter, who made it seem sensible. It does not matter that what he said deserves little sustained analysis. Carter sounded omniscient; he persuaded literally millions of listeners. He was so successful that the administration finally took action to get rid of so powerful an opponent. Carter's example served as a warning to those who followed. By the time that Swing and Davis were promoting interventionism, Carter was heard at unpopular times in just a few cities. In radio the hour and number of stations taking a program determines impact. Denied both, Carter's influence dwindled to nothing.

The student of Harold Thomas Henry Carter's life is left with a curious feeling. Here is a man whose origins are so concealed that his whereabouts before 1924 are hard to discover. Enormously popular for a few years, he was forgotten even before his early death in 1944.[94] Copies of broadcasts heard nightly by millions of listeners can now be found only in obscure places. Unlike Ozymandias, there is not even a pedestal warning the mighty to despair of Boake Carter's works.

Carter also made the controversial, opinionated news broadcast a phenomenon of the decade. Commentators like Swing, Davis, and Murrow may not have paid much attention to what Carter said, but the ready acceptance they found as news commentators depended in no small measure on public acceptance of independent radio news analysis, something pioneered by Carter. He, along with his competitor Lowell Thomas, established the commercial possibilities of news commentary before anyone else. This pioneering quality should not be overlooked no matter how much criticism Carter deserves for his unprincipled tirades against whatever the New Deal proposed to do at home and abroad.

NOTES

1. *Newsweek,* July 18, 1936, p. 26.
2. Harold L. Ickes, "Mail-Order Government," *Collier's,* February 18, 1939, p. 15; Ickes, *America's House of Lords: An Inquiry Into the Freedom of the Press* (New York, 1939), p. 114.
3. Paul Y. Anderson, quoted in *Time,* October 28, 1940, p. 47.
4. A.J. Liebling, "Boake Carter," *Scribner's Magazine* 104 (August 1938): 9.
5. Quoted in Boake Carter, *"Johnny Q. Public" Speaks!* (New York, 1936), p. 158.
6. Quoted in *Time,* October 28, 1940, p. 47.
7. Memorandum for James Roosevelt n.d. [December 15, 1937], Official File 2103, FDRL [hereafter OF, FDRL].
8. Telegram, Cordell Hull to American embassy, London, January 26, 1938, 811.108 Carter, Boake/1; telegram, Herschel V. Johnson, London, to Secretary of State, January 29, 1938, 811.108 Carter, Boake/2, both in Record Group 59, Department of State Files, National Archives, Washington, D.C. [hereafter RG 59]. Before 1917, Russia used a different calendar from Western Europe, hence the two September dates.

9. Maxine Block, ed., *Current Biography 1942* (New York, 1942), p. 138; *Who's Who in America 1936-37*, copy in OF 2103, FDRL. "Records of Leading Personalities in the United States," p. 10, an annual compilation of biographical sketches prepared by the British embassy in Washington for the Foreign Office, states merely that Carter "served for the Royal Air Force in 1918." See copy, Sir Ronald Lindsay, ambassador, to Foreign Office, August 4, 1939, A5562/5143/45, Correspondence of the Foreign Office, Public Record Office, London [hereafter FO].

10. M. M. McCrum, Headmaster, Tonbridge School, Tonbridge, Kent, England, to author, March 20, 1970.

11. R. F. Harrison, Registrar, University of Cambridge, Cambridge, England, to author, March 24, 1970.

12. James L. Houghteling, Commissioner, to Congresswoman Virginia E. Jenckes, December 31, 1937, *Congressional Record*, 75th Cong., 3rd Session, Appendix 1006 (March 14, 1938); Carter, "Whither America?", address before Washington Forum, January 25, 1938, in *Congressional Record*, 75th Cong., 3rd Session, Appendix 371. Carter became an American citizen on November 28, 1934.

13. This information has been pieced together from a variety of sources including Liebling, "Boake Carter," p. 9; Block, *Current Biography 1942*, p. 139; *Newsweek*, July 21, 1934, pp. 20-21; *Literary Digest*, April 17, 1937, pp. 29-30; dust jacket, Carter, *This is the Life* (New York, 1937); dust jacket, Carter, *"Johnny Q. Public,"* both in a collection of Franklin D. Roosevelt material assembled by Hunt L. Unger in the Northwestern University Library, Evanston, Ill.; *New York Times*, January 16, 1936, p. 18. The commentator was extremely sensitive about his stature. He claimed to be five feet six inches tall, but refused to allow any full-length publicity photographs to be used.

14. Liebling, "Boake Carter," p. 10.

15. *Ibid.*, pp. 9-10.

16. Mrs. Emily D. Stephens, Valley Forge, Penna., to Hoover, November 9, 1931, "Carter, B." folder, PSF 372, HHL.

17. Block, *Current Biography 1942*, p. 138; CBS Talent File (old) for Carter, CBS Program Information; *Literary Digest*, April 17, 1937, p. 30; folder 1, Station WCAU, Station Files, Federal Communications Commission, Washington National Records Center, Suitland, Maryland; John O. Downey, general manager, WCAU, to author, September 5, 1969.

18. Memorandum, James W. Baldwin, secretary of Federal Radio Commission, May 19, 1932; G. E. Sterling, Acting United States Supervisor of Radio, to Director of Radio Division, Department of Commerce, May 21, 1932; both in Box 438, Station WCAU, FCC Radio Division, Record Group 173, National Archives, Washington, D.C.

19. CBS Talent File (old), Carter, card 16, CBS Program Information; Virgil

H. Frazier, Air Defense League, Philadelphia, to Marguerite Le Hand, November 21, 1934, OF 95-E, FDRL; Carter's column, the *Boston Globe,* June 8, 1941, p. 20; June 16, 1941, p. 13.

20. Carter, "Battle of the Airlines," *The Commentator* 3 (February 1938): 87; CBS broadcast, October 27, 1936, Box 186, RG 122. These Ediphone transcriptions contain numerous errors in orthography and grammar.

21. CBS broadcast, May 7, 1936, Box 193, RG 122.

22. Harry C. Butcher, CBS vice-president, to Early, November 9, 1935, OF 2103, FDRL.

23. Hull to Carter, December 30, 1935, 611.563/339B, RG 59.

24. *Congressional Record,* 74th Cong., 2d Session, 6173 (April 27, 1936).

25. Recorded transcription of interview with Farley, February 14, 1936, Reel 9B, James A. Farley Collection, RSS-LC; Edward L. Bernays, *Biography of an Idea: Memoirs of Public Relations Counsel Edward L. Bernays* (New York, 1965), devotes Chapter 46, pp. 571-80, to his work with Carter and Philco; interview with Payne, February 15, 1936, printed in *Congressional Record,* 74th Cong., 2d Session, Appendix 2454; background information in Frank Russell, NBC vice-president, to Lenox Lohr, February 14, 1936, unmarked folder, NBC Box IV-A, Lohr MSS; for an acrimonious exchange between CBS and the Republican National Committee just before Carter began his series, see CBS, *Political Broadcasts: A Series of Letters Exchanged Between the Columbia Broadcasting System, Inc. and the Republican National Committee* (New York, January, 1936), n. pg., copy in Harry C. Butcher to Laurence Richey, January 23, 1936, "CBS Correspondence (10)" folder, Post-Presidential Subject File 67, HHL.

26. CBS broadcast, May 15, 1936, Box 189, RG 122.

27. "I recall that to trade up radio, which appealed to basically the lower socio-economic groups at the time, we made the suggestion that ambassadors appear on the radio. This was startling at the time." Bernays to author, January 14, 1974.

28. CBS broadcast, May 18, 1936, copy in Laurence Duggan to Sumner Welles, June 15, 1936, 032/Philco/18, RG 59; CBS broadcast, May 15, 1936, Box 189, RG 122; Bernays, *Biography of an Idea,* pp. 576-77.

29. Duggan to Welles, June 15, 1936, RG 59.

30. [Editors of *Fortune,*] "Philco," *Fortune* 40 (February 1935): 74 ff.; *Variety,* June 24, 1936, p. 54; Ruth Brindze, *Not to be Broadcast* (New York, 1937), pp. 112-13; [Editors of *Fortune,*] "The Radio Industry," *Fortune* 17 (May 1938): 120.

31. Documents concerning the Simpson case may be found in *Foreign Relations of the United States: Diplomatic Papers, 1936,* 2: 291-92, 293 [hereafter *FR: 1936*].

32. Hull to chargé in Germany (Mayer), July 29, 1936; Hull to Raymond H.

Geist, consul at Berlin, August 31, 1936, both in *FR: 1936,* 2: 295, 296-97.

33. CBS Broadcast, September 6, 9, 10, 1936, Box 203, RG 122.

34. CBS broadcast, September 18, 1936, Box 200, RG 122.

35. CBS broadcast, September 21, 22, 1936, Box 200, 201, RG 122.

36. Hull to Dodd, September 28, 1936; Dodd to Hull, December 1, 1936, in *FR: 1936,* 2: 301.

37. CBS broadcast, September 28, 1936, Box 199, RG 122.

38. Grant-Smith to Carter, September 30, 1936, Box 39, Correspondence II, Cordell Hull MSS, Manuscript Division, Library of Congress, Washington, D.C. [hereafter Hull MSS].

39. Carr to "G-S," October 8, 1936, Box 13, Wilbur J. Carr MSS, Manuscript Division, Library of Congress, Washington, D.C. Carr's Diary contains no references to either Carter or Simpson during this period.

40. Hull to Grant-Smith, October 3, 1936, Box 39, Correspondence II, Hull MSS.

41. CBS broadcast, October 21, 1936, Box 197, RG 122. The broadcaster seems to have had a special affinity for Nicaragua, possibly because of time spent there betwen 1921 and 1924.

42. Liebling, "Boake Carter," p. 10; based on five recordings of Carter's broadcasts in NBC warehouse, 136 W. 52d St., New York, N.Y. [hereafter NBC warehouse].

43. 78 rpm original transcription, CBS broadcast, June 18, 1936, Records 1543-4, Box 36-1; 78 rpm original transcription, CBS broadcast, June 19, 1936, Records 1541-2, Box 36-1, both in NBC warehouse.

44. 33 1/3 rpm original transcription, CBS broadcast, June 22, 1936, Record 2813, Box T36-19, NBC warehouse; CBS broadcast, May 28, 1936, Box 191, RG 122; column, the *Boston Daily Globe,* January 4, 1940, p. 15; MBS broadcast, June 26, 1942, "Radio News Comment on the Rubber Shortage," June 30, 1942, Box 1846, Records of the Office of Government Reports, Record Group 44, WNRC-Suitland [hereafter RG 44].

45. CBS broadcast, June 23, 1936, Box 188, RG 122; 78 rpm original transcription, CBS broadcast, June 18, 1936, NBC warehouse; CBS broadcast, October 22, 1936, Box 184, RG 122; MBS broadcast, March 5, 1942, "Daily Radio Digest No. 50," Box 1848, RG 44.

46. CBS broadcast, November 4, 1936, Box 184, RG 122; column, the *Boston Daily Globe,* July 8, 1940, p. 11.

47. CBS broadcast, March 11, 1938, in A. Craig Baird, ed., *Representative American Speeches: 1937-1938, The Reference Shelf* 10, No. 11 (New York, 1938): 98-99.

48. *Ibid.,* pp. 99-100.

49. CBS broadcast, November 18, 1936, RG 122.

50. CBS broadcast, October 20, 1936; see also October 23, 1936, both in Box 195, RG 122; and June 30, 1938, copy in Carter to Herbert Hoover, July 28, 1938, "Boake Carter" folder 339 (1), PPI, HHL.

51. CBS broadcast, November 13, 1936, Box 183, RG 122; 33 1/3 rpm original transcription, CBS broadcast, May 24, 1938, Record 5832, Box E-38-2, NBC warehouse.

52. Harrison B. Summers, compiler, *A Thirty-Year History of Programs Carried on National Radio Networks in the United States 1926-1956* (Columbus, Ohio, 1958), pp. 40, 46, 54, 62; CAB Crossley rating, February 25, 1936, July 28, 1936, 4-Q, BP-1969; "Boake Carter" folder, CBS Program Information; CBS Talent File (new) and (old), Carter, CBS Program Information; Paul Lazarsfeld, *Radio and the Printed Page: An Introduction to the Study of Radio and Its Role in the Communication of Ideas* (New York, 1940), p. 187 89.

53. Edgar Grunwald, ed., *Variety Radio Directory 1939-40* (New York, 1939), p. 3: 442; Hadley Cantril and Mildred Strunk, *Public Opinion, 1935-1946* (Princeton, N.J.: 1951), p. 514 (The commentator was more popular than Walter Lippmann or Westbrook Pegler); "Gallup and Fortune Polls," *Public Opinion Quarterly* 4 (June 1940): 351.

54. Richard Sheridan Ames [Boake Carter] "News on the Air," *Saturday Evening Post,* January 23, 1937, p. 38. Internal evidence indicates that Carter must be the author.

55. *Variety,* February 2, 1938, p. 35; Paul M. Lewis to Roosevelt, October 19, 1937, President's Personal File 1794, FDRL [hereafter PPF]; CBS Talent File (new), Carter, program card no. 1421, CBS Program Information. Philco's sponsorship had begun in January 1933.

56. Davies, in Moscow, to Hull, March 28, 1938, Box 42, Correspondence II, Hull MSS.

57. Albert Stanhope Brown to Philco Radio, July 15, 1937; cf., Rev. W. R. Robinson, House of Representatives, State of Washington, to Philco Radio, July 14, 1937; unsigned telegram, Los Angeles, Cal., to White House, n.d. (filed July 19, 1937), both in OF 2103, FDRL.

58. Notation of telephone call, Carter to White House, September 11, 1937; McIntyre to Carter, September 14, 1937, OF 2103, FDRL; Roosevelt to Rhoda Hinkley, December 16, 1937, Elliott Roosevelt and Joseph P. Lash, eds., *F.D.R.: His Personal Letters, 1928-1945,* 2 vols. (New York, 1949), 1: 733-34 [hereafter *Personal Letters*].

59. Memorandum, Messersmith to J. E. Saugstad, Division of Trade Agreements, November 12, 1937, 800.8830/607, RG 59.

60. Report from the Commissioner to Jenckes, *Congressional Record,* 75th Cong., 3d Session, Appendix 1005-09 (March 14, 1938).

61. Carter to White House, n.d. (filed January 18, 1938), OF 2103, FDRL.

62. Handwritten note, Pierrepont Moffat to Sumner Welles, n.d. [January 26, 1937], 811.108 Carter, Boake/1; Herschel V. Johnson to Secretary of State, February 2, 1938, 811.108 Carter, Boake/4, both in RG 59.

63. Carter, "Should the U.S. Establish an Alliance with Great Britain?," *The Congressional Digest* 17 (August-September 1938): 223.

64. Jay Pierrepont Moffat Diary, January 26, 1938, Houghton Library, Harvard University, Cambridge, Mass. [hereafter Moffat Diary].

65. Harold L. Ickes, *The Secret Diary of Harold L. Ickes,* 3 vols. (New York, 1953-1954), 3: 313 [hereafter *Secret Diary*].

66. Moffat Diary, January 31, 1938; members of committee to Philco, January 31, 1938, copy to Department of State, 711.00/787, RG 59.

67. Ickes, *Secret Diary,* 2: 430; Dr. William G. Hanrahan, Springfield, N.J., to L. E. Brubb, president, Philco Radio, February 8, 1938, copy in OF 2103, FDRL.

68. *Congressional Record,* 75th Cong., 3d Session, 3120 (March 9, 1938); *Variety,* March 2, 1938, p. 28.

69. *Congressional Record,* 75th Cong., 3d Session, 3320; a copy of the original resolution may be found in 811.108, Carter, Boake/6, RG 59.

70. *Variety,* April 13, 1938, p. 30; 33 1/3 rpm original transcription, CBS broadcast, May 24, 1938; 33 1/3 rpm original transcription, CBS broadcast, May 25, 1938, Record 5833, Box E-38-2, both in NBC warehouse; CBS broadcast, June 30, 1938, "Boake Carter" folder 339 (1), PPI 24, HHL.

71. Page to Chester, March 18, 1938, Box 42, Correspondence II, Hull MSS.

72. Page to Hull, March 28, 1938, Box 42, Correspondence II, Hull MSS.

73. Davies to Hull, March 28, 1938, Box 42, Correspondence II, Hull MSS.

74. Davies to Page, March 28, 1938, Box 42, Correspondence II, Hull MSS. There is nothing concerning Carter in the Joseph E. Davies MSS, Manuscript Division, Library of Congress, Washington, D.C.

75. *Time,* April 25, 1938, p. 11. Carter's columns may be found in the *Boston Daily Globe,* March 1-December 15, 1938; see also Stanley High, "Not-So-Free-Air," *Saturday Evening Post,* February 11, 1938, p. 76; *Variety,* September 21, 1938, p. 27.

76. Roosevelt to Arthur B. Sherman, April 6, 1938, *Personal Letters,* 2: 74.

77. Based on daily radio schedules in the *Chicago Tribune,* 1939-1941; *Variety,* September 13, 1939, p. 19; December 20, 1939, p. 24.

78. Based on daily radio schedules in the *New York Times* and the *Washington Evening Star,* 1939-1941; *Variety,* October 30, 1940, p. 40; November 12, 1941, p. 56. In 1944, the last year of Carter's life, he advertised Chef Boy-Ar-Dee products. His rating was 2.3. Summers, *A Thirty-Year History,* pp. 106, 112, 122 (cited above, note 52); Hooperatings quoted in Burke Herrick to H. V. Kaltenborn, December 11, 1942, Box 150, Kaltenborn MSS; program times in "Daily Radio Digest No. 46," March 30, 1942, Box 1848, RG 44.

79. Column in *Philadelphia Public Ledger,* March 11, 1940, in *Congressional Record,* 76th Cong., 3d Session, Appendix 1446.

80. Column in *Philadelphia Public Ledger,* July 20, 1940, copy in OF 2103, FDRL; same column in *Boston Daily Globe,* July 19, 1940, p. 19.

81. *Variety,* November 13, 1940, p. 38; Carter to "Dear Boss," November 9, 1940, OF 2103, FDRL.

82. Bruce Berckmans, general sales manager, Piel Brothers, to Early, January 30, 1941; file memorandum reporting White House response to telephone call, Berckmans to White House, January 31, 1941, both in OF 2103, FDRL.

83. F.H. Marling, advertising manager, Pure Oil Company, to Kaltenborn, March 21, 1942, Box 150, Kaltenborn MSS.

84. Henry M. Dawes to Marling, March 24, 1942, Box 150, Kaltenborn MSS.

85. *Congressional Record,* 76th Cong., 3d Session, 10732 (August 22, 1940).

86. Column, *Boston Daily Globe,* May 11, 1941, p. 22.

87. MBS broadcast, March 24, 1942, "Daily Radio Digest No. 67"; "Daily Radio Digest No. 50"; MBS broadcast, March 13, 1942, "Daily Radio Digest No. 57"—all in Box 1848, RG 44. There is important corroboration of details in OF 2103, FDRL, and "Boake Carter" folder 339 (2), PPI 24, HHL.

88. Copy of *Journal American,* August 23, 1942, in OF 2103, FDRL; *Variety,* June 20, 1940, p. 29; column, *Boston Daily Globe,* June 13, 1941, p. 6; David Horowitz, *Thirty-three Candles* (New York, 1949), pp. 287-300, 320-36, 369.

89. Form letter, Carter to Roosevelt, March 4 and March 7, 1943, OF 2103, FDRL; Moses Guibbory, *The Bible in the Hands of Its Creators: Biblical Facts as They Are* (New York, 1943), volume I, copy in Library of Congress, Washington, D.C. Guibbory refers to "Harold of the house of Israel" in the preface, p. xiii; *Newsweek,* August 24, 1942, p. 66.

90. Horowitz, *Thirty-three Candles,* pp. 444-84, 502.

91. Telegram, Hoover to Mrs. Boake Carter, Hollywood, California, November 17, 1944, "Boake Carter" folder 339 (2), PPI 24, HHL.

92. Sheelah Carter to Hoover, December 11, 1944, "Boake Carter" folder 339 (2), PPI 24, HHL.

93. Carter and Thomas H. Healy (New York, 1938); (New York, 1939); memorandum of telephone conversation, Carter with Laurence Richey, February 11, 1938, "Boake Carter" folder 339 (1), PPI 24, HHL.

94. Edward L. Bernays, who worked closely with Carter in 1936, put it this way in a letter to the author, January 7, 1974: "As I look back on Carter today, I would say that he suffered in his later years from overcompensatory inferiority. Here was an unknown character with an appealing voice and decided viewpoints, who all of a sudden as a result of the new instrumentality of radio found himself

with a huge audience that was enthralled by his staccato voice and point of view. He received so many letters that they had to be handled by a mailing bureau operation we set up. Naturally this adulation and godhead symbolism went to his head. And he suffered the consequences."

3 | H. V. Kaltenborn: The Gentle Art of Self-Publicity

"You fancy yourself a conversationalist and a raconteur. In reality you are a windbag and a bore." Although the *New Yorker* cartoon's caption did not refer to Hans von Kaltenborn, it might have. Kaltenborn lived for appearances, ever hopeful of impressing others. He proved extremely adept at promoting his name. He would not have been asked to play himself in the film *Mr. Smith Goes to Washington* had he not established a public image as the typical radio news analyst by 1939.[1]

What made him famous? His broadcasts lacked the logical, carefully prepared explanations found in Raymond Gram Swing's. Unlike Elmer Davis, Kalternborn seems never to have phrased a single thought memorably. There is so little solid content in his extemporaneous newscasts that they can scarcely be considered serious commentary. But during the 1930s most people thought differently. They knew he was intelligent, a good public speaker, and an experienced news writer. He had become radio's first regular news commentator. Above all, listeners understood that Kaltenborn's round-the-clock broadcasts during the Munich crisis in September 1938 established radio as the preeminent news source for foreign affairs.

WHAT SEEMED SOCIALLY ACCEPTABLE

Baron Rudolph von Kaltenborn-Stachau had settled permanently, if grudgingly, in Milwaukee, Wisconsin, when his son Hans was born on

May 2, 1878. The father grew up in the German state of Hesse-Darmstadt. After serving with the Hessian Guards during the Austro-Prussian War of 1866, he emigrated to Wisconsin. Three years later, Rudolph von Kaltenborn-Stachau returned to fight in the Franco-Prussian War. At its conclusion he sailed for the United States.

The father enjoyed being referred to as "Baron" in the United States, though his conspicuous lack of success made the title seem bitterly ironic. In 1872 he married Betty Wessels, whom he had met on board ship. She was on her way to America to teach German. They had one daughter and then Hans. The mother died at her son's birth.[2]

The widower found employment in a drugstore. Two years later he married again. This time it was the boss's daughter, American-born Clotilda von Baumbach. It was not a happy marriage. The new in-laws owned several successful pharmacies in Milwaukee. They considered the Baron an idler. The bride nagged her husband mercilessly. His response, as one delicate biographer puts it: "He grew fond of drink," and "it took hold in earnest after his first wife's death." For a time, von Kaltenborn-Stachau worked as a Standard Oil agent. In 1891, after losing his job, he moved his family to the booming sawmill town of Merrill, Wisconsin. His father-in-law provided enough money to open a building materials store. It did not prosper.[3]

In later years the broadcaster made much of his noble ancestry, though anti-German hysteria in America during World War I caused him to shorten "Hans von" to "H. V." The Baron told his children that the Kaltenborns were no parvenus, but belonged to the *Uradel,* Germany's ancient nobility. In fact an uncle, Hans Karl Georg von Kaltenborn-Stachau, served as German Minister of War from 1890 to 1893.[4] How embarrassing it must have been for the son to know that he came from a distinguished family, to be taught that pride in one's ancestors was desirable, and then contrast it with the reality of his father's many failures.

One effect was an unsettled childhood. Kaltenborn quit school at fourteen. He appeared on stage with a juggling act. He worked in his father's store in Merrill. When the Spanish-American War began, he joined the Fourth Wisconsin Volunteer Infantry. Before leaving, the Baron's son persuaded the editor of the *Merrill Advocate* to pay him as part-time correspondent while soldiering. The war ended before Kaltenborn ever left Alabama.[5] He later inflated his few months in training camp. "As an ex-drill sergeant," he declared in 1936, "I know that it takes pretty close to a year to perfect a man."[6]

Kaltenborn worked his way to Europe on a cattle boat in 1900. After visiting England and Germany, he traveled all over France on a bicycle selling stereoscopes and slides. In his autobiography, the commentator is quick to tell about his salesmanship and his job on the cattle boat. But he says nothing of his thoughts during these years.[7]

By 1905 the reporter felt the necessity of additional formal education. Twenty-seven at the time, he had never completed high school. Kaltenborn decided that Harvard would be a prestigious place to attend college. He was accepted as a special student and did extraordinarily well. Kaltenborn graduated *cum laude* in 1909, and a member of Phi Beta Kappa. At Cambridge the future broadcaster won the Boylston Oratorical Contest and was active in various plays. Upon graduation he was hired to tutor in pleasant surroundings. Kaltenborn boarded John Jacob Astor's luxurious yacht, the *Nourmahal,* for an extended cruise. He helped his employer's son prepare for Harvard.[8]

The college years suggest one of the commentator's distinguishing characteristics. He became adept at doing what seemed socially acceptable. But his enthusiasm for study seems to have stemmed mostly from a desire to impress others with where he attended school. Kaltenborn rarely simply ate lunch—he dined at the Harvard Club. His life was filled with pretense, in which very real accomplishments were used to promote some vision of a grander personage.

On a trip back from Europe in January 1908, he met Olga von Nordenflycht, his future wife. A formal letter of introduction to the girl's mother was deemed necessary, for this was the daughter of a very proper German consul. Kaltenborn finally traveled to Rio de Janeiro before receiving the father's permission. The marriage took place in Berlin during August 1910. The proud husband frequently let it be known that his wife had an aristocratic "von" as part of her maiden name.

In January 1914 Kaltenborn, who had worked for the *Brooklyn Daily Eagle* since 1902, went to Europe to reorganize the Paris bureau. At the outbreak of war the reporter was militantly pro-German. In a speech attacking British imperialism, he staunchly defended the Kaiser. By 1917 he decided that Germany was to blame for the conflict. He became the *Eagle's* war editor.[9] In 1921 he became an associate editor and stayed with the newspaper until 1930.

"HE KNOWS EVERYTHING"

Kaltenborn's first broadcast took place in 1921. He addressed a Chamber of Commerce luncheon in Brooklyn from an experimental station in Newark, New Jersey. With his usual flair for choosing topics his audience would appreciate, he explained "the value of a Chamber of Commerce to the community." On April 4, 1922, the newscaster made his first talk concerning current events. He broadcast over Radiophone WVP, the United States Army Signal Corps's station on Bedloe's Island, in New York Harbor.[10] The primitive-sounding name of the transmitter indicates how early Kaltenborn started commenting on the air.

The *Eagle* soon decided that circulation might increase through having Kaltenborn discuss current events on the radio. By October 1923 he broadcast for thirty minutes each Tuesday evening on New York's WEAF. Soon his talks were being picked up by distant receivers. A postcard from Danville, Illinois, in 1924 suggests the attitude of his remote listeners. "Think Mr. Kaltenborn most interesting—some one [sic] said 'He knows everything.' "[11]

Another listener, Charles Evans Hughes, thought otherwise. One evening the Secretary of State entertained a distinguished group of guests at home. He turned on the radio just in time to hear Kaltenborn vigorously attack his policy toward the Soviet Union. Hughes was furious at being criticized in his own home. He considered the broadcast an invasion of his privacy. Because there were no networks at this time, the Secretary called the president of the American Telegraph and Telephone Company, which provided telephone lines to connect New York with a Washington station. Hughes demanded that under no circumstances was the newscaster to criticize cabinet officials over the firm's facilities.[12]

During the twenties, Kaltenborn ran summer group tours for occasions such as the dedication of the Grand Canyon National Park or a centennial celebration in Brazil. Members of the party paid his vacation expenses. The news analyst also visited the Soviet Union in 1926 and 1929. He interviewed Chiang Kai-shek while traveling in the Far East in the summer of 1927. For "several years" during the winter months he taught journalism at the City College of New York.[13]

In 1930, after resigning from the moribund *Eagle,* Kaltenborn became a regular commentator for the Columbia Broadcasting System. He received a salary of one hundred dollars a week. A sponsor soon offered to augment his income. For thirty minutes each week, the broadcaster described the pleasures of travel for the Cunard Travel Club. "Last Friday," he began one broadcast,

> we voyaged across the Atlantic. Tonight we make our first landing in Europe. As our great liner draws near to the Old World, our eyes, eager for a sight of land after scanning the wide ocean for six days, see a green shore rising in the distance.
> We are approaching Ireland. What memories that name evokes![14]

Cunard chose not to renew.

Then for a number of weeks S. W. Straus, a New York investment company, sponsored his newscasts. Listeners were encouraged to write for a free copy of "The Road to Wealth" until the firm itself went under in 1931. Shortly thereafter Ex-Lax tried to hire him, but Kaltenborn refused "after prayerful consideration." He could not see himself "associated with a laxative, no matter what the reward."[15]

Instead, Kaltenborn, one of very few news commentators on the major networks during these years, offered an unsponsored newscast twice a week at a variety of times. He represented CBS at the national conventions in 1932. The broadcaster went to England during the summer of 1933 to cover the ill-fated London Economic Conference. A year later he even spoke on a Mussolini Black Shirt Band Program originating from the *S. S. Roma.* He served as the news department's utility infielder.

In 1934 a reporter described the news analyst as having a very loyal, if not especially numerous, following.[16] His lowly status at CBS as late as 1935 is suggested in a letter from a Toledo radio station manager to an irate listener, who complained that the network "Ha[d] moved him all over the face of the schedule." After yet another shift, this time to an undesirable hour early Sunday afternoon, CBS was reduced to justifying the change "in response to requests from many listeners."[17]

After each broadcast an announcer customarily mentioned that the commentator "could be engaged for a personal appearance."[18] Not yet a prominent radio personality, Kaltenborn made a good living as a speaker on current events. He appeared on "America's Town Meeting of the Air." The newscaster defended democracy against Norman Thomas and Madame Olivia Rossetti Agresti, a spokesman for fascism. In a less than rousing speech, he concluded that "the great task of democracy is to train that intelligent minority for leadership."[19]

Kaltenborn's first real break in radio came during 1936. While he was on his regular summer trip, this time to Europe, the Spanish Civil War began.[20] The traveler hastened to Irun. After briefly surveying the scene, he broadcast an assessment of the two sides:

> The rebels are led and controlled by the army officers and the aristo-crats, aided by the position and discipline of the Catholic Church. . . . The government motor car . . . was smeared on all four sides with the Communist hammer and sickle emblem and the initials of the radical syndicalist and labor unions that today dominate the Madrid govern-ment.[21]

His initial impressions changed after six days: "The Popular Front is much better organized than it was a week ago. I noticed how much more efficient it was; I noticed there are fewer Hammer and Sickle signs. . . ."[22]

On September 2 Kaltenborn broadcast radio's first live battle. The commentator set up his microphone on a piece of French territory that protruded into Spain near the city of Irun. Kaltenborn stood in neutral territory during the ensuing battle, yet could see and hear the fighting. After numerous frustrating technical difficulties, he finally received permission from CBS in New York to go ahead with the broadcast. Listeners could actually hear machine gun bullets whizzing overhead and the thud of bombs in the distance.[23] The newscast, however, came at a poor hour for most Americans.

In 1938 Kaltenborn was fifty-nine, with thinning hair, rimless glasses, and a comfortable paunch. A full moustache was set on a rather square face. Invariably, he displayed his Phi Beta Kappa key prominently across his vest. He resembled somewhat the stereotyped image of a humorless old German schoolteacher. The broadcaster's proud description of his wife's attentions intensified this impression: "Well, in the morning when I wake up she runs my bath, brushes my clothes, and cooks my breakfast. Then in the evening when I come home she brings me the newspapers, my bedroom slippers—and then she fixes the fire."[24]

To offset the results of this sort of life, Kaltenborn tried to keep his waistline respectable through regular activity, especially tennis. Photo-graphs show a faded, but loyal wife and her portly husband valiantly plopping tennis balls over a new—at a suitably fashionable country club.[25]

THE MUNICH BROADCASTS

In 1938, after taking control of Austria, Hitler demanded the cession of part of Czechoslovakia. When no unified opposition among Hitler's opponents developed, British Prime Minister Neville Chamberlain offered to meet with the Nazis to appease their desire for more territory. The result was three momentous meetings during September 1938, the last held in Munich, which led to the peaceful dismemberment of Czechoslovakia. Kaltenborn's rise to national prominence—and the beginning of radio as a major source of information for foreign affairs—occurred while Chamberlain bargained Czechoslovakian independence away in return for promises of peace in Europe. Day after day Kaltenborn slept in a New York CBS studio, commenting around the clock on the development and resolution of the Munich crisis. His facility with languages enabled him to translate and evaluate immediately speeches from French and German leaders as they came over the shortwave receiver. Speaking at 6:00 A.M. or as late as midnight, the commentator made 102 broadcasts in 18 days. CBS captured the major share of listeners with its comprehensive coverage. Kaltenborn received all kinds of awards and 50,000 letters of appreciation. He became a celebrity.[26]

In the immediate aftermath virtually everyone realized that radio had contributed something new to the ancient practice of diplomacy, though few were sure exactly what had happened. Langer and Gleason assert that "in many years the American public had not been so deeply stirred by foreign affairs as by the crisis of September, 1938. Day after day, excited radio commentators had provided an hour-by-hour account of the dramatic and frightening developments."[27]

The *Nation* published an article describing the enormous public interest in radio's handling of the crisis. "For the first time history has been made in the hearing of its pawns," the author declared. He claimed that the medium had established itself "as our dominant system of news communication."[28]

In October the networks eagerly published detailed information about the amount and cost of their news coverage. Between September 10 and 29, each major network offered about 150 shortwave pickups. Together they spent $160,000. More radio sets were sold during these weeks than in any previous three-week period in industry history. For the first time,

Americans found it fascinating to listen to foreign news from early morning until late at night.[29]

Public opinion surveys confirmed intense public interest. An American Institute of Public Opinion poll released in November 1938 showed that the Munich crisis had been twice as interesting to those questioned as any other event of the year. More specifically, an investigation of radio versus newspaper as a news source revealed a dramatic change between 1937 and 1938. Seventy percent of those questioned, divided according to income, both rural and urban, declared for the first time in October 1938 that they had preferred radio as a news source during the recent European crisis.[30]

Kaltenborn himself seemed confused by what had taken place during September. A rereading of Columbia's Munich broadcasts suggests that the commentator had little understanding of the long-range implications of what was happening. Radio's coverage of the crisis undoubtedly gave immediacy to a critical event in Europe for millions of Americans. In this sense broadcasting helped greatly in creating public awareness of European affairs. But Kaltenborn's own feeling that he had offered a routine performance seems correct. Probably the ability of a single person to survive eighteen days of almost continuous broadcasting is what captured the public's imagination, not the specific things said.

Kaltenborn afterward proudly explained that "every one of these talks was entirely unprepared."[31] As a result he frequently advocated diametrically opposed courses of action. On September 17 he noted that Roosevelt and Hull were apprehensive lest an "incautious word so arouse isolationist opinion" that Hitler would be certain of strict American noninvolvement. However, the newscaster added that should hostilities break out, the United States would "show at least benevolent neutrality" toward Britain and France. Two days later Kaltenborn declared that "the United States must stand aloof from a continent that for the moment is devoted to the glorification of force."[32]

Hitler made an important address at the *Sportpalast* in Berlin on September 26. Kaltenborn, in summarizing American press opinion concerning this speech, noted substantial agreement among journalists. They expressed a personal antagonism toward *der Führer,* he felt. As to the speech itself, Kaltenborn did not find in it either "logic or a clear conclusion." He did report, however, "each time I've met Hitler, each time I've heard him, that there is an absolute sincerity there."[33]

The next day he filled in some free space with an interview. Charles R. Hodges, dean of economics at New York University, had just returned from a vacation in Central Europe. The conversation was halting at best:

KALTENBORN: And I wonder whether you could give me perhaps just a few of your impressions about Germany?
HODGES: I made a very brief visit, Mr. Kaltenborn, to what was formerly Austria.
KALTENBORN: That is particularly interesting. . . . And you don't find the old Austrian spirit of cheerfulness?
HODGES: No, it's a pretty serious life down there now.[34]

Too often, this sort of thing appeared in the many slow moments seemingly inherent in round-the-clock broadcasting. One afternoon the commentator even analyzed the Archbishop of Canterbury's prayer for peace.[35]

By the end of the Munich crisis, Kaltenborn had presented an enormous quantity of rather confused analysis and speculation. If he believed that there would be no war, his audience would have had difficulty in so knowing. Until September 30, for instance, the newscaster never discussed what the dismemberment of Czechoslovakia might mean to the long-term chances for peace.

On October 9 he did. "The full importance of the defeat suffered by France and Britain at Munich is now gradually appearing," he stated.[36] His *I Broadcast the Crisis,* containing excerpts from the September newscasts, appeared near the end of October. In a postscript, Kaltenborn cited the comment of an eighteenth-century British statesman who had also kept the peace, but at heavy cost to future security. "Today we ring the Bells. Tomorrow they will wring their hands!" Robert Walpole had declared.[37]

The public impact of radio's Munich coverage became even more apparent a few weeks later. On October 30, 1938, CBS broadcast a modernized version of H. G. Wells's *War of the Worlds.*[38] Orson Welles updated the novel by having Martian invaders land in New Jersey. Many listeners tuned in too late to hear an announcer explain carefully that what followed was a Halloween play. A comprehensive public opinion poll reported that only a tiny number of persons heard the program. Of those questioned, only about 3 percent of the sample thought it to be a genuine news program.[39] Still, some citizens actually ran frantically from their homes. Radio stations received hundreds of telephone calls from people hysterically inquiring about the Martians' landing near Princeton. The FCC found nothing amusing about these public fears, nor did the network presidents. In Washington it was agreed that no further radio programs would use a " 'news broadcast' type of presentation.'' NBC promised not to ''accept news that will create mental anguish,'' particularly at ''meal times.''[40] Even if only a few hundred people actually believed that the Martians had landed, radio networks felt that they must be more careful to control the content of their programming, apparently believing that bad news, real or otherwise, was unacceptable. Undoubtedly the Welles broadcast would have frightened some listeners had it been presented at any time. But most observers have agreed that the excessive fear it engendered is in part explained by radio's coverage of the Munich crisis.[41] The *War of the Worlds* program offers additional evidence of how deeply round-the-clock news in September penetrated the public consciousness.

KALTENBORN LOSES A SPONSOR

In the aftermath of the Munich crisis, Kaltenborn for the first time had no trouble finding sponsors. On January 1, 1939, he began a weekly news program for General Mills. He discussed the final stages of the Spanish Civil War, in particular the shortcomings of pro-Roman Catholic factions. Threats by church pressure groups in America led the cereal company to cancel Kaltenborn's contract after only thirteen weeks.

General Mills was already heavily involved in sponsoring radio shows, mostly soap operas. The firm also ventured forth with a ''Hymns of all Churches'' program, and occasional ''Betty Crocker cooking talks.''[42] The decision to hire a news commentator thus represented a considerable departure from earlier practice.

The first evening, the corporation's chairman of the board told listeners that ''General Mills has pledged itself to preserve untrammeled . . . complete freedom of selection and expression.''[43] Kaltenborn presented the news, plus some institutional puffs of his own creation on Sundays at 10:30 P.M. over a large number of stations.

On January 29 Kaltenborn discussed Spain briefly. ''The capture of

Barcelona,'' he declared, ''changes the character of the civil war in Spain. The struggle is now revealed as a part of the Fascist International's drive for power. . . . Stalin probably realized that the Spaniard was too much of an individualist to be a good Communist.''[44] This alienated a considerable number of listeners. In fact, the extreme response suggests that Kaltenborn's well-known antipathy toward Franco, and his many earlier criticisms of the Spanish church, aroused strong opposition, rather than a few remarks on Sunday evenings in January 1939.[45]

The commentator particularly antagonized Thomas A. Lahey, associate editor of *The Ave Maria,* a Catholic weekly published in Notre Dame, Indiana. Lahey, in late January, wrote to Henry A. Bellows, director of public relations at General Mills. The latter had unusual qualifications for his position. A Harvard Ph.D., he had served on the original Federal Radio Commission, and as a CBS vice-president from 1930 to 1934.[46] In a corporation that spent a great deal of money on radio advertising, he clearly enjoyed considerable authority.

On February 1 Bellows wrote Lahey that Kaltenborn had explicit instructions ''to avoid expressions of personal views on all controversial matters.'' The commentator, after receiving a copy of this letter, informed the General Mills executive that this ''clearly contradict[s] the promise of complete freedom which I received and accepted on the opening broadcast.'' A stubborn man, the news analyst again talked briefly about the Spanish Civil War the following week. He noted that the ''collapse of Spanish Loyalist resistance'' meant ''a stronger position for the two dictators Hitler and Mussolini.''[47]

The next day, February 6, Lahey prepared a detailed criticism of Kaltenborn's broadcast. Writing ''frankly and with genuine friendliness,'' the associate editor minced no words. He claimed that a ''barrage of propaganda'' had unjustly maligned Franco's position. Lahey then put aside any pretense of ''genuine friendliness'':

> I fear very much, Mr. Bellows, that you and your organization will regret it for a long time to come if, as a result of any future broadcasts, your millions of Catholic customers get the idea that General Mills is ever so faintly associated with any activity supporting the Loyalist cause and what it represents in Catholic eyes.[48]

The same day, Bellows wrote to Kaltenborn enclosing his previous reply to the editor. He mentioned having received a number of similar letters but said that Lahey's was "a lot more intelligently expressed." The complaints were "definitely having an effect on some . . . Directors," he added.[49]

On February 8 Bellows informed the *Ave Maria* spokesman that he had warned his broadcaster "frankly that our company is much disturbed by such criticism." He also wired Kaltenborn:

> In handling Spanish news this week please remember many listeners sincerely and intensely believe Franco's victory a triumph for Christianity. While suggesting no limitations on your report and analysis of the news I believe this is a case where editorial comment or indication of personal bias should be avoided.[50]

Four days later, the news analyst opened his program with a lengthy eulogy of Pope Pius XI, who had conveniently died that week. "The world loses a vigorous champion of peace and tolerance," declared the commentator. He also hoped that "for the sake of the Spanish people," a "disastrous war would soon be brought to an end."[51]

The newscaster avoided the subject of Spain during the next few weeks. In spite of this, the board of directors at General Mills decided not to renew his contract. On March 7 a telegram informed Kaltenborn that "criticism received from listeners played no part in the board decision but it was felt that in view of constantly increasing emotional strain of national political situations sponsorship by us of any news commentator involves unavoidable dangers."[52]

On March 27 the newscaster signed a one-year contract with the Pure Oil Company, to begin April 10. Shortly after, he was attacking Franco in a way he had never done under the sponsorship of General Mills. On May 16 he informed his listeners:

> A word from Spain tonight is that General Franco has decided to retain 80,000 volunteer officers in active service as the framework for a possible Spanish army of two and a half million men. That looks like the creation of an elite Fascist guard on the Nazi model. Every dictator needs a private army to maintain his power.[53]

Following such comments, letters from angry Catholics poured in during June. Kaltenborn admitted to Pure's advertising director that he disliked the Spanish church but added: "There will probably be some occasion in the near future when I can say something nice about the Catholic church and its attitude here in the United States."[54]

From the evidence presented, it appears that Kaltenborn lost his contract with General Mills principally because of Roman Catholic opposition to his broadcasts. But there were other considerations. David Clark, during his investigation of Kaltenborn's relations with General Mills, recently wrote the firm concerning the broadcaster's dismissal in 1939. A company executive, after checking the records of the board of directors, stated that he did not think that Roman Catholic opposition had anything to do with the decision. Instead a threatened boycott of Gold Medal flour by German bakers, particularly in Minnesota, where the corporation had its headquarters, was responsible.[55] Because of this response, Clark offers no speculations as to which sort of pressure group—ethnic or religious—proved more effective. But since there is no correspondence from Henry Bellows concerning Germans in the Kaltenborn papers, it seems likely that the influential director of public relations worried more about Roman Catholics than Nazi sympathizers.

The news analyst told a colleague about the activities of both groups. Hendrik van Loon, in a letter to Roosevelt on April 18, 1939, stated: "Hans Kaltenborn writes me today that his sponsors too feel obliged to fire him on account of protests coming from local Nazis and the Church."[56] This suggests that the bakers were in part responsible. But in the absence of any correspondence, one can only assume that the Germans did not rely on a letter-writing campaign to make their views known.

Clark contrasts Pure's willingness to sponsor a commentator in spite of continued objections by certain listeners with General Mills's refusal. He concludes that the former company had a greater dedication to freedom of speech.[57] Events in Spain suggest another significant difference. In January 1939 Pierrepont Moffat described a "Lift the Embargo Week," with "enthusiasts pouring into Washington from all over the country."[58] To keep the Loyalists from losing the war, American supporters realized that arms and other goods were urgently needed. At such a juncture, those passionately in favor of Franco might be expected to oppose the rebels' critics with special vehemence. By April, when Pure's sponsorship began, the Nationalists had won. Franco's supporters knew that the United States no longer represented a danger to the rebel cause. Roman

Catholics could afford to start letting a commentator say what he wished. In addition, someone who had just lost a sponsor might well have been expected to remember "discretion" more easily.

A second difference concerns the companies involved and their products. Kaltenborn proved ineffective in his institutional promotion for General Mills. The company may have decided that it was a waste of advertising dollars to sponsor a program in which the many male listeners would scarcely rush out to buy Gold Medal flour. With gasoline it was a different matter. The news particularly appealed to those who would purchase automotive products. Pure also felt that Kaltenborn's commentaries would give prestige to a smaller company seeking a national image.[59] They were willing to take greater risks.

ENHANCING REALITY

Between 1939 and 1941 the newscasts of Kaltenborn and Lowell Thomas attracted the highest program ratings. A 1940 *Radio Daily* program poll named Kaltenborn the more popular.[60] One reason for such success was an ability to gain attention. By reading the commentator's broadcasts and following his public life—there was scarely any other— one quickly concludes that this was a perfect person for an industry prone to endless exaggeration. When one of the newscaster's books had sold very poorly, he created a special radio program to promote sales. After a flashy introduction including a "crescendo of rumbling . . . then sharp break," Kaltenborn simulated interviews with Mussolini and Hitler. He impersonated the dictators' voices as they answered his questions.[61]

The blurring of the line separating truth from something a little shy of it is exemplified in a letter the broadcaster wrote to his sponsor's advertising agency. He hoped to interest the company in paying for a little junket:

> I have decided against taking any vacation. The times are too serious and I would be unable to detach myself from the war in such a way would [sic] be necessary to really enjoy a vacation. . . .
> However, I should very much like to utilize a three weeks [sic] period of absence from broadcasting for the purpose of a quick study trip of Latin-America at war.[62]

Perhaps the news analyst really believed that he had described the truth. If so, he had enhanced reality until he no longer knew what was fact. The commentator believed personal interviews and frequent trips made for an informed understanding of foreign affairs. Mostly, however, he learned little from talking briefly with heads of state. Along with two other journalists, Kaltenborn interviewed Hitler in 1932. This soon blossomed into "anyone who, like myself, has repeatedly met and talked with Hitler knows . . ."[63]

Kaltenborn loved the trappings of wealth. There is admiration—and envy—in these lines used to open one newscast: "I flew in from Tulsa, Oklahoma this afternoon at over two hundred miles per hour in a $25,000 private plane. It was a beautiful all-metal monoplane with luxurious fittings that is the personal property of an oil magnate."[64] At the time he was sponsored by the Pure Oil Company.

In 1939, visitors heard Kaltenborn's voice in the Perisphere at the New York World's Fair. The broadcaster publicized the affair on a program with André Kostelanetz and his orchestra. The Ethyl Gasoline Corporation sponsored the show. The newscaster declared that the "petroleum industry" was one of the "research organizations of American industry" helping to create the World of Tomorrow. An announcer quickly agreed and went on to commend the "enterprise" of the oil companies for providing "the world's lowest gasoline prices."[65]

Besides praising business, Kaltenborn also loved to be seen with high society. In 1941 he met the Duchess of Windsor—probably one in a large crowd—and hastened to tell listeners about the world of fashion. "The Duchess' hat," he explained,

> looked like a skull cap with a black bow on the back. And just above the middle of her high forehead where her hair is parted was a diamond V-for-victory clip. There was another diamond clip at the front of her high dress. Her feet were tired, poor thing, for she kept wiggling her ankles the way children do when they don't like to stand. She carried sables and her corsage of six big red roses was flattened out to look like a giant camelia.[66]

Such descriptions stemmed directly from the newscaster's unwillingness to use a prepared script. Kaltenborn prided himself on his ability to speak extemporaneously. His handling of the Munich crisis was based on this talent. In general, however, few benefits accrued from not writing out broadcasts in advance. Kaltenborn often used the same evidence to draw exactly opposite conclusions without explaining why he had changed his mind. For instance, in May 1942 Kaltenborn described how "with rare propaganda skill, the administration is releasing its information on the Tokyo raids just a little at a time." Two days later he asserted that "this bombing of Tokyo, the Battle of the Coral Sea, and the Russians' push on Kharkov have all been given more emphasis than they deserve."[67]

Kaltenborn's opinions about the worth of the Soviet Union followed an especially erratic course during the months after the Nazi invasion in June 1941. On July 3, for no particular reason, Kaltenborn opened with a hammer-and-tongs assault. He proclaimed that "Stalin is just as much of a crook as Hitler." If the Soviets would "recall some of the skilled saboteurs the Communist International has trained and sent to other countries," he insisted, "they might be able to organize and execute his scorched earth policy."[68] Two days later, after approvingly referring to Herbert Hoover's statement that Russia was " 'a militant destroyer of the worship of God,' " the commentator suggested that "President Roosevelt's promise of help for Russia was political rather than practical." After all, he continued, "the Soviet Government has been a militant destroyer of the worship of God since it came to power in 1917." On July 10 Kaltenborn urged plain speaking between Soviet Ambassador Constantine Oumansky and Roosevelt on the subject of "Communist intrigues in the United States."[69]

Three days later, again for no apparent reason, the newscaster suggested that "it makes good sense, good strategy, good politics and good diplomacy to cooperate even with a Russian Communist regime for the elimination of Public Enemy Number One." On July 19 he returned to a more familiar theme. The news analyst explained that America did not offer assistance to Russia to "keep either Stalin or his Communist stooges in a place of power." He also hinted of internal subversion:

> Joseph Stalin's picture is being applauded in American motion picture houses. I was present yesterday when it happened on Broadway in New York City. It reminded me that we have a lot of people in this country who believe more fervently in Joseph Stalin than they believe in American democracy. People like that will bear watching.[70]

Gradually, this sort of comment became increasingly rare. By September 14 Kaltenborn supported proposals to supply Lend-Lease material to the Soviet Union. Having forgotten his extemporaneous tirades of months gone by, the newscaster put his beliefs in perspective: "That is why I always considered Hitler a greater menace to the outside world than Stalin. . . . Russia is so rich and powerful it can afford mistakes." [71]

Perhaps Kaltenborn's much-vaunted expertise as an extemporizer is best evaluated by seeing what a subject of his analysis thought of the commentator's ability. Professor Brooks Emeny presented his views on the "Town Meeting of the Air" in 1940. The broadcaster summarized what had been said. Emeny reacted vigorously: "Mr. Chairman, Mr. Kaltenborn's analysis of my own talk illustrates very well the danger of trying to put too many ideas into a small space of time. Because as a matter of fact, he misinterpreted every single statement that I made." [72]

"EE-TIS AN EE-PAWK-UL STEP"

Today, listening to a fifteen-minute Kaltenborn broadcast produces an immediate reaction of utter bewilderment. How could such a mannered style have been associated with serious news commentary? To say that he spoke rapidly in a clipped fashion, or that he minced his words, hardly approximates the reality of his pronunciation. "It is an epochal step" became "ee-tis an ee-pawk'-ul step"; "Russia" was "r-rush-shee-ia"— the "r" was rolled once. "Europe" came out "yuh-r-up"; "isola-tion," "isso-lay-shun"; "very" was "veh-r-ry." [73]

The news analyst's voice in no sense enlarged the content of the words he chose. Just the opposite. Though a distraction, Kaltenborn's unique speaking style increased public awareness of the commentator. Some listeners may have thought such precise diction indicated careful broadcast preparation. Others, detecting a foreign accent, believed that no true American could understand several languages. Many assumed that anyone who sounded so serious and authoritative must have known what he was talking about.

Such listeners would have overlooked ideas that seem less compelling in print. For instance, in 1939 Kaltenborn explained how to keep the peace: "But, one reflects, since we cannot enter a war until Congress actually votes to get us into it, it might be argued that with Congress adjourned there might be less chance of Congress voting us into war."

On another occasion the commentator reminded his audience: "Remember that ours is a land where religion is free and where each man has the right to worship God as he sees fit, and anyone who attacks a man because of religion or race, that man is false to the fundamental principles of American liberty.[74]

Such analysis was not enhanced by the homely advertising copy that preceded it. A typical Pure Oil commercial began: "Wherever there's fire or combustion, you'll find carbon. It doesn't hurt much in a fireplace, but in the innards of your motor excess carbon smothers performance. . . . It's molasses in January as far as pick-up goes."[75]

But Kaltenborn also had effective methods for encouraging his audience to take a greater interest in foreign affairs. He gave away war maps of Europe so listeners could find the location of places he discussed. He offered free handbooks on defense and the army to help make the problems of war production clearer to large numbers of people. Pure Oil dealers reported an enthusiastic response.[76] Although the advertising copy may have sounded unpolished, the booklets and maps were successful in making the listener concerned about foreign events and a regular part of the newscaster's audience.

Kaltenborn began with a clipped "Good evening." He then presented a talk based mostly on wire service reports. In fact, after moving to NBC in May 1940, his rough drafts consisted of teletype reports glued on sheets of paper with penciled comments added. When the commentator wished to emphasize something, he would raise his voice. Sometimes he would fairly shout a phrase such as the "entire world" so that the microphone would distort his voice momentarily. Occasionally he was filled with sarcasm as he pronounced a certain adjective: Russia "pretend[ed]" that Britain planned to attack her. He offered comment by adding an unconvincing little chuckle before such a word as "obligingly." At other times he spoke so quickly—up to two hundred words a minute—that the listener had difficulty comprehending just what was being said.[77]

Listeners had no problem detecting Kaltenborn's opinions. He spoke of one state governor as "too cheap and too second-rate for people to fall for." He condemned "the Nazi Jew Baiters" who had again "become a stench in the nostrils of peaceful decent men."[78] But these were single pungent references.

Sometimes he went on crusades, such as his comments concerning Franco's supporters. He became particularly outspoken on the subject of alleged abuses by organized labor. "I say to the leaders of union labor, the people still rule" was a comment in 1942. Such orations, more appropriate to the rhetoric of the stump speaker, led one Minneapolis labor publication to feature a front-page headline proclaiming " 'Keep Poor with Pure' Appropriate Radio Slogan for Kaltenborn.''[79]

After the war, Kaltenborn continued to comment over NBC. On November 4, 1948, he predicted Dewey's victory throughout the evening. The newscaster assured listeners that the farm vote would be decisive. Later, Truman brought him considerable publicity by mimicking his voice at an Electoral College banquet. Though by 1951 the news analyst had retired from active broadcasting, as late as 1958 he still spoke occasionally over NBC radio. He was eighty-seven when he died on June 14, 1965.

A HOUSEHOLD NAME

Like other commentators, Kaltenborn's impact cannot be measured by numbers of letters sent or conversations held with influential members of the administration. But his celebrity status following the Munich broadcasts meant that policy-makers in Washington knew of his pro-Roosevelt sympathies and listened to him on occasion. And such popularity ensured large numbers of listeners in other parts of the country.

Perhaps the cabinet official most appreciative of Kaltenborn's efforts was Roosevelt's elderly, conservative Secretary of War, Henry L. Stimson. Kaltenborn is the only broadcaster he mentions having talked with after taking office in June 1940. In his voluminous diary Stimson recorded that on Saturday morning, January 4, 1941, "Kaltenborn, a well-known radio commentator, came in to see me and we had a very pleasant talk. He seemed like a decent, fair-minded fellow.''[80]

Kaltenborn's relationship with Herbert Hoover is more fully documented. He had interviewed the Secretary of Commerce in December 1925. On several occasions he talked privately with Hoover during his presidency. In June 1938 Hoover invited Kaltenborn along on an annual group camping trip of prominent Californians known as the Bohemian Club. Hoover listened carefully to the commentator's broadcasts before Pearl Harbor. After 1945 the two became really close friends.[81]

If Hoover's friendship meant overlooking Kaltenborn's support for Roosevelt's foreign policy, the same cannot be said for certain congressmen. In April 1940 Hamilton Fish erupted on the floor of Congress: "[*Kaltenborn*] is more of a jackass than I thought he was—and that requires some stretch of the imagination." Fish referred to a "personal attack" the news analyst had made in one of his broadcasts.[82]

More serious were the efforts of Representative Karl E. Mundt two months later. He wrote the president of NBC, Lenox R. Lohr, complaining of excessive war hysteria in Kaltenborn's newscasts:

> I have already had a call from the Vice President of the Columbia Broadcasting Company assuring me of their sympathy toward my viewpoint, and giving me the gratifying information that they have discontinued the war broadcasts of Mr. Kaltenborn, due to the fact that he was going to excess in the matter of exciting people's emotions about the war.

Lohr was incensed. "The CBS comments cannot go unchallenged," he insisted.[83] He believed a competitor was trying to dump the entire problem of censoring news analysts into NBC's lap. The president's concern did not extend to his network's commentator. NBC did nothing to defend Kaltenborn against such charges, thus implicitly agreeing with Mundt. The newscaster's sponsor, the Pure Oil Company, remained silent as well. "In deference to the feelings of the articulate minority," wrote a representative of Leo Burnett, "we have admonished Mr. Kaltenborn to exercise more restraint in his broadcasts and he has agreed to do so."[84]

Others did so too. *Scribner's Commentator,* practically a house organ for America First, featured Kaltenborn's photograph in its November 1940 "Internationalist Hall of Fame." The magazine claimed "his broadcasts today are as packed with Go To War jingoism as any on the air-waves." Lord Lothian, British ambassador to the United States, expressed a similar sentiment, albeit from a different point of view. He wrote an official in the London Foreign Office in April 1940 that Kaltenborn was "inclined on the whole to be friendly to Great Britain in his radio talks which reach a vast audience and must be regarded as influential to a high degree.'' Wayne S. Cole mentions that America First tried unsuccessfully to shackle Walter Winchell and H. V. Kaltenborn by approaching their radio sponsors.[85] This suggests that the principal group opposing greater American involvement in foreign affairs considered him persuasive.

Kaltenborn's fellow broadcasters held the same opinion. William L. Shirer referred to ''our star foreign-news commentator'' in an offhand manner that suggests that this was a universally acknowledged fact. Elmer Davis was extraordinarily respectful. In September 1939 he wrote that Kaltenborn had covered the Munich crisis ''with outstanding brilliance.'' As late as November 1941 Davis protested to the *New York Times* the omission of his colleague's name in a story about radio reporters. This means that he still thought a good deal of his fellow commentator. Raymond Swing talked of Kaltenborn's having been a ''true gentleman.''[86]

What about the public at large? There are three ways of estimating the broadcaster's appeal to the average citizen. The first relates to his sponsorship by the Pure Oil Company. The firm had its headquarters in Chicago. Most of its sales were in the Midwest and South.[87] Pure did not want to pay for broadcasts where it had no outlets. As a result, Kaltenborn was heard in New York and Washington only once a week between 1939 and 1941. The commentator's impact, therefore, after the Munich broadcasts, should be considered as largely regional. For instance, the news analyst's free war maps of Europe were available only from Pure Oil dealers, who were not to be found in the East, nor west of the Mississippi River. This means that Kaltenborn's emotional support of Roosevelt was more important than it might otherwise seem. He broadcast much more frequently than Raymond Gram Swing in such places as Chicago. And his voice and name were better known according to polls of those years.

Such popularity stemmed primarily from the broadcasts of September 1938. After this date only a most dedicated listener would have located the hour of every Kaltenborn broadcast. In January 1939 he spoke once a week at 10:30 P.M. EST on Sunday night for General Mills. This was not a good hour even for the east coast. When Pure took over in April, he broadcast at the same time on Sunday and Tuesday. On September 25, 1939, the news analyst moved to 6:30 P.M. Monday, Wednesday, and Friday. In January 1940, in Chicago, he was speaking for CBS Monday,

Wednesday, and Friday at 5:30 P.M. CST. Tuesday and Thursday he commented at the same time but over another Chicago station, WIND. By May 1941 the commentator was heard in Chicago over NBC's WMAQ at 6:45 P.M. Tuesday, Thursday, and Saturday. Sunday afternoon he appeared on WIND. But the same month, in New York and Washington, he spoke only on Sunday afternoon at 3:25 P.M. For a time he even broadcast at 10:30 A.M., though exact details are lacking.[88]

For Kaltenborn it is possible to estimate which of his broadcasts particularly appealed to listeners. Earl S. Grow, Jr., examined more than fifteen thousand letters now in the Kaltenborn Papers to determine which of the commentator's broadcasts created the heaviest response.[89] Grow notes ten analyses between 1939 and 1941 that drew the greatest amount of mail. He feels that all consisted of issues that Kaltenborn had personally created. For two of them, this is hardly the case. Many broadcasts commented on the merits of providing more aid to Britain in early June 1940. And every commentator discussed Charles Lindbergh's September 1941 speech in which he connected the Jews with support for war in Europe.

Grow did not see that the broadcasts that attracted the greatest amount of mail were often those of an emotional nature. On September 22, 1940, listeners were delighted when the news analyst read a 1915 poem entitled "A Chant of Love for England." Even more responded when the newscaster gave the British lion's tail a vigorous twist. "We have no use for British imperialism in the Far East, or anywhere else," declared Kaltenborn on February 2, 1941.

Kaltenborn's emotional outbursts appealed to those who tuned in. The excitement of unsupported opinion freed the broadcaster from pedestrian facts. The platitudes enouraged some listeners to conclude that an understanding of foreign affairs was within the reach of all. In this sense Kaltenborn's impact differed from what he thought it to be. Instead of offering analyses he provided a measure of entertainment. Many people thought they were getting more.

In one sense they did. Kaltenborn provided a summary of the important news stories as they happened. After May 1940 he supported all major administration moves toward greater American involvement overseas. He saw nothing wrong with the secrecy surrounding the negotiations for the Destroyers-Bases Agreement. On August 22, 1940, he pointed out that "no one objects and no one sees anything out of the way in this procedure.''[90] When the agreement was made public on September 3, he termed it an ''epochal step in the history of this country.'' Four months later, during the debate over the Lend-Lease Act, Kaltenborn stood prepared to accept any strong legislation that passed Congress: ''The issue of war or peace does not depend on just what form our help to Britain takes—we are committed irrevocably to helping the British cause—that is the major fact.'' On April 24, 1941, he came out strongly in favor of convoying:

> Britain may lose the Battle of the Atlantic unless we can find some way to cooperate in getting war materials at least part way across the Atlantic. . . . It must be perfectly obvious to any thinking person that if we propose to keep German warships out of our side of the Atlantic by an effective neutrality patrol we must be prepared to take the risks that this involves.[91]

After the President's September 11 ''shoot-on-sight'' speech, in which he announced an undeclared war against German ships in the Atlantic, Kaltenborn insisted that neutrality had disappeared. He likened the supporters of isolationism to ''prohibitionists who insisted on preserving the Eighteenth Amendment even after it became a dead letter.'' On November 2, again referring to incidents in the Atlantic, the commentator openly called for a declaration of war against Germany: ''Why do both countries refrain from accepting the logical consequences of a situation that has involved acts of war by the navies of both powers?''[92] Regarding Japan he had been equally outspoken. He had favored strong measures against the Japanese since June 1939. On June 15, 1941, he went much farther: ''If I were responsible for our foreign policy I would run the risk involved in an immediate showdown with Japan.''[93]

In other words, full hostilities toward Japan and Germany met with Kaltenborn's approval well before Pearl Harbor. But such forceful statements must be placed within the context of his regular broadcast style—his penchant for opinionated appeals and his habit of presenting contradictory conclusions from the same evidence, such as his statements concerning the Soviet Union from June to September 1941. A systematic reading of Kaltenborn's broadcasts suggests that although after May 1940 he openly supported whatever Roosevelt proposed regarding Britain, Germany, and Japan, in general the erratic nature of his thought must have confused the careful listener.[94] Indeed since Kaltenborn did not analyze the news, it would be better to describe him as an "opinionator" rather than a commentator.

Such a conclusion ignores Kaltenborn's major contributions to the development of radio as a serious news source. After all, he really was the Dean of News Commentators, as he liked to refer to himself. He had the ingenuity and persistence to broadcast radio's first live battle from Spain in 1936. He spent thirty years promoting the occupation of radio news analyst in an industry where anything serious was considered taboo. And more than successful promoter, his abilities as extemporizer—however unfortunate, most of the time—gave him the ability singlehandedly to provide eighteen days of almost continuous broadcasting during September 1938. The Munich broadcasts represented Hans von Kaltenborn's greatest moment. In those dramatic days radio became the major source for overseas news. The newspaper "extra" disappeared—suddenly as out of date as an old washboard. For a "windbag and a bore" this represented quite an achievement.

The Munich broadcasts represented more than a personal triumph for Kaltenborn. In that month American isolationism received a blow from which it never recovered. Radio as a documentary medium showed that the European system really was disintegrating. The obvious conclusion, which took time to be understood, nevertheless, was that America had to be involved in the affairs of the rest of the world. In the next few years radio reported an abundance of news from overseas that suggested the wisdom of an American foreign policy based on more than simply doing as little as possible.

NOTES

1. The radio announcer's voice in Charlie Chaplin's *The Great Dictator,* made in 1940, is an obvious parody of Kaltenborn.
2. Giraud Chester, "The Radio Commentaries of H. V. Kaltenborn: A Case Study in Persuasion" (Ph.D. dissertation, University of Wisconsin, 1947), pp. 49-53; David Gillis Clark, "The Dean of Commentators: A Biography of H. V. Kaltenborn" (Ph.D. dissertation, University of Wisconsin, 1965), p. 50.
3. Clark, "The Dean of Commentators," p. 50.
4. H. V. Kaltenborn, *Fifty Fabulous Years 1900-1950: A Personal Review* (New York, 1950), p. 21. Essentially this account begins with 1898.

5. Chester, "The Radio Commentaries of H. V. Kaltenborn," p. 57; Kaltenborn, *Fifty Fabulous Years,* pp. 3-9.

6. CBS broadcast, November 15, 1936, quoted in Chester, "The Radio Commentaries of H. V. Kaltenborn," p. 60.

7. Kaltenborn, *Fifty Fabulous Years,* pp. 26-30.

8. *Ibid.,* pp. 37-53; Chester, "The Radio Commentaries of H. V. Kaltenborn," p. 70.

9. Kaltenborn, *Fifty Fabulous Years,* pp. 55-63; "Warum ich Deutschland liebe," cited in Chester, "The Radio Commentaries of H. V. Kaltenborn," p. 118.

10. Kaltenborn, *Fifty Fabulous Years,* p. 109; interview of Kaltenborn by Robert Trout, CBS broadcast, March 21, 1936, Box 198, Kaltenborn MSS; Chester, "The Radio Commentaries of H. V. Kaltenborn," p. 85.

11. January 2, 1924, quoted in Erik Barnouw, *A Tower in Babel: History of Broadcasting in the United States,* 3 vols. (New York, 1966-1970), p. 140.

12. Kaltenborn, *Fifty Fabulous Years,* pp. 112-13; David G. Clark, "Kaltenborn's First Year on the Air," *Journalism Quarterly,* 42 (Summer 1965), pp. 378-79.

13. Kaltenborn, *Fifty Fabulous Years,* pp. 105-109, 124-146. Publicity release, attached to Kaltenborn to George Akerson (Hoover's press secretary), January 12, 1931, "Kaltenborn" folder, PSF 534, HHL.

14. WABC broadcast (New York only), April 17, 1930 [1929?], Box 155, Kaltenborn MSS. Program cards for Kaltenborn in CBS Talent File (old) give the year as 1930; the manuscript is dated 1929. Three-by-five card, CBS Program Information.

15. CBS Talent File (old), Kaltenborn, CBS Program Information; Kaltenborn, "Reminiscences," p. 172, Columbia University Oral History Project, copy in Kaltenborn MSS.

16. CBS Talent File (old), Kaltenborn, CBS Program Information; Stanley Walker, *City Editor* (New York, 1934), p. 241.

17. J. H. Ryan, WSPD, Toledo Broadcasting Company, to Mrs. W. L. Kraus, January 22, 1936, Box 148; CBS broadcast, February 28, 1936, Box 198, both in Kaltenborn MSS.

18. For example, CBS broadcast December 10, 1933, Box 155, Kaltenborn MSS.

19. Kaltenborn, "Can Democracies Avoid Dictatorship?", February 18, 1937, *The Reference Shelf* 12, No. 2 (New York, 1938): 203.

20. Kaltenborn, "Reminiscences," pp. 191-94.

21. CBS broadcast, July 30, 1936, in Kaltenborn, "Radio Reports a Revolution," *Talks* 1 (October 1936): 47-48.

22. CBS broadcast, August 5, 1936, *ibid.,* p. 52.

23. Excerpts from this broadcast on CBS broadcast, July 10, 1937, presenta-

tion of National Headliners Club award to Kaltenborn, 78 rpm original transcription, both in Kaltenborn MSS; César Saerchinger, *Hello America!: Radio Adventures in Europe* (Boston 1939), pp. 224-25; CBS, *"We Now Take You To . . ."* (New York, February, 1937), copy in CBS Library; CBS Black Book, "Radio Programs 1936," CBS Program Information.

24. CBS broadcast, "Eddie Cantor's Camel Caravan," November 21, 1938, Box 155, Kaltenborn MSS.

25. There are numerous photographs of the commentator—and several of him playing tennis—in H. V. Kaltenborn, Iconographic Collection, State Historical Society of Wisconsin, Madison, Wisconsin.

26. See CBS, *Crisis: September 1938* (New York, 1938), a mimeographed transcript of all 102 broadcasts in 10 volumes.

27. William L. Langer and S. Everett Gleason, *The Challenge to Isolation, 1937-1940* (New York, 1952), p. 35.

28. James Rorty, "Radio Comes Through," *Nation,* October 15, 1938, pp. 372, 374; Allen, *Since Yesterday: The Nineteen-Thirties in America, September 3, 1929-September 3, 1939* (New York, 1940), p. 316. Allen devotes much of Chapter 12, pp. 314 ff., to Kaltenborn's Munich coverage.

29. *Variety,* September 21, 1938, p. 31; October 5, 1938, p. 1; Schechter, *I Live on Air,* p. 205; NBC, "A Tense World Speaks for Itself" (New York, October 13, 1938), copy in FD-NBC.

30. AIPO poll, October 17, 1938; poll, n.d. [1937], cited in Paul Lazarsfeld, *Radio and the Printed Page* (New York, 1940), p. 259.

31. Kaltenborn, *I Broadcast the Crisis* (New York, 1938), p. 9.

32. CBS broadcast, September 17, 19, 1938, CBS, *Crisis,* 3: 10, 4: 44.

33. CBS broadcast, September 26, 1938, *ibid.,* 7: 93, 95, 97.

34. CBS broadcast, September 27, 1938, *ibid.,* 8: 63.

35. Paul W. White, *News on the Air* (New York, 1947), p. 46.

36. CBS broadcast, October 9, 1938, Box 155, Kaltenborn MSS.

37. Kaltenborn, *I Broadcast the Crisis,* p. 255.

38. For a comprehensive discussion, see Hadley Cantril, Hazel Gaudet, and Herta Herzog, *The Invasion from Mars: A Study in the Psychology of Panic* (Princeton, N.J., 1940). See also Howard Koch, *The Panic Broadcast* (Boston, 1970).

39. AIPO poll, December 16, 1938, in Hadley Cantril and Mildred Strunk, *Public Opinion 1935-1946* (Princeton, N.J., 1951), p. 717. Only 12 percent of those questioned said that they had heard the program, and of this group only 26 percent (about 3 percent of the entire sample) said that they had considered it to be a news report.

40. Memorandum (prepared at Lohr's direction), n.d. [November, 1938], Box NBC III-B, Lohr MSS.

41. This is the conclusion of Cantril et al., *The Invasion from Mars.*

42. Earl Sidney Grow, Jr., "A Dialogue on American International Involvement, 1939-41: The Correspondence of H. V. Kaltenborn, His Sponsors, and His Public" (Ph.D. dissertation, University of Wisconsin, 1964), p. 307.

43. CBS broadcast, January 1, 1939, Box 155, Kaltenborn MSS. A somewhat different emphasis on the commentator's experience with General Mills can be found in David G. Clark, "H. V. Kaltenborn and his Sponsors: Controversial Broadcasting and the Sponsor's Role," *Journal of Broadcasting* 12 (Fall 1968): 309-21.

44. CBS broadcast, January 29, 1939, Box 155, Kaltenborn MSS.

45. See David H. Culbert, "Tantalus' Dilemma: Public Opinion, Six Radio Commentators, and Foreign Affairs, 1935-1941" (Ph.D. dissertation, Northwestern University, 1970), pp. 404-21.

46. Information in Box 148, Kaltenborn MSS.

47. Bellows to Lahey, February 1, 1939; Kaltenborn to Bellows, February [1-4, 1939]; CBS broadcast, February 5, 1939, Box 148, Box 155, Kaltenborn MSS.

48. Lahey to Bellows, February 6, 1939, Box 148, Kaltenborn MSS.

49. Bellows to Kaltenborn, February 6, 1939, Box 148, Kaltenborn MSS.

50. Bellows to Lahey, February 8, 1939; telegram, Bellows to Kaltenborn, February 8, 1939, Box 148, Kaltenborn MSS.

51. CBS broadcast, February 12, 1939, Box 155, Kaltenborn MSS.

52. Telegram, Bellows to Kaltenborn, March 7, 1939, Box 148, Kaltenborn MSS.

53. CBS broadcast, May 16, 1939, Box 156; see also April 3, 1938, Box 155, both in Kaltenborn MSS.

54. Kaltenborn to Francis H. Marling, Pure Oil Company, June 10, 1939; see also a series of letters sent in June 1939 protesting the commentator's anti-Catholic bias, all in Box 150, Kaltenborn MSS.

55. Clark, "Kaltenborn and his Sponsors," pp. 311-12, 321 fn.

56. Van Loon to Roosevelt, April 18, 1939, PPF 2259, FDRL.

57. Clark, "Kaltenborn and his Sponsors," pp. 317-20.

58. Moffat Diary, January 9, 1939.

59. Memorandum, Strother Cary, Treasurer and Director, Leo Burnett Company, February 25, 1970, in Leo Burnett to author, March 5, 1970; memorandum, Cary to Burnett, March 30, 1970, in Burnett to author, May 27, 1970.

60. "Matters for Action," January 19, 1940, p. 11, NBC Board of Directors Meeting folder, February 2, 1940, Box NBC I-A, Lohr MSS.

61. WABC (nonnetwork) broadcast, January 15, 1938, Box 155, Kaltenborn MSS.

62. Kaltenborn to Paul Harper, January 4, 1943, Box 150, Kaltenborn MSS.

Harper was an officer of the Leo Burnett Company, the agency that held the Pure Oil Company account.

63. NBC broadcast, May 20, 1940, Kaltenborn MSS.

64. CBS broadcast, May 2, 1939, Box 156, Kaltenborn MSS.

65. "Tune-up Time," CBS broadcast, April 13, 1939, Box 156, Kaltenborn MSS.

66. NBC broadcast, October 21, 1941, Kaltenborn MSS.

67. NBC broadcast, May 19 and 21, 1942, quoted in Giraud Chester dissertation notes, Box 214, Kaltenborn MSS.

68. NBC broadcast, July 3, 1941, Kaltenborn MSS. For his earlier comments about the Soviet Union, see Culbert, "Tantalus' Dilemma," pp. 471, 493-94.

69. NBC broadcast, July 5, 10, 1941, Kaltenborn MSS.

70. NBC broadcast, n.d. [July 13, 1941], July 19, Kaltenborn MSS.

71. NBC broadcast, September 14, 1941, Kaltenborn MSS.

72. "Must American and Japan Clash?", NBC broadcast, December 5, 1940, reprinted in *Town Meeting,* Vol. 6, No. 4 (New York, December 9, 1940), copy in Kaltenborn MSS.

73. 33 1/3 rpm original transcription, NBC broadcast, September 3 and July 23, 1940; tape recording 364A/4, April 2, 1955, all in Kaltenborn MSS.

74. CBS broadcast, May 3, 1939, Box 156, January 15, 1940, Kaltenborn MSS.

75. CBS broadcast, September 29, 1939, Box 156, Kaltenborn MSS.

76. F[rancis] H. Marling to Richard H. Mason, WPTF, Raleigh, N.C., July 29, 1941, Box 150, Kaltenborn MSS.

77. 33 1/3 rpm original transcription, NBC broadcast, July 23, 1940, Kaltenborn MSS.

78. CBS broadcast, January 31, 1936, Box 198; CBS broadcast, June 19, 1938, Box 155—both in Kaltenborn MSS.

79. *Time,* April 6, 1942, 78; *The Minneapolis Labor Review,* March 21, 1941, copy in Box 148, Kaltenborn MSS.

80. Henry L. Stimson Diary, January 4, 1941, Vol. 32, Henry L. Stimson MSS, Manuscript Division, Yale University Library, New Haven, Conn. [hereafter Stimson MSS].

81. Hoover to Kaltenborn, June 2, 1938, "H. V. Kaltenborn" folder 981(1), HHL. The same folder contains one 1940 broadcast that Hoover asked for; folders (2) and (3) contain the correspondence after 1945.

82. *Congressional Record,* 76th Cong., 3d Session, 4027 (April 4, 1940).

83. Mundt to Lohr, June 5, 1940; NBC interdepartmental cover memorandum concerning Mundt correspondence, June 10, 1940, Box 149, Kaltenborn MSS.

84. Paul C. Harper, Leo Burnett Company, to Mundt, June 12, 1940, in *Congressional Record,* 76th Cong., 3d Session, Appendix, 3992-93.

85. *Scribner's Commentator* 9 (November 1940): 17. Lothian to David Scott, Under Secretary in Charge of the American Department, Foreign Office, April 16, 1940, A3369/26/45, FO; Cole, *America First: The Battle Against Intervention 1940-1941* (Madison, Wis., 1953), p. 113.

86. Shirer, *Berlin Diary,* p. 178; Davis, "Broadcasting the Outbreak of War," *Harper's Magazine* 179 (November 1939): 580. Kaltenborn to Davis, November 27, 1941, Box 1, Swing MSS; Swing, interview with author, September 5, 1968.

87. Before 1941, Pure's sales were strongest in Florida, Georgia, Alabama, Ohio, and Michigan. Except for Minnesota, it did not market its products west of the Mississippi River. The company was looking for a national image, and this was its first use of a large advertising campaign. It was also Burnett's first major client (the agency was founded in August 1935). Memorandum, Strother Cary, Treasurer and Director, Leo Burnett Company, February 25, 1970, in Leo Burnett to author, March 5, 1970; memorandum, Cary to Burnett, March 30, 1970, in Burnett to author, May 27, 1970.

88. CBS Talent File (old) and (new), Kaltenborn, CBS Program Information; based on daily radio schedules in the *New York Times,* the *Chicago Tribune,* and the *Washington Evening Star,* 1939-1941; AIPO questionnaire Set 154-A, April 6, 1939, copy sent author by Professor Philip Hastings, The Roper Public Opinion Research Center, Williams College, Williamstown, Mass. [hereafter RPORC].

89. Grow, Jr., "A Dialogue on American International Involvement," pp. 183 ff.

90. NBC broadcast, August 22, 1940, Kaltenborn MSS.

91. A 33 1/3 rpm original transcription, NBC broadcast, September 3, 1940, January 12, April 24, 1941, all in Kaltenborn MSS.

92. NBC broadcast, September 11, November 2, 1941, Kaltenborn MSS.

93. NBC broadcast, June 15, 1941, Kaltenborn MSS.

94. For Kaltenborn's comments about most major overseas events, 1935-1941, see Culbert, "Tantalus' Dilemma," pp. 377-628.

4 Raymond Gram Swing: "He Isn't the Kind of Man You Would Call Ray"

At the time of Swing's death a colleague remarked: "He was the closest thing broadcasting ever had to a Walter Lippmann."[1] Shortly after Pearl Harbor a *New Yorker* cartoon expressed equal admiration but in a gentler way. The General Cigar Company sponsored the commentator. A fashionable suburban housewife, about fifty, was puffing on a cigar, to the obvious horror of her lady friends. Her comment: "Don't you think Raymond Gram Swing is just great!" In many places, loyal followers considered themselves something of a club. They knew that Swing prepared his analyses with greater care than almost any other newscaster. After 1939 surprising numbers of Americans began tuning in—those normally unwilling to listen to scholarly explanations. Swing's career as a radio commentator suggests much about the social history of America during the 1930s. The way he presented his material and what he said helps make clear what it was like to have depended on a radio newscaster for interpretation of foreign affairs. Swing became the most influential commentator on the air before Pearl Harbor for those seriously interested in foreign affairs—and the only newscaster with a worldwide audience.

Swing's broadcasts contained no sparkling epigrams. Nor was a sense of humor much in evidence. But he conveyed his enthusiasm for foreign policy with remarkable success. Listeners also heard a desperately earnest man refer to his deepest convictions on the air. The broadcaster openly admitted his approach to the news. "As the crisis which ended in World War II came to a head," he wrote, "I found myself growing patriotic to a degree I had never been capable of before."[2]

His moral righteousness did not please everyone. A cynical *New Yorker* profile emphasized the sometimes platitudinous quality of the newscaster's thought. The writer described Swing as a "hair-shirt character who relishes pain. . . . Failure strengthens him as prayer does lesser men. He owes his success to it."[3] Two journalists, struggling to capture Swing's spirit, settled for noting that even the commentator's close friends addressed him as Raymond: "He isn't the kind of man you would call Ray."[4]

A PERMANENTLY GUILTY CONSCIENCE

Raymond Edwards Swing was born in Cortland, New York, on March 25, 1887. His father was a professor of theology at Oberlin College, a small liberal arts school located near Cleveland, Ohio. His grandfather had taught theology at the same institution during its early years. A grandmother served as the first president of Mt. Holyoke College. An uncle, after graduating from Oberlin, became a distinguished social psychologist at the University of Chicago. Even Swing's mother taught at Oberlin for a time.

The son grew up in a family that demanded impossible standards in daily living. Seventy years later, he still had not forgotten the painfulness of his childhood. "It was something of an experience to pass one's father in the street," he recalled, "as I often did, without his saying a word, only silently nodding, and striding on without a smile or a halt." His parents insisted that he learn the "absolute truth."[5] Dinner table conversations centered on religious teachings about morality. Though Swing gave up Christianity and rebelled against his unbearably strict parents, he never forgot their emphasis on personal morality. He left home with a permanently guilty conscience.

In his autobiography the broadcaster reveals something of a fixation about personal sin by describing in minute detail his evil doings as a child. He smoked, "lied and cheated at home," and stole various things from drugstores in town. He even played cards against his father's express command. The final disgrace to his family came in 1906. Swing wanted to go to Amherst; his parents decreed that he would attend Oberlin. He failed his freshman year and had to leave school. He never received much additional formal education. He could not forgive himself for humiliating his father and mother.[6]

The family disgrace went to Cleveland to look for a job. He started as a night reporter for the *Cleveland Press*. In the next few years, he served as editor of tiny newspapers in Ohio and Indiana. In 1912 Swing ran the *Indianapolis Sun,* a new enterprise, and covered the campaign of the famous progressive, Senator Albert J. Beveridge. A photograph taken that year shows a young man wearing a bowler hat and a drooping bow tie. His hands stuffed in his pockets, he looks painfully ill at ease.[7]

Shortly after, a nervous breakdown forced Swing to give up his eighteen-hour days. The uncle at the University of Chicago offered to send his nephew to Europe for a year. Before departing, Swing married a young Frenchwoman whom his relatives had brought to Chicago to live with them. In 1913 he began working for the Berlin office of the *Chicago Daily News*. As he later recalled, Chicago newspapers were not much interested in printing stories about foreign affairs:

> One of my jobs was to keep a pleasant, homelike office where visitors from Chicago could come to read the *Chicago Daily News,* and sign their names on a register. And the only cables that went from that office in that year were these names, which were printed in Chicago, so that the friends of these tourists could keep track of them.[8]

When hostilities began in 1914, the young reporter accepted the German White Paper alleging Germany to be the victim of British and French provocations. Swing's "How Germany was Forced into War" appeared in the *Chicago Daily News* on September 4, 1914. The Germanistic Society of Chicago quickly reprinted the article. Although the reporter discovered soon enough the limitations of the White Paper as a scholarly source, Victor Lawson, publisher of the *Daily News,* was unconcerned. He claimed the article had saved his paper fifty thousand subscribers.[9]

Swing went to Constantinople in 1915. He watched the final naval engagement in the Dardanelles—to him by far the most exciting moment of his career as war correspondent. A few days later an English submarine surfaced in the Turkish Sea of Marmara and ordered the crew and him off a small freighter it planned to torpedo. The commander asked the ship's name:

> "Who are you." I took this quite innocently and landlubberly as being a personal question to me and said I was Raymond Gram Swing of the *Chicago Daily News*. Whereupon the commander replied, "Glad to meet you, Mr. Swing—but what is the name of your ship.''[10]

Rudyard Kipling, coming across a report of this dialogue in the submarine's log, wrote a story about the exchange. Swing claims that Kipling's version soon became "a favorite in naval messes in England.''[11] Although the commentator loved to tell the story on himself, his purpose was not to provoke laughter. His conscience demanded that even his radio audience know of his inability to say the right thing in a public situation.

Swing returned to the United States in April 1917. He had suffered a complete nervous breakdown. The broadcaster exposed the complexity of his mind when he described this period nearly fifty years later:

> I might say that being unemployed worked to my benefit, for during this time I went through a season of severe self-examination, and at the close of the period, I had learned better how to face up to the truth about myself and the problems of living. I have said earlier that I am not writing my confessions, and would not undertake to tell how I came to be the person that I am. All I am inclined to say now is that this period was to be of enormous value to me. I suffered and pondered and somehow gained insight and strength, an experience for which I have ever since been profoundly grateful.[12]

Swing apparently believed that self-comprehension demanded an intensity of anguish, even were it to remove him from the world of reality. He remained obsessed with what Elmer Davis once mockingly referred to as the Seriousness of the Situation.

Well before this breakdown Swing's first marriage had come to an end. The divorce became final in 1919. That September Swing handled publicity for the Hungarian Relief Commission, an organization that hoped to raise one million dollars to help feed starving children.[13] Before Christmas he returned to Europe as Berlin correspondent for the *New York Herald*. Two years later his friend Felix Frankfurter wrote to ask

him about German affairs. "Do not become too d— Americanized
[sic]," he jokingly added.[14] Shortly after Swing became one of the three
reporters whom the Soviet Union permitted to visit the famine-stricken
areas along the Volga River. He then moved to London to head the *Wall
Street Journal's* foreign service.

In the meantime he had married Betty Gram. In 1917 this militant
feminist was arrested in front of the White House while picketing for
women's rights. Betty Gram felt it degrading to take her husband's last
name as her own. For a time Swing and his wife registered at hotels under
separate names. However, even in liberal Weimar Germany few
approved of people with different names staying in the same room, even
though man and wife. Swing offered to take Gram as his middle name if
his wife would become Betty Swing. This arrangement lasted until their
divorce in 1944.[15]

The head of the *Journal's* foreign service quit in 1924 over a matter of
principle. The resignation stemmed from a quibble as to whether one of
his stories should have reported French francs in terms of their prewar
value or their depreciated postwar condition. This time it proved difficult
to find another position. Finally Swing became London correspondent
for the *Philadelphia Public Ledger.* He stayed with this newspaper until it
dissolved its foreign service in 1934.[16] Swing covered such important
European conferences as Rapallo during 1922. In England he sent his
children to Bertrand Russell's experimental school. Swing and his wife
were "somewhat alarmed" by what they had heard about "discipline in
the so-called public schools in Britain."[17] He traveled to the United States
to cover British Prime Minister Ramsay MacDonald's 1929 talks with
Herbert Hoover. In 1930 and again the following year, Secretary of State
Henry L. Stimson, while in London, invited Swing and a few leading
newspapermen to join him for luncheon briefings. After one of these
affairs the Secretary dourly noted that the journalists "told me that I was
human after all."[18]

When the London position disappeared in 1934, Swing was forty-
seven, with five children from two marriages. Reluctantly returning to
America, he served briefly as an editor for the *Nation.* His friendliness
toward the New Deal made him suspect to radicals on the staff. His
articles at first concerned domestic affairs—a subject not to his liking.
When he turned to foreign affairs his analyses seemed noticeably more
enlightening.[19]

Swing also worked on a series concerning American demagogues. In 1935 the essays describing such figures as William Randolph Hearst, Huey Long, and Father Coughlin appeared together in print. Walter Millis, reviewing the book for the *Saturday Review of Literature,* commented favorably, if not rapturously: "This is the case for believing that fascism lies ahead of us—a case put compactly, readably, and intelligently."[20] Swing's pessimistic conclusions failed to attract large numbers of readers.

A couple of weeks after giving up his editorial position, the journalist began a series on Alf Landon in the *Nation.* He described the governor as much closer to the New Deal philosophy than those who considered the Republican hopeful a "Kansas Coolidge." A *New York Times* editorial sarcastically noted that "Mr. Swing" was telling people that "Kansas is simple and good."[21] Many readers were appalled to see such a defense of Landon appearing in the *Nation.*

From January 1936 until late in 1937, Swing served as New York correspondent for the *London News Chronicle* and Washington correspondent for Britain's *The Economist.* He occasionally spoke to the Council on Foreign Relations and the Foreign Policy Association. Swing also discussed freedom of speech before groups concerned with broadcasting and freedom of the press. A December 1937 letter suggests that serious topics failed to interest every audience: "For the discouraging circumstances that confronted you when you arose to speak all of us present felt heartsick. . . . A number of those who left the room immediately upon the conclusion of Mr. Niles' singing came back to occupy seats in the balcony."[22]

By 1938 lecturing provided most of Swing's income. In a letter to his mother he described his hectic schedule:

This last week I spoke in Delaware University Monday night; in Philadelphia, Wednesday, and Chicago, Friday. Friday I did a broadcast for schools in Britain, and then my regular British broadcast Saturday night. . . . In Chicago I missed my train, the first time I've done anything like that for fifteen years. I had to fly. I wrote all but the last minute of my British broadcast in the plane, with the typewriter on my knee, finishing over Buffalo sometime after midnight.

This week I have a still harder schedule. I broadcast over WOR tonight. Wednesday I speak for the Foreign Policy Association in Bryn Mawr, lecture the next noon at the Cosmopolitan Club in Philadelphia, and then get back in the evening to speak at the Harvard Club in New York. The next evening I speak in Columbia University, and the following day do my broadcast to London.[23]

PAPA'S ELECTRIC TRAIN

Though living abroad through the 1920s, Swing had as much interest in radio equipment as any amateur in the United States. He spent so many hours tinkering with primitive receiving sets that his family talked of "Papa's electric train." Swing first spoke over the radio in 1930. He interviewed an English lecturer for the British Broadcasting Corporation. That April CBS hired him to comment on the London Naval Conference. Swing helped Columbia's European representative report British election returns for American listeners in 1931. Shortly after, he discussed United States affairs in a series of broadcasts for British schools over the BBC.[24]

In the fall of 1934 Sir John Reith, powerful managing director of the BBC, visited the United States. Roosevelt complained to Reith that his policies were consistently misrepresented in Europe. In Britain, for instance, Prime Minister Stanley Baldwin termed the New Deal an American dictatorship. The President suggested that the BBC and an American network exchange broadcasts to help remedy the situation. Reith agreed providing Swing got the job interpreting the United States to the British. Though the series did not last long in the original form, a year later Roosevelt still felt that "the idea is right."[25]

Swing began discussing what was "Behind the Week's Foreign News" for the "Columbia School of the Air" in 1935. Speaking at 2:45 P.M., he could hardly have reached large numbers of the general public. Indeed things were so relaxed that the commentator once had his wife read his remarks for him.[26] One CBS vice-president listened faithfully. Swing's content impressed him, but he could not stand the speaking voice. Swing was offered a position as Columbia's director of talks but refused when he learned that he would be unable to do any broadcasting. Edward R. Murrow got the job instead. At the Democratic national convention in 1936, Murrow asked Swing to offer a nightly summary. He "received a sharp order" saying that the former *Nation* editor was "not to be heard over CBS."[27]

Swing moved to Mutual in the fall of 1936. He received forty dollars a week for one newscast, heard only in New York City. Two years later there were few listeners to know that Swing had been in Czechoslovakia during the September 1938 Munich crisis—and unable to broadcast. When the commentator returned to America, he spoke with Cordell Hull and Pierrepont Moffat in Washington. The latter recorded in his diary that Swing "consider[ed] that it was [Georges] Bonnet personally who was responsible for the French betrayal of Czechoslovakia." Swing reports that he warned the Secretary not to let the American government take any credit for the Munich settlement.[28]

On October 18 the news commentator made his first radio address concerning the crisis. The excellence of his analysis led to an award from the Institution for Education in Radio, though there was little public acclaim. Swing minced no words:

> Tonight I have a sense of the almost pitiful limitation of the time at my disposal, and of my own mind in grasping the full measure of what has happened. . . . Try to think back six months ago when the crisis was first evident. If anyone had told you then that by tonight Czecho-slovakia was to be deserted by its allies, dismembered at their request, that Germany in this short time was to be given mastery of Eastern Europe and so of the European continent, that France would voluntarily step down from being a first class power to being shut up in western Europe with only Britain and no further allies to secure it, if anyone had said this would happen at the point of a gun, in terms of an ultimatum, and would be accepted by Britain and France without the firing of a shot, you would have thought such a prophet was mad.[29]

Swing believed that in part, Britain and France "preferred to live under Hitler's domination than to beat him with the aid of Soviet Russia. . . ." He also warned that Western European countries were merely "putting off the evil day when they themselves will be victims of German expansion." Swing declared that a war fought in the summer of 1938 would have been much easier to win than what would later take place.[30] In every way the commentator heaped opprobrium on those who had given in so readily to Hitler's demands. Swing's October 18 analysis stands well above the level of other radio broadcasts devoted to the Munich crisis.

In December he condemned Neville Chamberlain, but with sarcasm rather than vituperation. He noted that the Prime Minister had just reaffirmed the efficacy of his old methods. "Well, the policy of appeasement, if appeasement means giving things, has still plenty of scope," Swing dryly observed. His harshest comment about Chamberlain's policy came when the Nazis took over the remainder of Czechoslovakia in 1939: "One thing Hitler has achieved. He has stuck a dagger in that word appeasement, and it will not rise again soon to torment the consciences of the British and French democracies. Now we know that appeasement was the key to the door of conquest."[31]

In spite of such forceful comment, national prominence as a newscaster did not come until August 1939. In that month Swing's principal competitor, H. V. Kaltenborn, was in Europe and unable to broadcast daily. Swing found himself practically the only national news commentator offering regular analysis of overseas events. He tried to explain carefully why the chances for peace did not look good. By the last days of August he spoke as often as three times a day over a national network.[32]

When war began, *Variety* insisted that Swing sounded too scholarly for the average listener. The magazine's reviewer added: "Many of Swing's broadcasts are described in the trade as masterpieces of trenchant, satiric comment, but it is generally agreed that his style and manner have shot somewhat over the heads of the masses in this country." The General Cigar Company decided to sponsor the newscaster anyway. In 1941 White Owl cigars increased in sales twice as much as all other cigars of its type combined.[33] Apparently the "masses in this country" did listen. At least, the intellectual elite could hardly have smoked all of this mammoth firm's output.

What might someone have heard had he tuned in one of Swing's newscasts before Pearl Harbor? First, the CBS vice-president was right—Swing had a perfectly dreadful radio voice. One person remembers a "syrupy unctuousness." He insists that the broadcaster "sounded as though he were an undertaker."[34] An unfriendly reporter considered that Swing's "soothing whispery resonance" was "obviously the hallmark of a superior person." Overly precise pronunciations of foreign names at first sounded almost effeminate—and certainly affected. For instance, in 1938 Swing talked of "Fronhs" (France) with a good French "r." By 1941 things were different. The "Saigonh" of 1938 had become plain old Saigon.[35]

Swing exuded good intentions on the air. When he said, "I cannot begin to tell you the perplexity and despair," anyone could hear the honest desire—the utter sadness that no words could express what the commentator knew to be true. After 1939 he occasionally moved, if unintentionally, beyond commendable sincerity to fulsomeness. "Democracy is a hope, a trust in the future, the means of achieving something finer," he commented in December 1940. "I am not saying that faith is the easiest device with which to move a mountain," he told his listeners seven months later. "But as a shield it blunts the sharpest steel."[36]

Such comments seemed particularly out of place because of the advertising copy that accompanied them. At first *Variety* described the commercials as "typical thick cuttings of bologna." A great hearty voice boomed forth at the beginning of the broadcast with: "More men have enjoyed White Owls than any other cigar at any other price." Years later, the commentator had not forgotten this slogan. "The announcer had a deep, sonorous voice," he recalled, "and launched this declaration with compelling force."[37]

On the night that Hitler invaded the Low Countries, May 10, 1940, Swing forced the General Cigar Company to relinquish permanently an advertisement in the middle of his newscast. Even so there is a remarkable incongruity between the broadcaster's language, his speaking voice, and the surrounding hard-sell copy. The announcer might begin exuberantly: "Men! If you wanted to test the flavor of a real blended-with-Havana cigar, there'd be no better place to go than Havana itself! And that's what we did." Swing would follow immediately with a whispery, earnest "Good Evening! I hope I have your approval to talk about individuals. . . ."[38]

His prose was scarcely that of a polished professional writer, in spite of his many years as foreign correspondent. Swing expressed himself clearly, but in a strange personal idiom. He employed curious adjectives in his descriptions:

> He [Hitler] was trying to be just as disrespectful to Mr. Roosevelt as he could be without forthrightly lambasting him. He was being sarcastic, smart, humorous, adroit, I thought even insulting, having the kind of good time that a skillful man on a platform can have making a crowd titter. And those of you who know German and listened to the speech know that the Reichstag did titter, and Hitler had a thoroughly good time.

Listeners might well have been startled by the opening of one 1939 broadcast: "This afternoon a teaparty was given in Paris to which I should love to have been invited, or to have my ears invited."[39]

Swing's news analyses rarely sounded lighthearted. "Even when making a witty comment," concludes one student of the commentator's broadcast style, "Swing delivered it with unrelieved solemnity."[40] Occasionally he revealed a creative cleverness, if not actual wit. One talk began with an image that might easily have caught any listener's attention:

> Every child knows that a gas-filled balloon, if released, will sail off with the wind. And every diplomat knows that if there is any doubt about the direction of public sentiment, it can be measured by an experimental move of a public nature. Such a move is called a trial balloon.

This is scarcely "unrelieved solemnity." And yet Swing never sounded relaxed. His words seemed stilted and affected to those who did not hear the voice of a shy, ill-at-ease man. Leaving for a vacation, Swing offered a "personal word" to his listeners: "To those of you already on vacation I say: 'Here I come!' To those of you who aren't, I say, 'Join us soon!' "[41] The phraseology seems unfortunate, though expressed with obvious sincerity.

Swing's broadcasts lasted for fifteen minutes. He read each word distinctly and carefully. If the commentator received his information from an individual, he clearly indicated his source. "Ralph Ingersoll, editor of *PM*," he would say, "has just flown back from two weeks in London and has begun a highly informative series of articles in that paper."[42] The news analyst placed no stock in conspiratorial explanations. He once told listeners he would swear that "the inside story, the really true story, almost always is ten times duller than any rumor about it."[43] Broadcasts frequently included some personal touch.[44] Swing sincerely wanted listeners to know exactly how and why he had arrived at certain opinions. He carefully explained just how reliable his sources seemed to him. In content and preparation his talks were truly scholarly.

THE LIBERAL AS COMMENTATOR

Historians have difficulty agreeing on a definition of the word "liber-

al.'' The dictionary mentions a commitment to "nonrevolutionary progress and reform" and "policies that favor the freedom of individuals to
act or express themselves in a manner of their own choosing." Nothing is
said of which groups should bring about reform—in particular the role of
the state in achieving change—a central concern of American reformers
in the twentieth century.

Several years ago Professor Tang Tsou suggested a special characteristic of American liberals in the 1930s. He described Raymond Gram
Swing as typical because of his inability to comprehend ideologies. Such
a conclusion does an injustice to Swing's pre-1941 broadcasts. But the
commentator has willingly admitted to being a "typical liberal."[45]

In March 1941 Swing devoted part of a broadcast to defining Chinese
communism. He asked his friend Evans Fordyce Carlson, the first
American military attaché to visit northwest China, to help him:

> I have pointed out that Chinese Communists are not precisely what the
> label means to many people. Having been challenged on that statement,
> I asked Major Evans Carlson to give me his definition of the Chinese
> Communists. . . . He says the Chinese Communist leaders study not
> only Marx, Engels and Lenin, but Rousseau, Jefferson and Sun Yat-
> sen. And the social order they set up where they have control is
> compounded of the philosophies of all six, leavened by their own
> thinking and experience, and their knowledge of their own people and
> customs. Politically, he says, they set up a representative government,
> since they elect their own officials. Economically, they believe in the
> state ownership of banks, mines and communications, but they pro-
> mote producers' and consumers' cooperatives. "By and large" he
> says, "they favor with amazing fidelity the type of state envisioned by
> Sun Yat-sen—a state belonging to all the people, controlled by all the
> people and with rights and benefits for the enjoyment of all the
> people." He points out that the Chinese Communist party does have
> representatives in the Third International. But this, he says, has not
> affected the application of an indigenous philosophy. . . . As to the
> reality of the political democracy in the Communist controlled districts,
> Major Carlson says the people actually do select their own village and
> county officials, and in so doing they have freedom of speech, press
> and assembly.[46]

Carlson's definition left a good deal to be desired, though it described a
Chinese communism Swing wanted to believe in. The Major offered

description instead of analysis. Phrases such as "belonging to all the people" could never be explained precisely. Carlson optimistically accepted a part for the whole: "People actually do select their own village and county officials and in so doing they have freedom of speech, press and assembly." Swing might have asked a less romantic observer for help. Even so, Carlson, himself a professed liberal, reveals in his explanation a groping toward some comprehension of ideology. He does not make the notorious claim of the war years—that Chinese Communists were only "agrarian reformers."

Swing's belief that communism could promote progress and reform had definite limits. He spoke favorably of the Soviet Union but explained that "some instinct kept him from stepping across into the ranks of fellow travelers." By "some instinct" Swing meant a definition of liberalism based on nonrevolutionary change. He made this clear in a 1941 commencement address where he eloquently defended the democratic tradition before a graduating class filled with many avowed Communists:

> If I understand correctly, some of the liveliest hours you have spent in Brooklyn College have been produced by a conflict between the advocates of Utopia and the defenders of an imperfect democracy. . . . But what is notable about this country of ours is not its completeness, but that the opportunity remains to complete it. The Utopians do not see this, for their blueprint is complete. . . . When they come to do the building *from* the blueprints they will be making imperfections, too, and their dialectical advantage will begin to melt away.[47]

Swing feared that a revolutionary threat from the right existed in America during the 1930s. His 1935 book, *Forerunners of American Fascism,* contained pessimistic conclusions about the potential for fascism in the United States. He saw a danger to personal liberties in such people as Father Coughlin and Huey Long. Swing voted for the Socialist Norman Thomas in 1936, convinced that the New Deal was not doing enough. Only events in Europe turned him into an ardent Roosevelt supporter after 1939.

The commentator claimed that "most Americans underneath are . . . kindly and believers in the ultimate good."[48] He predicted that "cultural values would of course become exciting" if only more "thought and affection" were put into "serious broadcasting." Swing felt no real commitment to that "momument of a prosperous, mechanized America, the buildings that make up Rockefeller Center in New York.''[49] He considered individual creativity the most important thing a person could achieve. He stated that to be a musician or poet was much finer than being a scientist.

Swing placed enormous emphasis on the necessity of moral commitment:

> But there is one loyalty which is still greater than loyalty to a cause or to a friend. Here I beg of you not to dismiss that word truth as vague, abstract, and subjective. Instead of truth, I nearly said moral values, that a greater loyalty than a cause or a friend is the loyalty of moral values. I also nearly said loyalty to oneself. For the sense I have of truth is that it is a personal judgment based on a sense of social obligation, as well as on a scientific appraisal of evidence.[50]

Germany's treatment of Jews aroused the commentator much more than it did many Americans. In 1938 a young Polish Jew assassinated a German embassy official in Paris. Swing served on a committee that promised to hire a leading lawyer in France to defend the accused. Shortly after, in a broadcast he made yet another reference to the Nazis' "cold-blooded medieval destruction of the Jews." And this at a time when the State Department's Pierrepont Moffat could state that "the Jews [in America] are demanding that we go more strongly to the bat [sic] . . . but no one likes to be subjected to pressure of the sort they are exerting and the American public does not like pressure in favor of one particular population or group."[51]

One of the most revealing indices of Swing's attitudes appears in a 1949 letter he wrote to Albert Einstein. He had interviewed the scientist and worked with him in publicizing the dangers of atomic warfare. "And I came to love your spirit, with its clarity, sincerity, and complete absence of vanity," Swing wrote, "as I have never loved the spirit of any public man. You have taught me much, which I hope to be able in part to learn. I left you with a sense of wonder and also with affection, and with abiding thanks."[52]

There are obvious difficulties in concluding that these sentiments sum up the credo of the typical American liberal. The word itself eludes careful definition. Swing fervently believed in reform. But he was no radical—he did not seek fundamental change outside established channels of authority. Nor did his zeal for reform extend to proposals for what to attempt. He accepted the state as the proper vehicle of change, yet placed the burden of moral commitment mostly on the individual. He never saw the contradiction.

In spite of these shortcomings, Swing's respect for honesty and creativity, his belief in the perfectibility of human nature, his patriotic love of the democratic way of life, his reluctance to glory in the triumphs of technology, his acceptance of the welfare state, Keynesian economics, and his feelings of the necessity of moral judgment and commitment constitute a rough system of belief. In this sense Raymond Gram Swing can be considered a typical liberal. For certain, the commentator believed the word "liberal" possessed special meaning and that it described himself.[53] This says something about the intellectual climate in America during the 1930s.

After 1945 Swing broadcast much less frequently. Listeners seemed to tire quickly of his decision to devote one newscast a week to the dangers of the atomic bomb. His national prominence ended. In 1951 he joined the Voice of America. Two years later he resigned, protesting the "spineless failure" of the Department of State to protect employees smeared by Joseph McCarthy. For several years Swing served as Edward R. Murrow's ghost writer. In 1957 he married a fourth wife. He retired on December 31, 1963. After writing his most engaging memoirs, he lived quietly in Washington until his death on December 2, 1968.

UNOFFICIAL SPOKESMAN FOR THE ADMINISTRATION

Swing had a major impact on both foreign policy-makers and the general public before 1941. Aside from news analyses on radio, he made himself known through addresses to prestigious foreign affairs groups. In the fall of 1937 he spoke before the *New York Herald Tribune's* Seventh Annual Forum on Current Problems in New York City.[54] He appeared along with Eleanor Roosevelt, Senators Claude Pepper and Arthur H. Vandenberg, Secretary of Agriculture Henry A. Wallace, and Constantine Oumansky, Russian ambassador to the United States. He was the only prominent broadcaster whose speeches were regularly covered by the *New York Times*.

The commentator occasionally sent letters to important officials in the Department of State. In January 1939 he told Cordell Hull that he had given him an "enthusiastic tribute in a broadcast devoted to your services to your country."⁵⁵ He urged Hull to talk with British and French leaders in hopes of changing their nonintervention policy toward the Spanish Civil War.

Two months later Swing telegraphed Under Secretary of State Sumner Welles. He requested that the United States grant asylum to six hundred Spanish intellectuals trapped in Madrid. The commentator was joined by such people as Albert Einstein. The next day Hull himself replied by wire. He promised not to remain "indifferent."⁵⁶

The broadcaster's militant wife made others aware of her husband's activities. One historian states that Betty Gram Swing was one of three friends who finally "clinched" William Allen White's decision to become chairman of the Nonpartisan Committee for Peace through Revision of the Neutrality Law in September 1939.⁵⁷ Mrs. Swing was an influential member of White's Committee to Defend America by Aiding the Allies, active in the Union Now movement, a lobbyist for the National Woman's Party, and instrumental in raising money for Spanish refugee scholars and artists. One of the commentator's children recalls her mother as having been more "radical" than Swing himself during this period.⁵⁸

A most revealing aspect of Swing's political activities concerns the Council for Democracy. Begun by Henry Luce on July 30, 1940, the group included the president of CBS and such prominent Roosevelt advisers as Robert Sherwood. Swing served as chairman of the board for this organization. Years later the broadcaster claimed that the committee's avowed purpose was "to spur US entry into war."⁵⁹ At the time he felt that it had the same goal as White's Committee to Defend America, although it particularly concerned itself with "studying, applying, popularizing, [and] stimulating the application of those democratic principles now endangered by the test of war."⁶⁰

In January 1942 the news analyst formed another committee, Citizens for Victory, based on the membership of the White committee and the Council for Democracy. The first goal of Citizens for Victory, described by Swing himself shortly after the Japanese attack, suggests clearly the news commentator's attitude toward the enemy: *"We are out to win the war—fully and completely.* No compromises—no lazy appeasement for the sake of an early but shaky peace. The war must go on, in cooperation with our allies, until the Axis forces of aggression are blasted out of their last foothold." This is scarcely the voice of moderation, or one primarily concerned with the preservation of democratic principles even in time of war. It breathes the spirit of the man who tried to join the Department of State on December 8, 1941.[61]

Roosevelt learned of Swing in 1934 when the BBC chose the commentator to explain the New Deal to Britain. The next year Swing met a dedicated presidential adviser, Harry Hopkins. The two became good friends. Before Hopkins's death, he asked Swing to help him with the biography Robert Sherwood eventually wrote. Sherwood described Swing as "one of the few" columnists and broadcasters with whom the Iowan was friendly. One of Roosevelt's speech writers stated that in October 1940 he talked with Hopkins about getting some additional help for the presidential campagin. "The major requisites," he adds, "were to be able to write clearly and forcefully, and to be fully in sympathy with the domestic and international policies of the President. The first name that we agreed upon was Raymond Gram Swing."[62]

In March 1942 Hopkins sent a memorandum to the President's press secretary. Roosevelt wanted a copy of one of the news analyst's broadcasts. Two months later Hopkins and the President listened to Swing present his evening commentary. At its conclusion Hopkins phoned the broadcaster and asked him to come over to the White House for a friendly private conversation with Roosevelt and himself.[63] Swing attended a number of White House press conferences. He says that Roosevelt knew his face and name. It seems likely, however, that this became truer in the months following Pearl Harbor, when the newscaster moved from New York to Washington.

Swing's commentaries were heard in many parts of the world by 1941, particularly in England and Latin America; the administration recognized the value of analyses so favorable to its point of view. To broadcast outside the United States necessitated official governmental approval. And why give such approval to someone who might prove a lukewarm supporter? The decision to let Swing be heard overseas says something significant about how he was viewed in Washington. In March 1941 the administration started sending daily Spanish and Portuguese translations of Swing's commentaries by shortwave to Latin America. A surviving example of one of these broadcasts, which also could be heard in English, suggests that Swing did not forsake his careful approach in evaluating rumors for a worldwide audience. Discussing talk of what the Japanese might be doing to promote peace in November 1941, he added that "this sounds almost too good to be believed and I am not reporting it with any recommendation for credence."

Swing enjoyed an enormous audience in England. His fortnightly Saturday broadcasts at 9:20 P.M. were taken very seriously by many influential persons. Members of Parliament "formed a 'Swing Club' to listen to the commentaries in the parliamentary lounge." The BBC rebroadcast Swing's analyses to members of the British Commonwealth. In January 1940 a phenomenal 30.7 percent of England's adult population listened to his newscasts.[64] A few months later, the News Department of the Foreign Office was "bombarded with enquiries" because of what Swing said in a broadcast. Ambassador John G. Winant, who arrived in London during February 1941, stated that Swing had a "large listening public in Great Britain" and that what he said proved "very helpful in explaining and interpreting American news." Such a response prompted one malicious writer to term Swing's the best-known voice in the world.[65]

Perhaps the best evidence for the value of Swing's broadcasts to the British Foreign Office can be seen from the way a rumor concerning Swing was handled. In May 1940 Lord Lothian, British ambassador to the United States, reported that he understood that the BBC intended to terminate Swing's broadcasts because he was allegedly a "hostile influence." Lothian strongly denied the accusation:

> He is one of the most powerful voices on the radio in the United States and is genuinely friendly. We regard his influence as favourable especially because he is temperate and carries conviction. He is definitely regarded as pro-Ally here, though he is very independent, which is the reason for his influence. During the last two weeks he moved within limits of radio code far [sic] in the direction of un-neutrality.[66]

T. North Whitehead, assigned to the British embassy in Washington when the war began, and in the American Department in London after November 1939, noted that in America he "listened regularly" to Swing. He added that he "consistently listened" to Swing's English broadcasts. A superior noted that he too had "listened consistently" to Swing. He added that "we must certainly find out what is toward and intervene with the BBC with all weight, if necessary. The matter *may* be urgent."[67]

It turned out that nothing was amiss, save that Swing's doctor had ordered him to take a longer summer vacation. John Balfour, head of the American Department, suggested that "it be privately conveyed to Mr. Swing how much the British public relish his talks and how much their enforced interruption will be regretted."[68]

Before 1941 the commentator also contributed a "Weekly Cable on America" to the *London Sunday Express*. Since this paper's daily edition in 1939 had the largest circulation of any newspaper in the world, the news analyst's ideas in print reached an enormous number of readers, even if not everyone finished the column. In December 1941 the Minister of Information answered a Parliamentary Question by "quoting the opinion of an impartial commentator. In a recent newspaper article, Mr. Raymond Gram Swing wrote. . . ."[69]

While in London during July 1941, Swing was given a special dinner, attended by numerous government ministers, honoring his contribution to British understanding of America. Swing's factual—though optimistic—broadcasts meant a great deal at a time when England still doubted that the United States would assist her war effort enough. Winston Churchill invited Harry Hopkins and Swing to a small luncheon during this visit. After the meal the Prime Minister and the commentator had a long intimate conversation.[70]

Swing aroused considerable feeling in his American listeners. As he wrote Herbert Hoover in August 1940: "You would be amazed at the storm of protests that my broadcasts have brought me. In a sense, that bespeaks only the quick resentment of people at any thought of injuring Britain. I have been roundly abused and accused of taking Nazi money. . . ."[71] In the rest of the world, he was the only American commentator heard regularly. As such he enjoyed immense influence. In America he had a smaller audience. In June 1940 Swing received a Hooperating of 14.5, extremely high for a newscaster, and comparable to ratings received by entertainment shows (a 6.0 on this commercial rating scale was considered good for news analysts).[72] The broadcaster spoke at 10:00 P.M. for the East; 9:00 P.M. for the Midwest. Both of these were good hours for reaching a large audience. However, the Mutual system was by no means as effective as CBS or NBC in many cities. MBS had powerful affiliates in New York and Chicago; the Washington outlet was certainly adequate. But Swing attracted fewer listeners in small towns than commentators on the more powerful networks.

The news analyst spoke once a week, and only in New York City, from

1936 until October 1938. In September 1939 he was sponsored nationally twice a week. By October 1940 he broadcast Monday through Friday in New York and Washington. In Chicago, where the *Chicago Tribune* owned the Mutual outlet, he spoke only twice a week. Isolationist Colonel Robert R. McCormick had no choice but to present the viewpoint of an archenemy on nights when Swing had a commercial sponsor. As late as November 1941 the newscaster broadcast Monday through Thursday in New York and Washington but still only twice a week in Chicago.[73]

Of those commentators on the air before Pearl Harbor, Swing was definitely taken the most seriously by administration leaders. Roosevelt's confidant, Harry Hopkins, kept in frequent communication with the broadcaster. Swing and his wife also played active parts in two of the most prominent pressure groups advocating greatly increased American involvement overseas. As head of the Council for Democracy, Swing lobbied for full hostilities from July 1940 on. As a commentator, however, he made his feelings less public.

Swing's conception of liberalism demanded specific attitudes in his broadcasts. He believed in the rights of organized labor. During 1940 and 1941 commentators such as Kaltenborn and Fulton Lewis, Jr., frequently accused labor of unpatriotic strikes that, they insisted, hindered efforts at national defense. Most of the time Swing rarely mentioned the possible conflict between labor's right to strike and the need for a unified national effort toward defense preparedness. But one comment, made in October 1941, suggests where his sympathies lay: "Because of public opinion, management is encouraged to play up every labor dispute as disastrous to defense production, and to fly the stars and stripes in resisting legitimate labor demands."[74]

In June 1938, before many persons had begun debating such matters, Swing delivered a hammer-and-tongs assault on isolationists. Persons of this persuasion, he claimed, accepted a "narrow, strictly non-ethical, morbidly suspicious and fundamentally militarist philosophy." He added that "the isolationist, the hater of foreigners, the suspicious provincial, the man who doesn't care what happens to anybody else . . . has helped create the world as it is today."[75] As a liberal, he felt a moral obligation to care about what happened overseas. Two months later he warned that "it is impossible to talk about Europe as though it were a detached phenomenon." Boake Carter saw any American involvement overseas as meddling; he felt the United States should simply do nothing about what went on in the rest of the world. Swing knew otherwise. He declared that even isolation "would be an *active* policy; one needing *action.*"[76]

As early as February 1939 Swing declared that the Rome-Berlin axis "has a third dimension, it links up with Tokyo." A month later he became more explicit: "After all, there is only one conflict going on in the world today, a struggle for supremacy in power by one group of states over another."[77]

In July 1940 Swing justified Roosevelt's decision to restrict the export of scrap iron and oil to Japan as "not belligerent and not specifically anti-Japanese." He claimed that this step was "not an embargo" though he did not explain why.[78] During the next eight months, and as late as the middle of July 1941, Swing made a number of references to the existence of a moderate Japanese faction that had no desire for hostilities with the United States. On August 25 he gave up on moderation:

> Time and again since the invasion of China, the United States has been told that Japanese moderates were just on the verge of getting control over their extremists. And each time the extremists succeeded in exploiting the gain the moderates made in Washington.

As he explained in October:

> American opinion toward Japan is less blurred than toward the European war. War with Japan is less dreaded than involvement in war in Europe. . . . War between the United States and Japan would bring the United States into the European war too. It would put an end to the mental twists and insincerities of present day popular thinking. People would sigh with relief that things had become simple and clear.[79]

"Simple and clear"—that is what Swing strove to provide in his broadcasts. The best example is his unswerving support for each move Roosevelt made in the area of foreign policy after May 1940. Swing termed the Destroyers-Bases Agreement of September 3 a "signal act of intimacy and mutual assistance."[80] He praised the passage of the Lend-Lease Act. In May 1941, when some accused the President of vacillation regarding a decision to provide convoys, Swing proved most understanding: "Impatience with Roosevelt in American political life now paradoxically becomes part of the Roosevelt strategy.'' A couple of days later he explained that if the President openly declared himself in favor of '' 'taking' the country into war, the public would turn on him later.''[81] Yet Swing termed the occupation of Iceland on July 7 a ''logical development'' in American policy. Roosevelt's September 11 ''shoot-to-kill'' [sic] speech, the broadcaster claimed, was ''about right'' for the ''majority'' of Americans.[82]

An extreme example of Swing's faith in Roosevelt is provided by the President's Navy and Total Defense Day address on October 27, 1941, and his press conference the following day. Roosevelt aroused considerable furor by claiming to have proof of Nazi intrigue in the Western Hemisphere—evidence that American security was clearly endangered by Germany. According to Langer and Gleason, Roosevelt stated ''that he had in his possession a secret map, made in Germany for the Nazi Government, which allegedly revealed a Nazi plan to divide South America into five vassal states, one of which would have included the Republic of Panama.'' Unable to believe that the President would knowingly use a fraudulent map to promote a declaration of war against Germany, the historians suggest only that ''Mr. Roosevelt had before him an item of clumsy propaganda wholly unworthy of the notice he gave it.''[83]

Swing took a more understanding view. In his broadcast the following evening, he not only fully accepted the authenticity of the map—indicating the extent of his credulity about Nazi agents in Latin America—but demonstrated just how far he was prepared to go in supporting the President. Swing emphasized Nazi press coverage of Roosevelt's speech:

> The excerpts chosen were mostly those telling about the secret map of a Nazi-fied Latin America and the plans for a Nazi church to replace all other religions. These were branded as forgeries, as the President had foreseen they would be. In Washington Mr. Roosevelt at his press conference today did not throw more light on these two disclosures. The Latin American map, he said, could not be published because notations on it would reveal its source. That, he said, might jeopardize the source and perhaps eliminate a fountainhead of valuable information. He also said he could not make public the religious documents. . . . The President's speech, I should add, pleased the British.[84]

And well it might have. Some Englishmen probably hoped it might become another Zimmermann Note.

The map serves as an extreme example of Swing's decision, after May 1940, to become an unofficial spokesman for the Department of State and the President. Criticisms leveled at the administration became criticisms of Swing's broadcasts. On December 31, 1941, he summarized America's foreign policy in the months leading up to Pearl Harbor: "Our changeover did not come on December 7th, as we may be tempted to think. December 7th came because of our changeover." He explained that "step-by-step" progress had been necessary. "If a nation was going to see the issues of the war," he added, "this was the way the panorama could be taken in."[85] Roosevelt would have agreed fully.

Swing took his job most seriously. He felt an obligation to enlighten. He believed fervently in what he said on the air. Such intense convictions helped make especially persuasive his assessments of American policy broadcast to Britain and many other parts of the world. Swing "made journalism a high calling" because of the care with which he prepared his commentaries.[86] Compared to other radio news analysts, such as Elmer Davis or Boake Carter at the height of his public career, Swing never reached such enormous numbers of listeners in the United States. Only conditions abroad frightened Americans enough so that millions, even those with little formal education, paid attention to his scholarly, sometimes dry, sometimes dull explanations. Roosevelt found it extremely useful to have someone not officially a member of the administration offer such deeply felt support for his "step-by-step" progress toward war.

Swing had a consistency in his broadcasts that also made him unique. He had reported the rise of fascism in Europe and believed a similar phenomenon had threatened America in the form of Father Coughlin and Huey Long. As early as 1938 he began his campaign against isolationism in its various guises. A true Wilsonian, Swing felt America was directly involved in the fate of the rest of the world; he delighted in showing how the day's events made such a conclusion logical. Swing simplified the world struggle so as to give listeners an easy either-or decision. Either support Roosevelt and aid Britain in every way possible, or look for fascism's inevitable triumph throughout the entire world.

Swing did not invent internationalism, or interventionism. But he could not conceive of Amerca's not being involved in the affairs of other nations. To him the support of liberal ideas throughout the world was America's high duty. From today's perspective the difficulty in trying to impose political and social order on the entire world is all too clear. To Swing, and this is what makes him a significant spokesman for his generation, there was a simple way of eradicating threats to liberalism: full-scale war on fascism all over the world. Such a belief led Swing to willingly abandon the journalist's obligation to serve as independent critic. With the entire world threatened, there was no time for false objectivity; instead America needed a sense of commitment—of moral zeal. Swing's sorrow was the cautious way Roosevelt seemed to respond to demands for bolder action; Swing's joy was the declaration of war in December 1941; Swing's pity was that as a journalist he had been unable to do more.

NOTES

1. Fred W. Friendly, quoted in obituary, *New York Times,* December 24, 1968, p. 23.
2. Raymond Swing, *"Good Evening!": A Professional Memoir* (New York, 1964), p. 301.
3. Richard O. Boyer, "The Voice," *New Yorker,* November 21, 1942, p. 28. In 1964 Swing said that the *New Yorker* profile was "gay but maliciously inaccurate." *"Good Evening!"*, p. 264. In 1968 he claimed that Boyer was a "Communist" and that they were "ideological enemies." Interview with author, September 5, 1968, Washington, D.C.
4. Jack Alexander and F. I. Odell, "Radio's Best Bedside Manner," *Saturday Evening Post,* December 14, 1940, p. 15.
5. Swing, *"Good Evening!"*, pp. 3-15. The broadcaster's memoirs include a superb account of his Oberlin years. Raymond and Peter Swing, H. V. and Rolf Kaltenborn discussing "Youth Problems," Mutual Broadcasting System broadcast, June 30, 1939, 78 rpm original transcription, Kaltenborn MSS.
6. Swing, *"Good Evening!"*, pp. 15-31.
7. Photograph in Alexander and Odell, "Radio's Best Bedside Manner," p. 82.
8. Swing, *"Good Evening!"*, p. 32; Swing, address before the American Newspaper and Foreign News Correspondents Association, May 31, 1938, Box 1, Swing MSS.

9. Swing, *"Good Evening!"*, p. 47; Raymond E. Swing, "How Germany was Forced into War," [Chicago, 1914], Germanistic Society of Chicago, Pamphlets Dealing with the War in Europe No. 3.

10. MBS broadcast, October 18, 1939, Box 8, Swing MSS; the same story, using slightly different words, is in Swing, *"Good Evening!"*, p. 97.

11. Swing, *"Good Evening!"*, pp. 61,64.

12. *Ibid.*, p. 128.

13. Telegram, Swing to Hoover, September 27, 1919, "Raymond Swing 1919" folder, Pre-Commerce Correspondence File 5, HHL.

14. Frankfurter to Swing, February 2, 1921, Box 106, Felix Frankfurter MSS, Manuscript Division, Library of Congress, Washington, D.C. [hereafter Frankfurter MSS].

15. Swing, *"Good Evening!"*, pp. 122-40; John Hohenberg, *Foreign Correspondence: The Great Reporters and Their Times* (New York, 1964), p. 269; Betty Gram Swing, obituary, *Washington Post,* September 4, 1969, p. B6.

16. Swing, *"Good Evening!"*, p. 147; Hohenberg, *Foreign Correspondence,* p. 277.

17. Swing, *"Good Evening!"*, pp. 155-56.

18. Stimson Diary, July 29, 1931, 18: 153. See also August 27, 1931, 17: 186; February 17, 1930, 13: 41, Stimson MSS.

19. Swing, *"Good Evening!"* pp. 165, 172; cf. *Nation,* September 12-December 12, 1934, for Swing's articles.

20. Swing, *Forerunners of American Fascism* (New York, 1935); Millis review in *Saturday Review,* May 11, 1935, p. 5.

21. Swing, "Alf Landon is not Cal Coolidge," *Nation,* January 8, 1936, pp. 39-41.

22. C. S. Marsh, executive secretary, Second National Conference on Educational Broadcasting, to Swing, December 3, 1937, Box 1, Swing MSS; Swing, *"Good Evening!"*, pp. 184-85.

23. Swing to Alice Mead Swing, October 29, 1938, quoted in Swing, *"Good Evening!"*, p. 206.

24. Earl Sparling, "Let's Listen to Swing!", *Reader's Digest,* 37 (August 1940): 44; CBS Black Book, "Radio Programs 1930," CBS Program Information; Swing, *"Good Evening!"*, pp. 169, 191; César Saerchinger, *Hello America! Radio Adventures in Europe* (Boston, 1939), pp. 191-92.

25. Swing, *"Good Evening!"*, p. 191; list of news commentators, commercial and sustaining, 1935, 1936, in "Talent Radio" folder; CBS Black Book, "Radio Programs 1935," "Radio Programs 1936," all in CBS Program Information; letter to Harry C. Butcher sent with memorandum, Steve Early to Cordell Hull, June 7, 1935; Roosevelt's own notation on memorandum, Marvin McIntyre to Marguerite Le Hand, June 6, 1936, both referred to in White House cross reference, Box 1, CBS 1935, OF 256, FDRL.

26. Note on CBS broadcast, December 6, 1935, Box 3, Swing MSS. Swing said this was the only time it occurred. Interview with author, September 5, 1968.

27. Swing, *"Good Evening!"*, pp. 191-93.

28. Moffat Diary, October 13, 1938; Swing, *"Good Evening!"*, p. 203. The broadcaster carefully reminds his readers that he was but one person who gave this advice.

29. MBS broadcast, October 18, 1938, Box 5, Swing MSS; reprinted with almost no changes in Swing, *Preview of History* (Garden City, N.Y., 1943), pp. 19-24; Swing *"Good Evening!"*, p. 200.

30. MBS broadcast, October 18, 1938, Box 5, Swing MSS.

31. MBS broadcast, December 13, 1938, Box 5, Swing MSS; MBS broadcast, March 16, 1939, in Swing, *How War Came* (New York, 1939), p. 33.

32. *Ibid.*, pp. 195, 200.

33. *Variety,* August 30, 1938, p. 26; Boyer, "The Voice," November 14, 1942, p. 28.

34. The author's assessment of Swing's voice is based on listening to recorded broadcasts, October 18, 1938-July 28, 1941, RSS-LC; G.M.R. Dougall, former deputy director, Historical Office, Department of State, luncheon with author, August 20, 1969, Washington, D.C.

35. Boyer, "The Voice," November 14, 1942, p. 28; MBS recorded broadcast, October 18, 1938; February 11 and 14, 1941, all in RSS-LC.

36. MBS recorded broadcast, October 18, 1938, RSS-LC; quoted in Clarissa Lorenz, " 'And, Now—Mr. Swing,' " *Christian Science Monitor Magazine,* December 28, 1940, p. 6; MBS broadcast, July 29, 1941, Box 15, Swing MSS.

37. *Variety,* September 27, 1939, p. 26; MBS recorded broadcast, February 10, 1941, RSS-LC; Swing, *"Good Evening!"*, p. 197.

38. Quoted in Boyer, "The Voice," November 14, 1942, p. 26; MBS recorded broadcast, July 25, 1941, RSS-LC.

39. MBS broadcast, April 28, 1939, Box 6; January 10, 1939, Box 5, Swing MSS.

40. Robert Rutherford Smith, "The Wartime Radio News Commentaries of Raymond Swing, 1939-1945" (Ph.D. dissertation, Ohio State University, 1963), p. 109.

41. MBS broadcast, February 18, 1941, Box 13; July 14, 1939, Box 7, Swing MSS.

42. MBS broadcast, November 18, 1940, Box 12, Swing MSS.

43. MBS broadcast, April 20, 1939, Box 6, Swing MSS.

44. For instance, in January 1938 Swing explained one reason for his interest in China. He stated that his father had been a professor at Oberlin College and that he had permitted his son to have many conversations with a young Chinese student then attending Oberlin. H. H. Kung had often visited the Swing home. The broadcaster added that Chiang Kai-shek's brother-in-law was now China's

Finance Minister and that during the summer of 1937 he had "looked him up in New York City." MBS broadcast, January 7, 1938, Box 4, Swing MSS.

45. Tsou, "The American Political Tradition and the American Image of Chinese Communism," *Political Science Quarterly* 77 (December 1962): 570-600, revised slightly in Tsou, *America's Failure in China, 1941-50* (Chicago, 1963), pp. 219-36, in particular, pp. 224-45. Tsou's analysis of Swing, it should be noted, is based on a single broadcast.

46. MBS broadcast, March 7, 1941, Swing MSS. Box 38 of the Swing MSS contains seventeen detailed letters from Carlson to Swing, the earlist dated January 26, 1942.

47. Alexander and Odell, "Radio's Best Bedside Manner," p. 14; "Utopia versus Democracy," Brooklyn College, Brooklyn, New York, June 23, 1941, in Swing, *Preview of History,* p. 241.

48. Swing, *Forerunners,* pp. 14-21; Swing, *"Good Evening!",* p. 229; MBS broadcast, December 27, 1938, Box 5, Swing MSS.

49. "Radio as a Present Day Force," address presented at the Second National Conference on Educational Broadcasting, November 30, 1937, copy in Box 1, Swing MSS; "Youth, War, and Freedom," commencement address at Olivet College, Olivet, Michigan, June 16, 1940, reprinted in *Nation,* June 22, 1940, pp. 749-50.

50. Swing, "Utopia versus Democracy," p. 241.

51. *New York Times,* November 16, 1938, p. 9; MBS broadcast, December 6, 1938; Moffat Diary, October 29 and 30, 1938.

52. Swing to Einstein, August 14, 1949, Box 38, Swing MSS.

53. Swing, interview with author, September 5, 1968.

54. The forum was held on October 4-5, 1937, brochure in Box 1, Swing MSS.

55. Swing to Hull, January 19, 1939, Box 44, Correspondence II, Hull MSS.

56. Telegram, Swing to Welles, March 31, 1939; telegram, Hull to Swing, April 1, 1939, 852.00/9090, RG 59.

57. Walter Johnson, *The Battle Against Isolation,* (Chicago, 1944), p. 41.

58. Alexander and Odell, "Radio's Best Bedside Manner," p. 84; Betty Gram Swing, "This Happened in Europe," *Independent Woman* (March 1939): 88; John Temple Swing (replying for Sally Swing Shelley) to author, January 20, 1970; Professor Peter Gram Swing to author, December 9, 1969.

59. Swing, *"Good Evening!",* p. 216; Mark Lincoln Chadwin, *The Hawks of World War II* (Chapel Hill, N.C., 1968), has almost nothing on the Council for Democracy. *New York Times,* October 10, 1940, p. 22; Swing, interview with author, September 5, 1968.

60. Form letter, Swing to Fred I. Kent, January 30, 1942 [dated January 23], Folder S, Box 4, Fred I. Kent MSS, Manuscript Division, Princeton University Library, Princeton, N.J. [hereafter Kent MSS].

61. Memorandum, Swing to Kent, January 30, 1942 [dated January 23], Folder S, Box 4, Kent MSS; William L. Langer and S. Everett Gleason, *The Challenge to Isolation, 1937-1940* (New York, 1952), pp. 710-11; Swing, *"Good Evening!"*, p. 229.

62. A folder on Swing, Correspondence Files, 1941-1945, Harry L. Hopkins MSS, FDRL, contains only a few letters, the earliest dated February 11, 1943; Swing, "Harry Hopkins: Whipping Boy or Assistant President?", *Atlantic Monthly* 182 (November 1948): 89; Robert E. Sherwood, *Roosevelt and Hopkins: An Intimate History* (New York, 1948), pp. xi, xvi, 835; Samuel Rosenman, *Working with Roosevelt* (New York, 1952), p. 228.

63. Hopkins to Early, March 18, 1942, Box 8, Misc., OF 136, FDRL. Box 8 contains Swing's March 16 broadcast—the one requested. Cf. Swing, *"Good Evening!"*, pp. 231, 229. According to Swing, the meeting, "the only intimate time" he ever spent with Roosevelt, took place on May 24, 1942.

64. Teletype copy of WRCA shortwave broadcast, November 21, 1941, Ministry of Information to Foreign Office, F12692/86/23, FO; *Variety,* March 12, 1941, p. 30; Swing, *"Good Evening!"*, p. 194; *Time,* January 8, 1940, p. 34.

65. Typed jacket precis, P. Dixon, American Department, Foreign Office, May 30, 1940, R6407/58/22, FO. Swing made the broadcast on May 29; John G. Winant, *Letter From Grosvenor Square: An Account of a Stewardship* (Boston, 1947), p. 164. He adds that this was during the "early period" before December 1941; *ibid.*, p. 163; Boyer, "The Voice," November 14, 1942, p. 24.

66. Telegram No. 785, Lothian to Foreign Office, May 22, 1940, A3028/131/45, FO. As early as May 15, 1939, the Director of the BBC, F. W. Ogilvie, wrote Sir Alexander Cadogan, Permanent Under Secretary of State, that Swing was "the broadcaster whose sense of American feeling we have hitherto found to be trustworthy." A3509/27/45, FO.

67. Ink notation on precis jacket concerning telegram 785, A3028/131/45; ink notation on precis jacket, John Victor Thomas Woolrych Tait Perowne, American Department, May 24, 1940, A3028/131/45, FO.

68. Ink notation on precis jacket concerning telegram 785, A3028/131/45, FO.

69. See copy of Swing article, September 21, 1941, in A7697/355/45, FO; "Report on the British Press by Miss Cowles," n.d. [1942], 19-20, Box 16, PSF, FDRL; Mr. Bracken, in response to question of Hamilton Kerr, M.P., December 3, 1941, printed copy in A9860/118/45, FO.

70. Swing, *"Good Evening!"*, pp. 211-14.

71. Swing to Hoover, August 12, 1940, "Raymond Gram Swing" folder 1825, PPI 185, HHL.

72. *Broadcasting,* August 1, 1940, p. 76, cited in Smith, "The Wartime

Radio News Commentaries," p. 23; Swing, interview with author, September 5, 1968.

73. Based on daily radio schedules in the *New York Times,* the *Washington Evening Star,* and the *Chicago Tribune,* 1937-1941.

74. Column, *London Sunday Express,* October 31, 1941, copy in Box 1, Swing MSS.

75. "What of Collective Security?", pp. 39-40, address given at Beloit College, Beloit, Wisconsin. Though undated, the copy in Box 1, Swing MSS, speaks of the war in Spain as nearing the end of its second year.

76. MBS broadcast, August 30, 1938, Box 5, Swing MSS.

77. MBS broadcast, February 11, March 25, 1939, Box 5, 6, Swing MSS.

78. MBS broadcast, July 26, 1940, Box 11, Swing MSS.

79. MBS broadcast, August 25, 1941, Box 15; Column, *London Sunday Express,* n.d. [c. October 16, 1941], copy in Box 1, both in Swing MSS.

80. MBS broadcast, September 3, 1940, Box 12, Swing MSS.

81. Column, *London Sunday Express,* n.d. [c. May 1, 1941], copy in Box 1, Swing MSS; column, *London Sunday Express,* May 11, 1941, copy in Group 13, 1941, Box 7, PPF 1820, FDRL.

82. MBS broadcast from London, July 7, 1941, Box 15; column, *London Sunday Express,* September 12, 1941, copy in Box 1—both in Swing MSS.

83. Langer and Gleason, *The Undeclared War,* p. 595.

84. MBS broadcast, October 28, 1941, Box 15, Swing MSS.

85. MBS broadcast, December 31, 1941, Box 16, Swing MSS.

86. Editorial, *Washington Post,* December 24, 1968.

5 | Elmer Davis: Radio's Hoosier

His appearance lent itself to easy caricature. Those enormous black beetle eyebrows, the little black bow ties, the baggy pepper-and-salt suits. Others saw a resemblance to handsome Cordell Hull, Franklin D. Roosevelt's Secretary of State. His reply to would-be admirers: "We both look like Harding."[1] This was Elmer Davis, the Indiana Hoosier with such a comfortable first name. If how the man looked tells us nothing of his mind, the reply to flatterers suggests something of his personality. For two reasons Davis was unique among the major news commentators broadcasting before Pearl Harbor: he was a professional writer in the finest sense of the word, and he possessed a superb sense of humor.

On the air Davis exuded common sense. Though intensely committed to all aspects of Roosevelt's foreign policy after May 1940, the commentator did not lose his facility for discussing sensitive problems in a calm, deliberate manner. Listeners felt they could trust his judgment. But there were limitations. "Although . . . for many years an active journalist," a Nazi propagandist noted, "he has had from his youth on very little contact with the broad masses."[2] In other words, Davis sought to interpret the life and good sense of the average person without having experienced important aspects of what he wished to describe. If so, perhaps the news analyst's constant deprecation of his first name was a device to hide lingering embarrassment over his origins.

HIS MIND SET HIM APART

Elmer Holmes Davis entered the small, peaceful, optimistic world of

125

southern Indiana on January 13, 1890. Village names reflected a bound-less faith in the future. Aurora, his birthplace, was just a few miles up the river from Rising Sun. Even today, towns in the vicinity such as Patriot, North, and Centersquare suggest a homely rural society concerned with the problems the commentator was to leave behind, if never entirely escape.

Elam Holmes Davis was fifty-six at the birth of his youngest son. Born in Jefferson County, Missouri, in 1834, the father came to Aurora when five years old. A devout Baptist, he had been licensed to preach the gospel in the early 1850s, but "never actively entered the ministry because he believed that a minister should be better educated than he was."[3] For years he served as cashier of the First National Bank of Aurora, an important position in a bank with but three officials. By 1890 the family occupied a substantial home in one of the middle tiers of houses that rose steeply from the Ohio River.

Outwardly, the father seemed cautious and taciturn—the picture of the conservative small-town banker. Nevertheless, he had a bit of Mark Twain's Colonel Beriah Sellers in him. He became a director and trea-surer of the River View Cemetery Association and director of the Aurora Coffin Company. Another investment involved a whiskey distillery. Before his death, this superintendent of the Sunday school learned that a promoter's instincts and religious scruples made poor bedfellows.

In 1888, years after his first wife's death, Elam Davis married Louise Severin, daughter of a German who had made his way to Aurora after the Revolution of 1848.[4] A couple of letters she wrote her only child help suggest the formal, insular spirit of the mother, who became principal of the local high school. After years of financial security, the father was nearly ruined when a company in which he had speculated collapsed in 1910. Louise wrote "Dear Holmes:"

> I feel that his misfortune is, to some extent, at least, a judgment on him for engaging in making whiskey barrels. Maybe I am a temperance crank, but I believe that professing christians [sic] have no business to engage in any business that will help the liquor traffic, in any way.[5]

Though Davis's protective mother emphasized the value of education, she indicated her intellectual horizons in a letter to her son two years later: "Today's paper gave a picture of the Prince of Wales, and said he is . . .

supposed to mingle with the other students on terms of equality. Don't get too intimate with him, for he might wish to come home with you.''[6]

The son of a schoolteacher and a father who felt keenly his lack of formal education, Davis learned early that he should do well in his studies. In addition, he was quite sickly and had to spend many of his first fourteen years at home, often in bed. Short of books, he read every bound volume in his father's complete file of *Harper's Magazine*. Louise Davis taught her son when he could not attend class regularly. He soon showed himself to be an exceptionally gifted student.

His one outside activity, save an abiding interest in sports, seems to have been music. He did not demonstrate noticeable talent in either field. Years later he talked of having been buried in the back row of a male chorus where nobody could hear him. As a member of an Interurban Orchestra that played up and down the Ohio, Davis insisted he ''just managed to get under the wire.''[7]

At sixteen he entered Franklin College, a small school nearly as old as the state, about twenty miles south of Indianapolis. He achieved a brilliant record in the classics. His extreme seriousness also earned him the nickname of ''Deacon.''[8] At college, Davis still talked about excelling in athletics rather than scholarship. Only gradually did he realize that his mind set him apart from his fellow students. After graduation he taught Latin at the high school in Franklin for a year.

He began to question his Baptist upbringing. Disparaging remarks concerning the relation of prayer to success in study brought an indignant reply from his father: ''It makes you appear as speaking contemptuously of prayer, and sounds like you were apeing [sic] some of the idiotic sayings of the Chicago university professors.''[9] Davis apparently did not enter a Baptist church again save on his wedding day. But his continuing concern with the problems of religion resulted in a number of articles and one full-length novel.

Then came a chance to leave Indiana for good. He won a Rhodes scholarship, proving that even at this time not every candidate had notable athletic ability. When Davis enrolled at Queen's College, Oxford, in October 1910, it was only the sixth year that the scholarships had been given. By thriftily arranging passage for all forty-eight American Rhodes Scholars on the same boat, he received a free pass for himself.

At Oxford, he prepared for an examination in the classics, which required proficiency in both Greek and Latin. For the rest of his life many of his best essays contained references to the history of Greece and Rome. Indeed, it has been said that much of the vigor of his broadcast style resulted from his knowledge of Greek syntax. Aside from regular study, Davis spent his time debating such timeless questions as whether residence at Oxford involved a subtle disintegration of moral fiber. Along with John Crowe Ransom and Christopher Morley, he formed a group determined to write a special sort of novel. Each member contributed a chapter with the aim of making the plot so complex that the next writer would be unable to solve it. By the time Davis left Britain, he had decided to become a professional writer.

During these years he traveled extensively. Trips through the Balkans and much of Central Europe interested him in the problems of minority groups. Unfortunately, the condition of his father's health forced Davis to attempt his B.A. exams in June 1912, a year before it was customary to do so. He just missed taking a First.[10]

In 1914 he became a reporter for the *New York Times*. An early assignment offered a fine opportunity for one with an eye for the amusing. Davis joined the group of correspondents who set sail on Henry Ford's peace ship on December 4, 1915. Apparently the young reporter could not keep his irreverent thoughts to himself. He so angered certain delegates that they wished him put off the ship. Although more proper— the journalist did not forget what paper he represented—Davis's coverage of the ill-fated attempt to bring peace might be compared with another account of a ship filled with the well-intended, the voyage of the *Quaker City* described in *The Innocents Abroad*.

But the sobriquet of "Deacon" existed along with the wit. A conscientious son, he brought his mother to live with him in New York. He worked so hard that he began writing queer things to his fiancée. "Are you really so strange," his future wife asked, "or are you sitting up too late, and working far too hard to have any normal thoughts."[11] When he finally married Florence MacMillan, his best man was dour Edward Klauber, later a Columbia Broadcasting System vice-president noted for his extreme reserve and bluntness.[12] For the rest of his life Davis projected in his writings an optimism and good humor—if sometimes a bit malicious—while often being personally despondent. It is as though one

Elmer Davis remained in Indiana and poked gentle fun at the pretensions of another ambitious and deadly serious person who got his start in Aurora but developed fully in New York.

The serious and creative side of Davis was often frustrated by the demands of being a journalist. For a time he attempted two occupations, working for the *Times* by day, writing novels in the evening. His first of fourteen books, *The Princess Cecilia,* was published in 1915. Rereading it in the 1960s, Roger Burlingame, himself a professional writer, patronizingly—but accurately—dismissed it as "light reading in the romantic tradition." After the United States entered the war, Davis sought to become a European correspondent. Instead, the *Times* kept him in New York. He often spoke of his frustration, even claiming that he really would "like to get a shot at the Boche."[13]

In 1920 Davis created a memorable character to help cover the Democratic national convention in San Francisco. Godfrey G. Gloom, of Amity, Indiana, emerged as "the oldest living conventioneer." Fellow *Times* correspondents, who had covered the proceedings with appropriate dignity, so enjoyed Mr. Gloom that they called for another Davis Cup. Every four years this aged Hoosier returned to comment until a fatal accident occurred in 1936. His creator gave Gloom a proper obituary in the *New York Times.*[14]

Davis's newspaper sent him to cover the Washington Conference in late 1921. After describing the proposals made by Secretary of State Charles Evans Hughes on the opening day, Davis settled down to listen to endless droning speeches. His story for January 18, 1922 appeared under the title "Statesmen Show Great Endurance." He claimed to have experienced eternity.

Throughout the 1920s, Davis attacked impractical and idealistic offers to guarantee peace, particularly if they emanated from Senator William E. Borah, whom the writer considered a humbug and a fraud. When the "Lion of Idaho" proposed to outlaw all war, the Indianan remarked: "If he will only add a clause providing that on and after January 1 next sin, sorrow and suffering shall be forever prohibited, I am with him."[15]

By the time Davis quit his newspaper position on January 1, 1924, he had moved from reporting to the editorial page. During those years he covered all sorts of events, from sports to diplomatic conferences to national conventions—even reviews of books about ancient Greece—

with equal competence. In 1921 he produced the official *History of the New York Times, 1851-1921,* if not with wit or enthusiasm, at least in a scholarly and straightforward manner. In sum, Davis had shown himself proficient in so many areas that he could truly call himself a professional writer. For the rest of his life he demonstrated journalistic excellence in his articles and broadcasts about current events. And of course, during his tenure with the *Times* he polished his sardonic sense of humor.

After he left the newspaper, most of his books, as opposed to his serious pieces, continued to be frothy and lighthearted. *I'll Show You the Town* in 1924 and *Friends of Mr. Sweeney* in 1925 were gay effusions that ladies could keep comfortably on a bedside table. Of a much more serious nature was *Giant Killer,* published in 1928. This historical novel, which Davis considered his best, announced on the first page that only Fundamentalists still believed that David killed Goliath. *Giant Killer* did not prove a great success. The characters failed to come alive. But the book was expert in construction, offered an ingenious explanation of who actually killed Goliath, and represented much labor in describing politics in the eleventh century before Christ.[16]

In 1933 Davis and a friend attempted another potboiler, *Bare Living,* which described life in a nudist camp. The last novel, *Love Among the Ruins,* appeared in 1935. Davis made his living by producing fiction for popular magazines, along with occasional serious pieces. An instance of the former was "She Needs an Older Man." The story described an ex-brain truster named Adam Adams who late one summer met an intelligent sweet young thing. Perhaps the author's own sense of advancing middle age appeared in passages such as: "We swam; and when she talked communism I listened patiently."[17]

Davis insisted that no writer was responsible for his characters and that therefore he revealed nothing about himself in his fiction. Such a belief helps to explain the faintly sterile quality of his carefully constructed prose. The idea of waiting patiently before returning to an old job appeared in other articles of the 1930s. "Come and Eat Lunch Against Franco," published in 1938, purported to be a humorous or, at least, a whimsical piece. It was filled with the sense that we are all developing paunches and just cannot afford to be as upset about injustices as we were in our salad days. This feeling certainly appeared in a sentence such as "Once for example, when I was lunching indignantly against the Southern cottonmill [sic] owners, or the war-mad Japanese militarists, or somebody of the sort. . . ."[18] There was a suggestion of tiredness totally absent two years later.

Davis's son has said that his father projected an image of failure at home during these years, in spite of the way he seemed to acquaintances and in print. He felt that he had been unable to achieve anything important as a writer. In his son's words: "We felt he was great, but that we needed to explain why. That his achievements, though solid and really impressive to those who understood the game, had to be reviewed at length before he could get recognition."[19]

After Davis began his radio career, he openly expressed a feeling of accomplishment. Other changes occurred as well. The comparison of a book review in May 1939 with an editorial in 1940 points up one difference. Rarely did anyone receive a more sardonic review than Charles and Mary Beard for the third volume of their *Rise of American Civilization*. Davis claimed his fellow Hoosiers' intellectual history "leads up into a rarefied realm of political thinking where the theorist has no rival but Mary Baker Eddy." As to the future of America: "The Beards know too much to guess at the answer, but they might have spared us this hint that God is keeping watch above his own. Maybe He is, but somebody else had better do something about it too." He complained that an Indianian had forgotten the hallmark of the Hoosier, "a congenital inability to Realize the Seriousness of the Situation."[20] A little over a year later someone else had forgotten his Hoosier heritage. Davis ordained that Hitler was no laughing matter; therefore Charlie Chaplin's *The Great Dictator* was not amusing. He described himself as "one who has no time to read books unless they deal with the Situation."[21] It was a passing phase.

A "LOUSY AND MONOTONOUS" VOICE

"Why don't you take some voice Culture," an angry listener once demanded. "Your voice is as lousy and monotonous as Luella Parsons."[22] The orthography may be somewhat deficient, but the person who found Davis's speaking voice disagreeable had just cause. Writers of solemn mien have noted that journalistic excellence, not voice quality, was the prime consideration in hiring radio commentators during the late 1930s. Those who heard Davis for the first time considered that a classic understatement. The flat, dry, dull Indiana accent seemed anything but that of the ideal radio broadcaster. But an easiness about Davis's speech projected abundant common sense. And the flatness turned out to be an effective device for delivering quiet bits of humor, even within the confines of a five-minute newscast. Covering Wendell Willkie's campaign in 1940, Davis quoted the Republican nominee's description of Senator Hiram W. Johnson of California as a "fighting, fearless liberal." Without change of tone he added: "Two days ago in Kansas he said that about Walter Johnson." In 1942 the commentator discussed General Douglas MacArthur's supporters in America, and their idea of who was to blame for shortages in war production. The problem could be resolved, the newscaster noted, if "MacArthur should return to this nation and overturn the Hopkins's [sic], the Frankfurters, and the Reds inside the Government."[23] Listeners quickly learned to distinguish the broadcaster's interpretation in one or two words or even the slightest change in modulation.

Though the dryness of the speaking voice proved excellent for sardonic effects, in general the newscaster seemed completely oblivious to the aural aspects of broadcasting. Reading Davis was the same as hearing him—hardly the compliment some well-wishers have assumed.[24] Listeners heard a rational discussion, but logic is sometimes better comprehended in written than in spoken form. Davis was a distinguished journalist who also talked on the radio. He never understood, as did his colleague Edward R. Murrow, that words can increase intensity of meaning when broadcast.

An old wives' tale describes James Watt as a small boy watching steam rise from a tea kettle. To explain Elmer Davis's career in radio there is no analogous story from his youth. Throughout the 1930s virtually every news commentator save Murrow began as a journalist. Davis possessed impeccable credentials: reporter, then editorial writer for the *New York Times,* 1914-1924, and intermittent contributor to that paper thereafter. He had the additional advantage of an early friendship with Edward Klauber, a fellow *Times* reporter and best man at his wedding.

According to CBS records, Davis's first radio appearance came in 1930. Few tuned in late in the evening to hear "What is College For" or

"Optimism." In May 1932, the next time Davis broadcast over CBS, he described an enormous beer parade in New York. At least one listener considered it exceedingly clever.[25]

While H. V. Kaltenborn visited Europe during the summer of 1937, Davis replaced him for seven broadcasts. *Variety* reported that his first attempt got cut off in the middle by a Roosevelt speech. Davis "did not . . . sound quite as incisive as he manages to be in print," concluded the critic. After the seventh newscast, the reviewer praised Davis, claiming he should continue even after Kaltenborn returned.

The real opportunity in radio materialized two years later. Kaltenborn again had gone to Europe. On August 22, 1939, as the likelihood of war grew increasingly apparent, the director of news at CBS asked Davis to help out as a commentator.[26] From then on, he broadcast virtually every day.

At first things sounded a little rough. Each newscast contained numerous distracting "uhs." The Hoosier's pronunciation of foreign names left the listener confused as to which person was being discussed. Davis offered considerably more opinion (and a few wild guesses) than two or three months later. Even so, Edward R. Murrow, with good reason, wrote his colleague on September 15 to congratulate him for the best "fair, tough minded [sic], interesting talking" he had heard.[27]

Davis led an incredibly hectic life after the war began. In addition to several kinds of newscasts, he contributed frequently to the *Saturday Review of Literature,* even becoming an editor in early 1940. He was best known, however, for a five-minute summary and interpretation of the news that formally began on September 24, 1939. CBS broadcast Davis over most of its network seven days a week at 8:55 P.M. EST. For a number of months in 1939 and 1940, he also presented a fifteen-minute commentary Monday, Wednesday, and Friday at 6:30 P.M. over WABC in New York. Finally, he offered extemporaneous analysis on occasion, as during late August and early September 1939.[28]

Davis developed the ability to compress news commentary into a five-minute period. Since he gained such acclaim for these brief newscasts, stylistic description is in order. After an ebullient announcer extolled Gillette's sharper cleaner edges—almost jamming a blue blade through the listener's ear in the process—the commentary began without a single word of introduction. For five straight minutes Davis moved briskly from one topic to another, occasionally adding a sardonic touch. For instance, in February 1941 he referred to some group (possibly opponents of Lend-Lease) as "gratuitous asses," a comment that made skittish CBS executives wish they had not hired someone with such a sharp tongue.[29]

Davis took pains to be scrupulously accurate. He would say "quote" and "end quote" before and after using another's words. He mentioned by name sources such as *Harper's,* or Raymond Clapper, or the *New Republic,* from which he had gotten specific information. When he felt uncertain he would admit it: "I can speak only from hearsay."[30]

The fifteen-minute newscasts allowed for more detail and occasionally larger amounts of humor. In 1940 a listener commented on a broadcast since lost: "Your satire on the Railway Station bombing gave us a hearty laugh—and laughter is *so* rare these anxious days." The same spirit pervades an analysis made on the air five years later that does exist. Davis described the testimony of Ambassador Patrick J. Hurley before the Senate Foreign Relations Committee:

> The crowd enjoyed the exchanges between General Hurley, the handsomest of all our ambassadors, and Chairman Connally, most Senatorial-looking of Senators; but they were apparently on the Ambassador's side, and applauded him when he shouted that he didn't want his government pussyfooting. He shouted a good deal, including declarations that he wasn't aggressive, belligerent or emotional. However, after he had been talking some three quarters of an hour Senator La Follette interposed to ask just what was the issue.[31]

Davis's written style contained two particular characteristics. Both appeared regularly in the fifteen-minute newscasts—less often in the short broadcasts. Davis loved classical analogy; few other political commentators in twentieth-century America have known enough ancient history to feel comfortable drawing comparisons between the Peloponnesian War and World War I. In 1917 Davis published an excellent analysis of the Treaty of Brest-Litovsk. The *Times* reporter compared it to the Peace of Nicias, which Thucydides felt had settled nothing. In an essay published in October 1939, Davis claimed Thucydides offered much that would illuminate the difficulties of another war. During May 1940 he changed analogies to indicate a fundamental alteration of the European situation. Not Thucydides but a Roman historian now provided perspective for Hitler's invasion of the Low Countries:

> "Who is so worthless or so indifferent," Polybius asked his readers, "as not to want to know how and under what system of government it happened that in less than fifty-three years almost everything in the inhabited world was subject to the sole rule of the Romans?"[32]

Classical analogies remained more than set pieces to be wheeled out in troublous times; they became part of Davis's mental process. When the broadcaster visited London in May 1941, he made notes to himself concerning the "restoration of immediacy" in England that had been known to ancient civilizations, but lost since the Renaissance.[33] Fascination with the classics, however, meant total respect. Davis, so alert to the amusing aspects of current politics, thought of the distant past in terms of rational and stately discourse. Perhaps he believed in the Greeks too earnestly—and in the process cut off the humor that so enlivened their culture.

Everyone recognized Davis's wit. It sometimes took the form of religious allusions. His 1938 review of a book describing how to sell vacuum cleaners included phrases such as: "If the end product of his [the salesman's] labors is such an appalling slaughter of the innocents as is going on at this writing in Barcelona" or the reviewer's feeling that he should go "into the wilderness to live on locusts and wild honey" after reading about salesmanship. Davis's essay about his disappearance and presumed death during the New England hurricane of September 1938 included another gentle spoof on religion: "No cataclysm of nature, except possibly Noah's flood, ever afflicted a region populated by so many professional writers; and most of them were prompt to cash in on it, especially if they carried no wind insurance."[34]

The Indianan occasionally tried a different sort of irony. That same essay concerning the hurricane employed a device that, if not carefully used, turns into the chuckling we're-all-too-human spirit of the *Reader's Digest:*

> How often when I was a young reporter have I called up a bereaved family for information about the deceased, to be told that he was one of Nature's noblemen and the kindest husband and father that ever

lived. . . . A man who had read his own obituary will never be quite the same again.[35]

Davis occasionally relied on less subtle devices, including unfortunate puns. In an article about the La Follettes, he described Julius Heil as an inept Wisconsin politician who "usually puts his worst foot foremost. Nevertheless his worst foot was good enough to boot Phil La Follette out of office. . . ." In an impish mood, he actually responded to a silly listener's complaint about pronunciation. A man claimed Davis failed to say bauxite properly as "bo-zit." "As none of us here have [sic] ever had any personal dealings with Bauxite," replied the broadcaster, "we have to follow the dictionary."[36]

This sort of attitude, along with a compelling desire to comprehend the real import of political events, made Davis's broadcasts and writings before 1941 unique. Humor is extraordinarily difficult to handle properly. Too much destroys the seriousness of a subject. If too caustic, only a particular turn of phrase may be remembered. With infrequent lapses, Davis managed to lighten serious subjects without destroying the content. Few commentators have possessed his admirable touch.

THE MAKING OF AN INTERVENTIONIST

In 1938 not many Americans sensed any urgency about European affairs; in 1941 most did. In 1938 not many intellectuals felt committed to Franklin D. Roosevelt's foreign policy; in 1941 most did. Elmer Davis remained a noninterventionist—that is, he opposed greater American involvement overseas, including "all aid short of war" for Britain—until Hitler's invasion of the Low Countries in May 1940. Then Davis changed his mind. He joined the militant Century Dinner Group of William Allen White's Committee to Defend America by Aiding the Allies. He ceased functioning as an independent observer of the news and became, in matters of foreign policy, a Roosevelt partisan. The commentator's conversion turned almost entirely on European events; he generally ignored the Far East in his writings and broadcasts.[37]

Though Davis did not begin broadcasting regularly until August 1939, he published several assessments of European affairs before the beginning of the war. He contributed a series of articles to *Harper's* in which he placed particular emphasis on Czechoslovakian affairs. In June 1937 he noted that Britain and France seemed ready to make ever-greater conces-sions to Hitler. Davis felt that the Czechs could not hope to win against Germany alone and might therefore have to accept "surrender and alliance" with the Nazis.[38]

His mild disapproval turned to indignation following the September 1938 Munich crisis. Davis spent much of "The Road from Munich" indicting a "considerable part of the British governing class" for giving up Czechoslovakia "without a fight." Noting that Soviet Russia had been excluded from the Munich deliberations, he added that this was "good news for the English; especially the rich and well-born, who are ready to give him [Hitler] three cheers whenever he starts out against Russia, the enemy of God and property." After quoting a passage from *Mein Kampf* in which Hitler seemed to predict exactly how he would dismember Czechoslovakia, Davis drew an unflattering historical parallel:

> Europe . . . at the end of 1938 stands about where it stood at the end of 1811, with this difference: in 1811 England was not only the implac-able but the impregnable enemy of the man who dominated the Conti-nent. The England of 1938 is something else, strategically and morally.[39]

He turned to gentle sarcasm in a column for the *New York Times* on January 4, 1939:

> 1938 was such a big year for the Germans that it is not surprising that their language grows a little flowery. . . . Marshal Goering says that it "sticks out above the centuries like a granite obelisk, and overshadows all events in German history like a gigantic oak tree." Non-Germans may be inclined to feel that it sticks out like a sore thumb, and that if it is an oak, it is of the poisonous variety; but allowance must be made for the point of view.

The following month he published two pieces in the *New Republic* and the *Saturday Review of Literature* concerning the implications of Munich. Davis declared that American assistance to Britain could only strengthen Neville Chamberlain's government. That thought "makes me sick at the stomach," he admitted. Davis added that "before Munich I thought it would be less costly to stay out." Now he was certain that the British might sell their fleet to Germany to prevent war.[40] In a second article, he pointed to a dilemma confronting Roosevelt. If the United States did nothing to help France and Britain, both might become tools of Hitler. If assistance were offered, he continued, Chamberlain's forces might sell out America anyway. Davis sensed no "hysterical urgency" in coming up with a solution to this "Democratic Dilemma."

When the Nazis took over the remainder of Czechoslovakia in March 1939, Davis discussed the meaning of the action in a lengthy letter to the *New York Times*. "But always remember," he concluded, "that if Europe cannot save itself we cannot save it; that whatever we may find it necessary to do for England and France is done only for our own safety, and that we should help them no further and no longer than our own interest seems to require."[41]

Hitler's invasion of Poland in September 1939 and the Russo-Finnish War affected Davis's views. He now favored giving Britain "all aid short of war." But his conversion remained a bit uncertain. Writing in *Harper's*, he asserted that "the interest of the American people requires us to keep out of the war for two sound reasons: we have unfinished business of our own to solve; and furthermore, past experience makes it doubtful if we could do Europe much good." He then added an important qualification:

> Suppose the Germans win the war, or begin to win it. In that case, our policy would have to recognize that the world situation had completely changed, that some of the comfortable buttresses of our security have been pulled out from under us. If the British navy is defeated or seriously threatened with defeat, we had better think hard about what that will mean to purely American interests, and take whatever action might seem advisable to require complete participation in the war. . . . That any American interest would be served by again sending an army to Europe seems to me inconceivable.[42]

On April 4, two days before Hitler invaded Norway and Denmark, Stanley Hornbeck, the Department of State's political adviser on Far Eastern affairs, wrote Davis concerning this article. He urged the broadcaster to do "a lot more thinking" about his assertion that " 'there is no point in intervening' in a war 'again if the job has to be done over every twenty years.' '' Hornbeck pointed out that this sort of logic might lead one to stop ''eating breakfast'' since the same thing would have to be repeated at ''noon and again in the evening.''[43]

Davis replied that he was ''far from convinced'' by Hornbeck's analogy. He declared that ''if we have to fight in defense of our own interest, let's limit our action to what that defense requires, and not delude ourselves with the belief that we can effect anything like a durable settlement of the affairs of Europe.'' On April 22 Hornbeck wrote again. He repeated what he had said before, though agreeing that ''with regard to most matters there is and can be no such thing as complete and permanent crystalization.''[44]

On April 22 Davis discussed the possibility of changing his position. He told listeners that ''the American people want to keep out of the war,'' but then described

a general realization for the first time that the Germans may win this war. . . . Most people in this country want the Allies to win and believe that it will be on the whole to our interest if they do win. No doubt a good many of you who are listening do NOT feel that way, but I am talking about the majority opinion. And the unrecognized premise of a good deal of American isolationism was a conviction that the Allies were going to win anyway so we needn't worry about how the war would come out. That conviction, recently, has been shaken; and accordingly a lot of people are worrying, for the first time.[45]

A listener who opposed America's ever going to war praised the commentator's ''calm manner'' in this broadcast. She contrasted it with the '' 'Pro-British' '' remarks of ''The Kaltenborns, Swings, etc.''[46]

Four days later, Davis again discussed why the United States should not enter the war. He turned to the war debts argument, declaring that the Allies this time ''are getting supplies from us that they badly needed, but they are paying for them. The same day, he wrote another listener that ''it is clearly advantageous to us to keep out of the war. . . . [But] to give whatever help we can to the Allies without going to war is another matter, and seems to be a highly intelligent national policy.''[47] On May 6 he still believed America should stay out of the war, even though ''it looks as if the British, more likely than not, may lose the war.'' He returned to attacking England's upper class with its ''invincible ignorance'' for bringing about such a catastrophe. He also claimed that "there are millions of decent Germans who don't like the way the Nazis are behaving at home or abroad."[48]

In the next couple of days he wrote a review of Charles A. Beard's *A Foreign Policy for America.* Davis praised the historian's theory of Continentalism, which differed, he felt, from "head-under-the-bedclothes isolationists." The reviewer declared that Beard meant only that "the United States, either alone or in any coalition, did not possess the power to force peace on Europe and Asia."[49] He repeated that American policy would need major revision if German hegemony in Europe became likely.

The Nazi invasion of the Low Countries on May 10 forced Davis to face this eventuality. That evening he offered no special comment except to report that "the first day of the German *blitzkrieg* against the Low Countries seems to have met with only very moderate success." Three days later he quoted Churchill's phrase that he had nothing to offer but "blood, toil, tears and sweat [sic]."[50] The next night Davis declared that "in Washington there was a spreading realization that this country is none too well prepared for hemisphere defense." On May 22 he reported with obvious approval Edward R. Murrow's statement that "the British revolution occurred today peacefully and constitutionally when Parliament passed a bill giving the government full control over all individuals and property."[51] Davis now believed that America should formally enter the war against Hitler out of self-interest. But few listeners would have known about such a fundamental change in position from listening to his radio broadcasts.

Davis presented his new faith more openly in a *Saturday Review of Literature* editorial published on May 25. He explained that not Thucydides but Polybius offered understanding as to the May 10 invasions. He wanted every reader to realize that the Nazis, like the ancient Romans, would soon control " 'everything in the inhabited world.' "[52]

The broadcaster explained at greater length, in an article published on June 29, why he had changed his mind. He asserted that most Germans now approved of Hitler. The invasion of Norway, he felt, served as a "psychological turning-point" which convinced "a large part of the German population . . . that once more the *Führer* would bring home the bacon." He stated that May 10 had marked "the beginning of the other kind of war, the war that German and Italian leaders truly call the world revolution.'' There was a big difference, too, in Davis's attitude toward the British:

> It looks at this writing as if the survival of what has hitherto been called civilization must depend chiefly on the British and American peoples. . . . Under pressure the British have at last achieved that unity and resolution which we still have to attain. . . . We are far nearer that point, so far as popular sentiment goes, than would have been dreamed of by the wildest enthusiast six weeks ago. . . .[53]

Clearly this represented quite a transformation from what Davis had been saying in April. He now implicitly advocated full hostilities against Germany. He no longer accused the British of being controlled by a narrow upper class. He insisted that virtually all Germans supported Hitler. The "Democratic Dilemma" had been resolved—it had become possible to separate good from evil, with civilization the good that Britain and the United States together could preserve. For the first time he spoke openly of an Anglo-American alliance. He placed no limits on what form the partnership should take, or how closely the two countries should work. He left those decisions to Roosevelt and Churchill.

Davis's conversion does not reveal remarkable powers of analysis. Once having changed his mind, he accepted a set of arguments to accompany his new position. He became an administration booster in the process. When he talked of "unity and resolution," he also meant suppressing "wrong" opinions and conflicting counsel. He demonstrated the truth of Randolph Bourne's belief that "War is the health of the State."

Davis demonstrated his continuing support for Roosevelt's foreign policy repeatedly in the months after May 1940, though he found the Chief Executive's handling of the third-term nomination most distressing. At the convention, the President devoted his acceptance speech to a careful discussion of problems that America might have to face in its relations with the rest of the world. Davis praised the speech, but believed its spirit weakened by political maneuvering.[54] Davis felt that the Destroyers-Bases Agreement of September 3 represented another example of the devious methods Roosevelt employed to gain his ends. The commentator did not oppose the agreement, but considered it "regrettable" that the President did not "get a Congressional vote."[55]

Following the November elections, Davis stopped making any sort of criticism of the President's methods. After the fireside chat of December 29, when Roosevelt talked of America's becoming the "great arsenal of democracy", the news analyst declared that such an obligation had already been "generally accepted by the American people." He explained that "the American people have recognized in the past few months a sudden wholly unforeseen danger to American security."[56]

On February 11, 1941, Davis reported the testimony of Wendell Willkie in support of Lend-Lease. The broadcaster insisted that only Hitler could determine whether increased aid to Britain would result in full hostilities. He wrote Philip F. La Follette about the sort of person who opposed giving aid to Britain. The former governor replied: "If I correctly get the 'burden of your sermon,' it is this: My opposition to the President's foreign policy has put me in bad company."[57]

In May Davis spent three weeks in England. On June 14, 1941, the *Saturday Review* reprinted his broadcast summing up his impressions of Britain and what America's duty should be. Davis declared that he knew of no "informed person who doubts that an eventual collapse of England would seriously endanger the security of the U.S." As to convoys, he said that their use might "mean shooting, but if Hitler should win this war, there's likely to be some shooting afterwards which would no longer be on the other side of the Atlantic."[58] In short, he did not seem alarmed by the possibility of full hostilities. Three months later he belittled talk of Roosevelt's September 11 "shoot-on-sight" speech as being particularly provocative. Davis stated that the President had spoken "only of shooting in the protection of the waters essential to the defense of the United States."[59] His support of whatever Roosevelt wanted to do did not waver before December 7.

Shortly after Pearl Harbor, Davis proved his wartime patriotism by giving up broadcasting to enter government service. He became director of the Office of War Information, charged with regulating war news for the home front as well as information about America to foreign listeners. He did not prove a conspicuous success. His lack of administrative experience, plus his feeling that people within the agency acted insubordinately, led to the resignation of gifted employees and strong opposition in Congress.

After the war Davis presented newscasts for the American Broadcasting Company. He no longer spoke daily. He lectured more frequently at college campuses. As he explained to his friend Felix Frankfurter in 1953:

> I have been very academic lately—Yale, then the New School, then the Phi Beta Kappa oration at Harvard. (As my colleague Mr. Winchell would say—Oration? Huh!) However, it seems to have been a success, as one of my listeners said to me afterward. "That was a marvelous speech, Mr. Rice."[60]

The following year Davis finally published a best seller, *But We Were Born Free,* ironically not the novel he had attempted so often, but a series of essays in defense of freedom. Davis told Americans frightened by McCarthyism, "Don't let them scare you." It was an eloquent book, and full of sensible ideas. It is also what a later generation remembers most about the Hoosier. Davis did not attempt to be clever. He considered freedom of the mind, like ancient Greece and Rome, a serious topic. Occasionally he sounded a bit too earnest—even waving the flag in a few places—which suggests one reason why he had used humor before 1941. In this sense, these essays, though filled with steadying judgment, do not represent his finest writing.

During the last few years little was heard of the person who when asked by a reporter if he had a nickname, once replied: "No. Why should I? Isn't Elmer enough?" Afflicted with a variety of illnesses requiring serious operations, Davis felt the doctors were needlessly prolonging his life. He died on May 18, 1958; the funeral took place at the Washington Cathedral. As the minister intoned "The Lord giveth and the Lord taketh away," a microphone crashed to the floor. Raymond Swing said he could not help thinking Davis himself had given it a hearty shove.[61]

FIVE-MINUTE UBIQUITY

Franklin Roosevelt, like most listeners, was first attracted to Davis's newscasts because of their cleverness. Robert Sherwood quotes a particular broadcast, made in early 1942, which delighted the President:

> There are some patriotic citizens who sincerely hope that America will win the war—but they also hope that Russia will lose it; and there are

some who hope that America will win the war, but that England will lose it; and there are some who hope that America will win the war, but that Roosevelt will lose it!

The Chief Executive thought this marvelous. Besides repeating it to friends, he mentioned it several times in letters sent shortly after Pearl Harbor.[62] A couple of months later, Roosevelt needed someone to head the Office of War Information. He thought of "the fellow with the funny voice. Elmer—Elmer something." It is possible that the President himself decided on a man without administrative experience to head the new agency. But perhaps a couple of Davis's friends had more to do with the decision. Felix Frankfurter wrote Roosevelt on March 12, 1942: "Much as I love Bob Sherwood, even he could not seduce me with a suggestion unless I truly believed it to be right. And so when he suggested Elmer Davis to head up Information something clicked in me and I just know it is right—and right for you from every angle."[63] Davis got the job.

He had other influential supporters. By 1937 he was well acquainted with the State Department's Stanley K. Hornbeck. In August 1940 the latter described him as a "brilliant expositor—with a real sense of humor." In April 1941 Hornbeck sent Davis an extended memorandum he had prepared recently. The news analyst thanked him for "hav[ing] begun my education on the Far East." In the next two years Hornbeck provided the commentator with excerpts from books and articles he found informative.[64] Each held the other in high esteem, though Hornbeck's enthusiasm and concern for the Far East did not lead Davis to increase the amount of space he devoted to Japan and China in his broadcasts.

Many in the administration listened to Davis as well. In August 1940 Henry Morgenthau, Jr., particularly liked one of the Hoosier's newscasts. He asked the Assistant Secretary of the Treasury to locate a copy for Roosevelt. During August 1941 Davis sent a detailed memorandum to the President's press secretary urging less British censorship of war news.[65] The newscaster was too practical a man to have prepared such a statement had he known that nobody would ever read it. Two months later Henry Stimson and Davis exchanged a couple of letters. In the early part of 1942 Sumner Welles praised Davis for his commentaries. "One of your constant listeners—when present conditions make it possible," he declared. A few months later Felix Frankfurter told Davis about "a close reading of much that you have written during the last twenty years."[66]

In June 1940 Davis demonstrated his support for a declaration of war against Germany. He joined the twenty-two-member Century Dinner Group, the more militant part of the Committee to Defend America. The only radio commentator in the group, he proved particularly useful in publicizing their beliefs. But he later had second thoughts. Mark Lincoln Chadwin, in *The Hawks of World War II,* states that by the winter of 1940 Davis was one of several members who felt "their usefulness as objective analysts of foreign affairs would be impaired by continued association with a "pressure group." "[67]

A reading of Davis's broadcasts indicates that in spite of what he might have done privately, on the air he tried to avoid extreme British partisanship. Of course it depended on who listened. No reader protested when the *Nation*'s pro-British literary editor, in May 1940, said that Davis and Swing were the two best news analysts, particularly because of the "remarkable" objectivity in their broadcasts.[68] Actually Davis's sympathies lay with the British. It is not surprising that by early 1941 the BBC broadcast commentaries by both Swing and Davis to a "large listening public" in Great Britain.[69] An August 1941 example of what Davis told his English audience at 9:20 P.M. on Saturday evenings suggests that for the BBC he abandoned all constraints in expressing his feelings about the necessity of American intervention in the war. "It's becoming plainer and plainer," he declared, "that what is going on in South America, and in South-Eastern Asia, is directly related to the war in Russia, for they are all parts of one single Great World War." He claimed that the Japanese occupation of Indochina on July 25 was "certainly encouraged, if not directly arranged by Hitler." He urged changes in the Department of State:

> There is an increasing demand that the President and Secretary Hull get rid of the unteachable group in the State Department of men who have not learned, after ten years of experience, that appeasement has never worked anywhere, at any time. The second plain fact is that every bold step by the Administration gets overwhelming public support.

When Davis announced that "moderation and appeasement have never stopped Japan yet," he, like Swing, was telling the English what they wanted to hear.[70]

Davis's written work increased his radio audience in two important ways. His frequent contributions to *Harper's* and the *Saturday Review* made his name familiar to readers of these two influential magazines. And both periodicals reprinted broadcasts or described his radio career, along with urging subscribers to listen. Unlike other newscasters, Davis had a couple of articles reprinted in *Reader's Digest*. Thus, even as a writer, he occasionally reached an enormous audience.

His chief impact on the average citizen came through his nightly five-minute broadcasts. Davis rose to national prominence with amazing swiftness. In October 1939, *Variety* felt that next to Swing, "the man who has most imprinted his personality on the public as a result of broadcasting war news this fall is probably Elmer Davis."[71] In other words, though having joined a group of prominent newscasters, he had not yet become a household name. A *Fortune* survey in January 1940 asked the respondent to name his favorite radio news commentator. Davis came in seventh. But another poll from the same period put him in third place behind H. V. Kaltenborn and Lowell Thomas.[72] Obviously the two surveys contradict each other; the surprising thing is that any national poll could indicate this much awareness of a newscaster who had been on the air for only three months.

At least part of the explanation, aside from the quality of reporting, stems from the mechanics of broadcasting. Davis spoke daily—more often than any other news analyst—with the resultant increase in public exposure. Since he appeared on CBS, he was assured of a large number of powerful stations all over the country. He had the same hour every day and a good one for the East, Midwest, and West. Finally, the brevity of the program made his comment uniquely different from others on radio.

By December 1940, a Hooperating reported a phenomenal 24.3 for Davis. His commentary was heard an average of 3.6 times per week. Compared with ratings for other newscasters, it seemed incredibly high, particularly during this year. Advertisers took note. Colgate Palmolive Peet signed a contract in March 1941. The company agreed to sponsor Davis over ninety stations six days a week. *Variety* commented that it represented the first time CBS had ever had a "contract for news broadcasts of such proportions."[73] Businessmen knew who was reaching millions of citizens nightly.

Davis was one of the two best-prepared radio commentators discussing foreign affairs before 1941. If he often slighted events in the Far East, he showed great concern over American policy toward Europe. Before May

1940 he doubted whether America should play an active role in European affairs. After Hitler's invasion of the Low Countries, Davis consistently favored more aid for Britain than Roosevelt provided. He did not differ from other influential Americans; before December 1941 he never explicitly advocated sending an army overseas. But his summaries of the news subtly led listeners to look favorably on such a point of view. Sumner Welles sensed Davis's complete support for administration foreign policy. "I have yet to remember an instance when you have rocked the boat," he wrote the commentator shortly after Pearl Harbor.[74]

It is hard not to admire a man who expressed himself so well. Davis's greatest contribution, however, came from his ubiquity during the twenty months before Pearl Harbor. He broadcast more often and over stronger affiliates than any other commentator. His conversion to militant interventionism provides a good example of what happened to many Americans—both intellectuals and average citizens. Davis expressed the shared assumptions of many liberals in an exceedingly lively fashion. This makes the study of his style very important. He used his wit to point up serious subjects. Otherwise he would be remembered as a humorist, not as a political commentator who could turn a phrase with such felicity.

Davis's contribution to the making of foreign policy is similar to that of his colleague Raymond Gram Swing. Davis had a much larger audience at home; he was heard less frequently in other parts of the world. Davis was not considered the unofficial voice of the State Department, though his support for Roosevelt's foreign policy was no secret. Davis did not make foreign policy, but like Swing, he made an interventionist foreign policy possible by relating the events of the rest of the world to the need for American involvement. An independent commentator, he too abandoned objectivity in the twenty months before Pearl Harbor. He used his wit to lampoon those who dared to suggest that America had too many problems at home to worry about the rest of the world. The careful listener had no difficulty telling what Davis favored. He consistently showed the need for an end to isolationism. Davis and Swing contributed importantly to the shift in public mood from isolationism to interventionism, because both not only reported the overseas news but explained specifically what such news meant for American foreign policy.

Davis was fully committed, but thanks to his sense of humor he successfully maintained his persona as an independent commentator who happened to believe in what Roosevelt wanted to do. This indirect support proved far more valuable in combatting isolationism than direct propaganda. Davis with complete honesty could say that only the world crisis had made him abandon isolationism. Nightly he explained to listeners that the facts demanded American involvement overseas.

NOTES

1. Richard Lauterbach, "Elmer Davis and the News," *Liberty Magazine,* October 23, 1943, p. 55, copy in Box 1, Davis MSS.

2. Wilhelm Arntz, "Der Direktor der 'Traum-' Fabrik," *Die Wehrmacht,* May 26, 1943, p. 2, copy in Box 10, Davis MSS.

3. Obituary for Elam H. Davis, Box 4, Davis MSS.

4. Roger Burlingame, *Don't Let Them Scare You: The Life and Times of Elmer Davis* (Philadelphia, 1961), p. 22.

5. Louise H. Davis, Aurora, to Davis, Oxford, England, December 29, 1910, Box 1, Davis MSS.

6. Louise Davis, Aurora, to Davis, Oxford, October 26, 1912, Box 1, Davis MSS.

7. Davis, "Constant Reader," *Harper's* 200 (October 1951): 161; Davis, commencement address, Aurora High School, June, 1951, cited in Burlingame, *Don't Let Them Scare You,* p. 23.

8. Arntz, "Der Direktor der 'Traum-' Fabrik," p. 2.

9. Elam H. Davis, to Davis, March 15, 1910, Box 1, Davis MSS.

10. Burlingame, *Don't Let Them Scare You,* pp. 37, 46, 51; advertisement, *Saturday Review,* July 15, 1939, p. 19.

11. Florence MacMillan to Davis, October 22, 1914, Box 1, Davis MSS.

12. *New York Times,* February 6, 1917, copy in Box 53, Burlingame MSS.

13. Burlingame, *Don't Let Them Scare You,* pp. 68, 78.

14. *Ibid.,* p. 92.

15. *New York Times,* January 18, 1922, p. 2, November 18, 1925, p. 22, both cited in Philip Chalfant Ensley, "The Political and Social Thought of Elmer Davis" (Ph.D. dissertation, Ohio State University, 1965), pp. 53, 54.

16. These opinions concerning *Giant Killer* are similar to those expressed in a review by Stephen Vincent Benet, "The Two-Edged Blade," *Saturday Review,* October 27, 1928, p. 293, cited in Ensley, "The Political and Social Thought," p. 13.

17. *The Saturday Evening Post,* January 4, 1936, p. 13.

18. Author's Note, *Giant Killer* (New York, 1943), p. vii; *Harper's* 176 (May 1938); 665.

19. Robert Lloyd Davis to Roger Burlingame, June 19, 1960, Box 8, Burlingame MSS.

20. Review of *America in Midpassage*, Charles A. And Mary Beard, *Saturday Review*, May 20, 1939, p. 4.

21. Davis, "No Time for Comedy?", *Saturday Review*, November 9, 1940, p. 8.

22. H. D. Wenzel to Davis, April 8, 1951, Box 9, Davis MSS.

23. CBS broadcast, September 18, 1940, reel 224, Phonoarchive; CBS broadcast, April 1, 1942, "Daily Radio Digest No. 46," Box 1848, RG 44.

24. See E. B. White's comments quoted with obvious approval in Burlingame, *Don't Let Them Scare You*, p. 334.

25. CBS Talent File (old), Davis, (Sustaining), CBS Program Information; Stanley Walker, *City Editor*, (New York, 1934), p. 240.

26. CBS Black Book, "Radio Programs 1937," CBS Program Information; *Variety*, July 21, 1937, p. 34; September 1, 1937, p. 36; Davis, "Broadcasting the Outbreak of War," *Harper's* 179 (November 1939): 581.

27. See comments by Davis after Adolf Hitler's Reichstag Speech, CBS broadcast, October 6, 1939, 33 1/3 rpm original transcription Kaltenborn MSS; CBS broadcast, September 14, 1939, reel 999, Phonoarchive; Murrow to Davis, n.d. [1939], Box 1, Davis MSS.

28. CBS Talent File (new), Davis, Sustaining and Sponsored, CBS Program Information; see also the daily radio schedules in the *New York Times* for this period.

29. Raymond Lee to Davis, February 19, 1941, Box 50, Kaltenborn MSS.

30. A 33 1/3 rpm original transcription, CBS broadcast, October 6, 1939, Kaltenborn MSS; CBS broadcast, April 22, 1940, Elmer Davis MSS, Special Collections, New York Public Library, New York, New York [hereafter Davis MSS, NYPL]; CBS broadcast, August 15, 1944, Box 13, Davis MSS.

31. Harold Abbot Titcomb to Davis, April 12, 1940, Davis MSS, NYPL; ABC broadcast, December 5, 1945, Box 13, Davis MSS.

32. Davis, "Required Reading," *Saturday Review*, October 14, 1939, pp. 3-4 ff.; and "To Polybius for Perspective," *Saturday Review*, May 25, 1940, p. 10.

33. Notes taken by Davis in Britain, April 29-May 19, 1941, Box 5, Davis MSS.

34. "Mousetraps for Mice and Men," review of *Tested Sentences that Sell* by Elmer Wheeler, *Saturday Review*, April 23, 1938, pp. 14-15; Davis, "On Not Being Dead, as Reported," *Harper's* 178 (April 1939): 538.

35. *Ibid.*, p. 537.

36. Davis, "The Wisconsin Brothers," *Harper's* 178 (February 1939): 268;

G. H. C. Winston, Hampden-Sydney, Va., to Davis, April 8, 1940; Davis to Winston, April 15, 1940—both in Davis MSS, NYPL.

37. For further information concerning Davis's change in political thinking, see Alfred Haworth Jones, "The Making of an Interventionist on the Air: Elmer Davis and CBS News, 1939-1941," *Pacific Historical Review* 42 (February 1973): 74-93.

38. Davis, "Czechoslovakia: Bridge or Barricade?", *Harper's* 175 (June 1937): 85.

39. Davis, "The Road from Munich," *Harper's* 178 (December 1938): 42, 45, 43-44, 40.

40. Davis, "Topics of the Times," *New York Times,* copy in Notebook, "Times," p. 13, Box 53, Burlingame MSS; Davis, "Is England Worth Fighting For?", *New Republic,* February 15, 1939, pp. 35,37.

41. Davis, "Democratic Dilemma" review editorial of *Men Must Act* by Lewis Mumford, *Saturday Review,* February 18, 1939, pp. 8-9; *New York Times,* April 14, 1939, copy in Box 4, Davis MSS.

42. Davis, "The War and America," *Harper's* 180 (April 1940): 449-62, abridged in Davis, "This 'Pot-and-Kettle' War," *Reader's Digest* 36 (April 1940): 17, 21-22.

43. Hornbeck to Davis, April 4, 1940, Stanley K. Hornbeck MSS, Manuscript Division, Hoover Institution on War, Revolution, and Peace, Stanford, Cal. [hereafter Hornbeck MSS].

44. Davis to Hornbeck, April 7, 1940; Hornbeck to Davis, April 22, 1940, Hornbeck MSS.

45. CBS broadcast (fifteen minutes), April 22, 1940, Davis MSS, NYPL.

46. Miss M. E. DeEster, Seymour, Conn., to Davis, n.d. [April 23, 1940], Davis MSS, NYPL.

47. CBS broadcast (fifteen minutes), April 26, 1940; Davis to B. L. McCullough, Seattle, Wash., April 26, 1940, Davis MSS, NYPL.

48. Davis, "The God of Hitler and Spinoza," *Harper's* 171 (July 1940): 189, 190. On p. 189 he begins: "As I write (May 6th) . . ."

49. Davis, "America and the War," review of *A Foreign Policy for America* by Charles A. Beard, and *Isolated America* by Raymond Leslie Buell, *Saturday Review,* May 18, 1940, p. 5.

50. CBS broadcast, May 10, May 13, 1940, reel 186, 187, Phonoarchive.

51. CBS broadcast, May 22, 1940, reel 190, Phonoarchive.

52. Davis, "To Polybius for Perspective," editorial, *Saturday Review,* May 25, 1940, p. 10.

53. Davis, "War on the State of Mind," review of *The Strategy of Terror* by Edmond Taylor, *Saturday Review,* June 29, 1940, pp. 5, 17.

54. Davis, "Contradiction at Chicago," editorial, *Saturday Review,* August 3, 1940, p. 8.

55. CBS broadcast, September 3, 1940, reel 224, Phonoarchive.

56. CBS broadcast, December 29, 1940, reel 3701, Phonoarchive.

57. CBS broadcast, February 11, 1941, reel 263, Phonoarchive; La Follette to Davis, February 24, 1941, Box 1, Davis MSS.

58. CBS broadcast n.d. [May 31, 1941], Davis, "Report from London," *Talks* 6 (July 1941): 1; Davis, "To the *SRL* Reader," *Saturday Review,* June 14, 1941, pp. 17, 9.

59. CBS broadcast, September 11, 1941; Davis, "A Half-Hour Later," *Talks* 6 (October 1941): 2. For a fuller discussion of Davis's comments on overseas events, see David H. Culbert, "Tantalus' Dilemma: Public Opinion, Six Radio Commentators and Foreign Affairs, 1935-1941" (Ph.D. dissertation, Northwestern University, 1970), pp. 377-628.

60. Davis to Frankfurter, June 13, 1953, Box 51, Frankfurter MSS.

61. Lauterbach, "Elmer Davis and the News," p. 57 (cited above, note 1); Swing, interview with author, September 5, 1968.

62. Robert E. Sherwood, *Roosevelt and Hopkins: An Intimate History* (New York, 1948), p. 437; for instance, Roosevelt to Russell C. Leffingwell, March 16, 1942, *Personal Letters,* 2: 1298-99.

63. Lauterbach, "Elmer Davis and the News," p. 13; Frankfurter to Roosevelt, March 12, 1942, in Max Freedman, annotator, *Roosevelt and Frankfurter: Their Correspondence, 1928-1945* (Boston, 1967), p. 651.

64. Telegram, Davis to Hornbeck, October 17, 1937; Hornbeck to Davis, October 18, 1937; Hornbeck to "To Whom it May Concern," August 29, 1940; Davis to Hornbeck, n.d. [dated April 19, 1941, by Hornbeck's secretary], Hornbeck MSS.

65. Herbert E. Gaston to Roosevelt, August 19, 1940, Box 1, OF 4040; Davis to Early, August 16, 1941, Box 2, OF 144, both in FDRL.

66. Davis to Stimson, October 11, 1941; Stimson to Davis, October 24, 1941, both in Box 389, Stimson MSS: Welles to Davis, March 6, 1942, Box 1, Davis MSS; Frankfurter to Davis, June 18, 1942, Box 51, Frankfurter MSS.

67. William L. Langer and S. Everett Gleason, *The Challenge to Isolation, 1937-1940* (New York, 1952), pp. 710-11; Mark Lincoln Chadwin, *The Hawks of World War II* (Chapel Hill, N.C., 1968), pp. 113, 67.

68. Marshall, "Notes by the Way," *Nation,* May 4, 1940, p. 570.

69. John G. Winant, *Letter from Grosvenor Square: An Account of a Stewardship* (Boston, 1947), p. 164.

70. Typed transcription of BBC broadcast, "American Commentary by Elmer Davis," August 2, 1941, A6312/44/45, FO.

71. Review by Robert J. Landry, *Variety,* October 18, 1939, p. 24.

72. Hadley Cantril and Mildred Strunk, *Public Opinion 1935-1946* (Princeton, N.J., 1951), p. 707; *Radio Daily,* January 19, 1940, in Box 2, OF 228, FDRL.

73. *Variety,* December 18, 1940, p. 34; "Colgate Buys Elmer Davis on 100 CBSers," March 26, 1941, p. 27; *CBS Program Book* (New York, December 1941), copy in Box 2, OF 256, FDRL; based on daily radio schedules in the *New York Times, Chicago Tribune,* and the *Washington Evening Star,* 1939-1941. Davis was heard only rarely in Chicago before Pearl Harbor.

74. Welles to Davis, March 6, 1942, Davis MSS.

6 | Fulton Lewis, Jr.: "We Never Put 'Em to Sleep!"

A journalist who worked with Lewis during the early 1930s considered him "the most verbose human being now inhabiting the earth. . . . A helpless gabbler."[1] In 1949 a fellow reporter offered an only slightly more flattering assessment: "Fulton, for all his bloated sermonizing on the touch-me-not purity of The American Way is a shrewd and tireless reporter. . . . He's a terrific guy with the negative stuff—I mean he really rises high when he can lambaste something or other."[2] Drawing no such distinction, the commentator himself once proudly described his radio style: "We never put 'em to sleep!"[3] Controversial news presented in such a manner brought a fanatical following. The broadcasts also aroused intense hatreds.

Those who still remember Lewis's name probably recall his notoriety during the early 1950s. He was one of Senator Joseph McCarthy's most vigorous defenders. In those years some writers made much of the newscaster's opposition to American entrance into World War II. They remembered how he had encouraged Charles Lindbergh to make his first radio broadcast in September 1939. Others, incensed by Lewis's tactics, recalled his series of broadcasts for the National Association of Manufacturers in 1941. For them, that was enough to damn the news analyst. Such passions are misplaced when considering Lewis's activities before Pearl Harbor. He did oppose Roosevelt's foreign policy, he did offer fawning apologias for big business under the auspices of NAM, he did find much favor with a certain stripe of congressman. Lewis's career demonstrates the techniques and commercial benefits of sounding controversial. But before 1941 his national audience was rather limited.

153

Raymond Gram Swing's opinion seems sound. Before Pearl Harbor his colleague was "a phenomenon more than an influence."[4] Lewis was an isolationist who lacked an audience.

A WASHINGTON SOUTHERNER

On April 30, 1903, Fulton Lewis, Jr., was born in Washington, D.C. His father enjoyed a lucrative law practice. The family owned a substantial home in Georgetown and a summer residence on the grounds of what is now the Washington Cathedral. A maternal grandfather had been Lincoln's Chief Clerk of the Treasury, a position corresponding to today's Treasurer of the United States.

Like many other long-time Washington residents of the period, the Lewises considered themselves Southerners. When their son was ready for college, the University of Virginia seemed a natural choice. He entered in the fall of 1920. The following spring, unwise speculations by the father temporarily placed the family in straitened circumstances. Lewis, Jr., remained in Washington the next year for lack of funds.[5] An indifferent student, he chose to leave college in 1924 without graduating. A part-time position playing a theater organ in a local movie house seems to have been his chief memory of the Charlottesville years. In an authorized biography, Lewis recounted how, though never having played an organ in his life, he got the job:

> He looked over the controls, found the one which—he hoped—would disconnect the foot pedals, pulled out all the rest. Then he ripped into "Margie."
>
> As he beat the bass keys with his left hand, his feet literally danced on the disconnected pedals. Music boomed out in the cavernous empty theater, and the manager couldn't keep his amazed eyes off those flying feet. When Fulton finished, the theater man shook his head in admiration and awe. "Gee," he breathed, "you really can play those things!"
>
> Fulton got the job, to begin the next day. From the theater he went straight to the organ at the University chapel and sat down at the console. He cut all classes, missed all meals, and got no sleep that night, but when he reported for work the next day, *he could play the organ!*
>
> It has been like that ever since.[6]

It was. He showed an impressive ability to bluff his way through almost any situation. His career as newscaster was a "cinch"—the only requirement was an ability to talk.[7] A quick person could learn enough to play a theater organ in a day—as long as the manager or audience was sufficiently ignorant.

In the fall of 1924, Lewis enrolled in the George Washington University School of Law. He quickly decided that his father's career would not be his. He became a reporter for the *Washington Herald,* at eighteen dollars a week. His industriousness, self-confidence, and general ebullience served him well. In three years he was city editor. In 1928 he became part of the Washington Bureau of Hearst's International News Service.[8]

The following year he met his future wife. Alice Huston was the daughter of Claudius Hart Huston, a Chattanooga millionaire who once served as chairman of the Republican National Committee. Before the Great Crash, Alice allegedly had a million dollars in her own name. Lewis met her while covering an important tennis match at the exclusive Chevy Chase Country Club. The sporting event was his story alone: he was the only reporter in Washington who belonged to the club. Through his fiancée he came to know President and Mrs. Hoover. When the marriage took place in June 1930, the First Lady and the Vice-President of the United States attended the ceremony. A few notes Mrs. Hoover sent to Alice Lewis suggest that she felt a genuine fondness for the younger woman.[9]

Shortly after his marriage, Lewis began gathering information concerning the manner in which Postmaster General Walter F. Brown and large airlines worked together in handing out airmail contracts. Through most of 1930 and 1931 the journalist collected data proving collusion and fraud. Thinking his research had provided a major story for his employer (and made him famous in the process), he was terribly disappointed when Hearst not only refused to publish his findings but took offense at what the young reporter had uncovered. It turned out that Arthur Brisbane, Hearst's leading editorial writer, was the Postmaster General's close personal friend. The investigator sensed that his tenure as a Hearst employee would be limited.[10]

Still upset by this turn of events, Lewis finally gave his 398-page report to Senator Hugo Black in 1933. The Alabamian used its contents in an investigation of airmail contracts that fall. The following February,

Roosevelt, with calamitous results, ordered the army to fly the mail. The journalist then persuaded the chairman of the House Committee on Military Affairs to suggest his name to the President for membership on a committee to study the "whole problem of aviation under the Black Bill."[11] Nothing happened.

A rare surviving letter from Lewis to his wife provides a further indication of the reporter's intense ambition during these years. He had been sent to Cuba by Hearst in 1933.

> Today I'm to interview President Machado, as you probably will have found out by the papers before this reaches you. . . . Mr. Hearst is very much interested in this thing personally, and I believe strongly the job may do us much good. He might even want to talk over with me about what I have seen and found out here. I am informed indirectly that Sumner Welles, whom I have talked confidentially with many times, is very much pleased with the investigating I did, and wants me to see the President when I get home. That of course would come about on invitation from the White House, but wouldn't it be swell if it did?[12]

Lewis continued as a Hearst employee. He wrote a syndicated column, "Washington Sideshow," filled with inside information, much of it pure gossip. A story about Hoover's vice-president, Charles Curtis, out of office, suggests the reporter's style: "He has a lackadaisical law-office down town. Lonely. Not much company these days. Lunch at a drug counter. Sandwich and coffee. Chats with the soda-jerker. After all, has to have somebody to talk to."[13]

Two articles concerning Cordell Hull suggest Lewis's willingness to express any opinion that might be salable. In 1934 he prepared a story describing the Secretary as "a kindly, lovable, monumentally sincere man." There were no takers. The journalist tried another tack. A more ambitious piece, "Cordell Hull: Errand Boy," was also returned. The editor of the *American Mercury* felt "it fail[s] to go deep enough into the man. It is . . . not a sufficiently sage analysis."[14]

Early in 1936 Lewis published "How the Republicans Hope to Beat Roosevelt" in reactionary Bernarr Macfadden's *Liberty Magazine.* The journalist suggested that the Democrats could be defeated "if the Great American Voter grows sufficiently weary of the towering beanstalk of national indebtedness, [and] if his breathing becomes labored in the stratosphere of brain-trust theories.'' In a thoughtful touch, Lewis then concluded that Macfadden was one of seven "real probabilities" for the Republican nomination that year.[15] Though the prediction proved inaccurate, he was asked to contribute to *Liberty* on later occasions.

In sum, the Hearst employee tried his hand at many things during these years. He spent a great deal of time helping to expose John Semer Farnsworth, an honor graduate from Annapolis convicted of selling naval secrets to the Japanese in 1936.[16] As in the case of the airmail scandals, he received little recognition for his careful investigation. The reporter decided that he possessed special abilities to uncover wrongdoing—with unfortunate results. During his radio career Lewis led many crusades. He rarely found especially worthy subjects. Many of his later exposés were believable only to listeners convinced that there were conspiracies all about, especially in the highest government echelons.

SUBSTITUE GLOBE-TROTTER

Lewis's first contact with radio apparently came in 1927. He read *Herald* "news flashes" over a Washington radio station. Nine years later, a chance to do a complete news broadcast materialized. Hearst's Washington Globe-Trotter always read a poem during the middle of his fifteen-minute program. When the regular man took his summer vacation, Lewis offered to substitute without pay. Instead of poetry, he tried something more exciting:

> Fulton took a microphone to the Department of State. He read the straight news part of the program. Then, instead of reading a poem, he brought before the mike a department code clerk with a message from the cruiser. It was in code—not a secret code, but a kind of wireless shorthand—and the clerk read it as it came in, then translated it for the radio audience. It concerned the actual rescue of American citizens in war-torn Spain.[17]

He handled the newscasts so effectively that William B. Dolph, manager of Mutual's Washington outlet and director of radio for the Democratic National Committee in 1936, decided to test Lewis as a radio personality.

The reporter, having recently quit Hearst's International News Service to try public relations, gladly accepted Dolph's offer.

Lewis's first program concerned fishing, not the Department of State. He offered his talks intermittently over WOL during the fall of 1936. Listeners learned that star-drag reels could be had for less than four dollars.[18] Attempting a light touch, the angler wrote "laugh" into his own scripts. After not broadcasting for several weeks, he began: "It seems like three months instead of three weeks since we last went fishing over the air; this old microphone here almost has cobwebs, so far as I'm concerned."[19]

Lewis's regular news commentaries began on October 28, 1937. He started on a local station at twenty-five dollars a week. By December he had gained a number of additional Mutual outlets. Though speaking at 7:00 P.M., he could not get a sponsor. Years later, the broadcaster explained why:

> It was only after a long, long time that I realized what the trouble was. My competition on the other three networks at that time was Amos and Andy, Easy Aces, and Fred Waring's Pennsylvanians, and I was the only person in radio stupid enough to take that time slot.[20]

Not until October 1939 did his news analyses find a buyer. Detrola Radio, a Detroit firm, purchased the program over fourteen stations. A *Variety* reviewer felt that Lewis, who read his own commercials, had "the knack of not saying anything very new or very controversial, yet making it listenable. That's usually considered commercial."[21]

ADJECTIVES ARE NOT THE NATURAL ENEMIES OF NOUNS

In 1949 the following seemed a good description of the commentator's broadcast style:

> His favorite preliminary tactic in attack and counterattack consists in characterizing the enemy as something like "a piddle-paddle, double-talking, CIO-Communist backed, left-wing crackpot." (Lewis has never subscribed to the theory that adjectives are the natural enemies of nouns.) If his target should be an academician, Lewis commonly

includes in his initial thrust "inexperienced, impractical, theoretical college professor." A man known as an aesthete is likely to bob up as a "thyroidal poet" or "Greenwich Village expert on art and culture with a capital C." When he is genuinely aroused about someone, Lewis generally adds "shyster," "bum," "gibble-gabble phony," or a "shilly-shallying fuzzy-duzzy."[22]

Such colorful language, made with equal parts of slang and cliché, proved immensely appealing to some. But this is the mature Lewis in action.

Broadcasts before 1941 were a different matter. In 1939 Lewis talked about a "ten-dollar word." He introduced a topic with "and while this is not generally known." A boat was "designed to dish it out but not to take it, as one naval expert told me today."[23] By the fall of 1940 he had started using a theater organ selection to begin and end his program. He spent a major part of one newscast describing a small theater in Virginia (the topic alone suggests one difference between broadcasts done this year and several years later) in an unconvincingly lively fashion:

> The American theatre was tottering from a combination of malnutrition of the box-office [sic] as a result of the depression and body blows from the booming movie business. The lights were going out on Broadway. Because the theatre was one of the first luxuries, Mr. America pared it off the family budget.[24]

A year later, after carefully explaining that Roosevelt had refused to give him background information at a press conference, Lewis told his listeners: "I got the background from other Washington sources by long distance telephone." On December 8, 1941, he covered Roosevelt's "Day of Infamy" speech. He familiarly described "Jimmy" Roosevelt helping his father up the aisle. Shortly after the President finished his remarks, Lewis turned to "a most amusing experience here, ladies and gentlemen" and began discussing in detail whether he did or did not have the right to broadcast congressional debate over a Declaration of War.[25] His technique needed polishing.

A 1946 transcription of a newscast devoted in large part to the sins of Henry Wallace shows the fully developed Lewis rhetoric to good advantage. The commentator directed his remarks to those "State [Department] pink-tinged frustrates" busy with their "mission for

Moscow." Numerous clichés helped pad out the rapid tumble of words: "So the jig was up and [Chester] Bowles threw in the sponge"; "how does that jive," and "set that one." The voice—clipped and insistent— conveyed a sense of presenting information from special sources a- vailable nowhere else. Someone listening might have pictured Humphrey Bogart playing a particularly tough gangster.

The commentator breathed hatred in his venomous attacks. A popular article on Lewis titled "Voice with a Snarl" captured the way he said "admiiiire." When the news analyst employed sarcasm, he offered a deprecatory little chuckle or lingered over a syllable. He said "appoin- tive" in such a manner that the listener understood that only loafers and time-servers were appointed to office. Words came so quickly that the newscaster often stumbled as he read. His pronunciation was generally unaffected, though "order" became "oughter"; "rather," "rahtheh"; and "article," "oughtikle." Lewis liked alliteration. He emphasized the same initial sound in "put off the politics," "piece of parchment," "Baltic and Balkans," and "mirror in the moving."[26]

Before 1941 and in numerous instances thereafter, regular broadcasts often seemed tedious.[27] Long descriptions of machines and their products failed to fascinate every listener. The "helpless gabbler" revealed him- self in a broadcast concerning the Pratt & Whitney Company and its problems with machine tooling. Lewis mentioned that "it's been impos- sible to know just what the facts really are and that's the reason I went yesterday to Hartford, Conn., to try to get a first-hand picture for you as to just what the real story is." He then expanded his travelogue:

> First of all, by way of giving you a general picture, that [Pratt & Whitney] plant is now turning out about 800 engines a month, which may sound like a very small number. You may picture the plant as one little medium-sized building, with a group of men using hand tools.
> Get that thought out of your head, right now. The actual buildings of that factory cover 30 acres of ground—that's the actual ground space— and the daily pay roll is 13,000 men. Thirty acres is a good sized farm in some parts of the United States.[28]

In May 1941, the NAM hired the commentator to present a series of testimonials concerning big business and its efforts toward national defense.[29] Each Wednesday at 2:00 P.M., Lewis's programs originated from a different plant. He was one of many doing the same sort of thing.

As a *Variety* reviewer noted, it was hard "to be able to speak admiringly of a radio program devoted to 'propaganda' for business. So many of the radio attempts have been either transparently biased and smug or cautious to dullness."[30]

Broadcasting from the Van Norman Machine Tool Company "in the historic city of Springfield, Massachusetts," Lewis demonstrated the latter defect:

> LEWIS: And what about the floor space, sir?
> SCOTT: [president of the company] Well, we've added 12,000 square feet to the building and six months ago we bought another factory with 200,000 additional square feet. . . . Our oscillating grinder is used by all manufacturers of ball bearings.

A few minutes later, the commentator indicated why some considered him a tool of the NAM: "Mr Scott confided to me this afternoon that he is just 39 years old—from blueprint boy to president at that age—a little real life answer to those who will want to tell you that today there is no opportunity for American youth."[31] Speaking from the Swift meat packing plant in Chicago about a month later, Lewis found kind words for his host: "This is headquarters for the luscious beef steaks and the thrifty, nutritious cuts, and the hickory smoked hams and bacon, that make the American people the best fed on the face of the earth . . . a notable monument to the American system of free enterprise."[32] Had this typified all of his broadcasts, he might have gained a reputation as radio's most effective soporific.

A good example of the news analyst at his best—both because of the subject matter and the manner of presentation—involved a 148-page pamphlet published by the Department of Agriculture in 1943. It was hard for the administration to talk of a critical paper shortage while its own agency came out with a copiously illustrated publication, "The Fleas of North America." Lewis could scarcely restrain himself:

> Oh, wait a minute. Listen to this carefully, because this proves that ALL government scientists and writers are not extremists or exaggerators . . . this fellow is a conservative from way back:
> "Fleas are probably best known as household pests. Their presence in house [sic], UNDER CERTAIN CONDITIONS, *MAY* cause the occupants great annoyance. . . . In the United States (mind you, this

is no reckless generalization . . . we're confining ourselves to the
United States)— In the United States, fleas are serious pests of dogs,
cats, and poultry. Dogs may be greatly annoyed by fleas, and when
attacked, spend much time, gnawing . . . the back near the root of the
tail.''[33]

Listeners relished this exposé, though it proved difficult for Lewis to
find more monumental examples of wrongdoing by government officials.

Lewis devoted many broadcasts to reports of his private investigations.
Though related to the theme of official bungling or boondoggling, the
actual instances proved inconsequential. In 1944 the commentator made
a flying visit to Mexico City. He promised to explain his findings ''just as
soon as it is safe to reveal them.'' Two years earlier, Mrs. Roosevelt had
been behind some crackpot scheme in which the Office of Civilian
Defense ''hired Miss Mayris Chaney to teach dancing to the nation's
youngsters so that they might be better able to protect themselves against
bursting bombs.'' In June and July 1942 he devoted endless broadcasts to
discussions of how to manufacture synthetic rubber. Seventeen complete
analyses were reprinted in the *Congressional Record,* but few listeners
can have been as fascinated as some congressmen apparently were.[34] In
fact, those whose minds tended to wander would not have been regular
listeners to Lewis's programs. The talks were too detailed to interest the
average housewife unless she, like the broadcasters, had an inexhaustible
enthusiasm for stories meant to embarrass New Dealers.[35]

At the end of the war, the Writers War Board, consisting of such
authors as Clifton Fadiman and Franklin P. Adams, summed up Lewis's
contribution to the war effort. They termed his ''radio period '*a shock-
ingly isolationist, intolerant and divisive program.*' '' No official action
was taken. The news analyst went on to greater successes as the friend
and confidant of Joseph McCarthy. In 1954, when Edward R. Murrow
openly attacked the senator on ''See it Now,'' his immensely popular
television program, McCarthy chose Lewis's radio newscast to offer a
formal rebuttal.[36] Critics later remarked that it was the last time radio had
been used to present a major news story.

In this comment lies part of the broadcaster's commercial difficulties
in the later 1950s. His television show enjoyed some success for a time.
But an unsmiling Lewis—with his long face, Roman nose, and slicked-

down hair—looked ill at ease on the newer medium. He apparently refused advice about how to improve his image. The broadcaster's mouth drooped open, accentuating a well-developed jowl. Undercover agents appeared on television with him. Investigators such as Major Racey Jordan looked so furtive that it proved doubly hard to believe their incredible tales of how Roosevelt and such traitors as Harry Hopkins and Harry Dexter White had given uranium and atomic secrets to the Soviet Union in 1944.[37]

A diminishing group of the faithful avidly followed the radio analyses. Lewis described his supporters in a 1958 television interview with Mike Wallace:

> You use the term, "extreme right." I prefer the term "conservative." But I find a very considerable amount of lunatic fringe that adheres like lint to the coattails of the conservative side of the American picture. Why I can't say. Unfortunately, Mike, you cannot control who follows you down the street or who writes you letters.[38]

By 1960, he had to travel from city to city looking for sponsors.[39] His open espousal of McCarthyism made advertisers leery of buying his program. At the time of his death, on August 21, 1966, he still found favor with a certain sort of person. Some of the more prominent gathered in Washington in 1962 to honor the commentator's twenty-fifth anniversary on radio. J. Edgar Hoover paid homage to the one broadcaster who had vigorously opposed communism in the United States. Most Americans were unaware that Lewis was still on the air.

MUTUAL'S ISOLATIONIST: THE LINDBERGH BROADCASTS AND INTRIGUE IN HAVANA

Not a great many pre-1941 Lewis broadcasts have survived. Of those that have, quite a few concern the need for national defense—a topic on which all found it easy to agree. Aside from these NAM-sponsored programs, there are testimonials from senators and representatives commending Lewis's distaste for Roosevelt's foreign policy and the New Deal in general. The newscaster's name was often mentioned on the floor of Congress. It is not difficult to demonstrate Lewis's isolationist sympathies.

At first he did not strongly ciritcize Roosevelt. For instance, he sent a fish to the fellow angler in 1935. The President was apparently delighted: "Just a note to tell you that Black Bonito was perfectly delicious. They have been very elusive when I have tried to catch them. Thank you ever so much." The following year, Lewis won the admiration of other reporters, and the President as well, by predicting in a press pool that Roosevelt would win every state except Maine and Vermont. The reporter's son was born the same year. He told his fellow journalists that he had another President. Shortly after, a photograph arrived from the White House inscribed: "To Fulton Lewis III, as one President to another. Franklin D. Roosevelt."[40] In January 1940 the Chief Executive began his press conference with some general banter. He wanted a copy of a recent Lewis dinner speech because he "could then steal a few of the quips." He added: "You know, I have no scruples about stealing things, absolutely none."[41]

The President's comments might have been less lighthearted had he realized that just four months earlier, Lewis had arranged for Charles Lindbergh to make his first radio appearance opposing American intervention in the European war. William R. Castle, Under Secretary of State during Hoover's administration and a bitter Roosevelt opponent, held a dinner at his Washington home on August 23, 1939. He invited Lindbergh, recently returned from Europe, and the broadcaster.[42] His two guests enjoyed each other's company. As Lindbergh reports in his *Journals,* the three felt the same way about dangers inherent in the crisis:

> We are disturbed about the effect of the Jewish influence in our press, radio, and motion pictures. It may become very serious. Lewis told us of one instance where the Jewish advertising firms threatened to remove all their advertising from the Mutual system if a certain feature were permitted to go on the air. The threat was powerful enough to have the feature removed.[43]

On September 10 the aviator, who had long resisted all attempts to persuade him to talk on the air, decided to accept Fulton Lewis's offer.[44] Two years later, when this story appeared in *Life,* some sponsors dropped the newscaster temporarily.[45] But a survey of the coverage of Lindbergh's initial speech by *Variety* and newspapers in several large cities shows that nobody mentioned Lewis's name, not even the *Chicago Tribune.* Only

Time credited the commentator with helping to arrange the broadcast.[46] Mutual hoped to have an exclusive, but Lindbergh insisted that CBS and NBC be included. In the end all three major networks carried his remarks though he spoke from an MBS studio.[47] Once again Lewis was denied the publicity he had sought for so long. No wonder Roosevelt sounded jovial about Fulton Lewis, Jr., in January 1940. He knew nothing of the latter's connection with Charles Lindbergh.

Within a few months Lewis's true feelings about the Roosevelts became better known. In April 1940 he broadly hinted that the American Youth Congress, one of Eleanor Roosevelt's projects, was a Communist-front organization. Lewis noted that the "main horde" that poured into Washington included mostly "Polish or Russian" names. Those who had come did not simply listen to Roosevelt on the White House grounds, "they swarmed the south lawn in a misty drizzle." Accusing the group of having done more in "three days to prove the Dies Committee charges" than Congressman Martin L. Dies had been able to do in two years, the writer concluded that "altogether, the Youth Congress champions— except for unflagging Mrs. Roosevelt—began to have their doubts about its [sic] guiltlessness of Communism which she had, in effect, guaranteed.[48]

If the syntax was garbled, the meaning was clear. Mrs. Roosevelt promoted the cause of subversive Communist organizations in America. Lewis's conclusion fit nicely with the magazine's lead editorial that issue. Publisher Bernarr Macfadden warned his readers that only those who favored "dictatorship" would vote the New Deal.[49]

On July 4, 1940, Lewis offered a special program devoted to foreign policy alternatives. Pretending it was 1776, he made obvious reference to the current political scene:

> As you well know, that caused a terrific controversy in Congress. . . .
> There are two widely separated factions . . . one is what you might call
> the isolationist group . . . they believe that we should break with the
> old world . . . we should live our own life, and we should NOT involve
> ourselves in affairs across the Atlantic and we should NOT submit to
> dictation and interference and meddling FROM across the Atlantic . . .
> these isolationists say that we should govern ourselves, and make our
> own place in the world . . . and they were the ones who have been
> supporting Mr. Lee of Virginia. . . .
> The other faction is what might be called the appeasement group . . .

it is the Tory party, really . . . they believe that we should try to reach a
peaceful settlement with King George.

The talk's popularity encouraged the broadcaster to present substantially
the same thing on later anniversaries of American independence.[50]

The climax of the Battle of Britain in September 1940 led many
Americans to sense a special urgency in sending additional assistance to
England. CBS correspondent Edward R. Murrow offered descriptions of
a city subjected to nightly air raid attacks. Lewis attempted to belittle the
damage. He described a "three-hour" interview with Major General
George V. Strong ("a wiry slender little fellow"), chief of the War Plans
Division of the Army and head of a Special Commission of American
Military Observers ("the picked brains of the Army") who had just
returned from a month in Britain. Lewis promised his audience "a bit of
cold hard fact as to what is the real situation in England." The commentator had to combat an image many Americans had come to accept:
"Now you've doubtless seen pictures of these various sites, buildings,
ruins and blazing fires because those are the only things photographers
take pictures of. There's no news interest in taking pictures of the
buildings that are not injured." He added that newsmen set up their
cameras to "show the damage most efficiently."

Lewis admitted that bombs hit London occasionally but that was "just
a tragedy." He quoted General Strong as saying that *"something less
than one percent"* of the city had been bombed. The German attacks
were "not nearly as efficient as they have been advertised." If somehow
glass shattered, no matter. It meant "a boom time for the glaziers."
Indeed the Nazis actually helped the business: "Glass mills are turning
out glass as fast as they can." Anyone listening to Lewis's account would
have thought that it was "business as usual" in London.[51]

Perhaps the commentator's most overt attempt at attacking Roosevelt
took place in July 1940. Lewis covered the second meeting of the Foreign
Ministers of the American Republics in Havana. On July 26 the German
chargé d'affaires in Cuba sent a long message to Berlin in which Kurt
Sell, embassy press adviser in Washington, discussed an idea of Fulton
Lewis, Jr.'s. The commentator allegedly wanted Hitler to address a short
telegram to Roosevelt, suggesting the President urge Churchill to give up
a hopeless fight. Roosevelt would of course make a rude reply, but it
would help keep America out of war.[52] Alton Frye, in his discussion

of Nazi intrigue in the United States before 1941, makes much of this report. He concludes that "the incident is an interesting revelation of a well-known American publicist's apparent readiness to cooperate with the Nazis in discrediting the United States President."[53] But Frye made no investigation of Lewis's influence before 1941.

A few weeks after the telegram of July 26 had been received, Berlin wrote Hans Thomsen, German chargé d'affaires in the United States, for information concerning Fulton Lewis, Jr. Thomsen's reply, which Frye discusses, should have encouraged the historian to look elsewhere for Nazi spies:

> He [Lewis] attempts to support the isolationist line in his commentary on foreign affairs. He takes an attitude toward Germany which is factual and unprejudiced, so that the proposal in question was certainly well meant. On the other hand, in contrast to some leading American commentators, no political importance is attached to L. The proposal in question, therefore, probably arises mostly from a desire on the part of the personalities involved to gain attention.[54]

In 1950 Hubert Humphrey publicized the July 26 telegram in hopes of making trouble for Lewis. The commentator, in a lengthy rebuttal, termed Humphrey's "statements . . . falsehoods out of the whole cloth."[55] The defense proved convincing only to Lewis's followers. Actually, there seems no question that such a telegram was sent to Berlin and that Fulton Lewis, Jr., made a suggestion to Kurt Sell to the effect that Hitler should wire Roosevelt. The message demonstrates the news analyst's interest in keeping the United States out of the European war and some extremely unethical behavior. But Thomsen's belief that the entire affair was a publicity stunt provides further proof that the commentator was not taken seriously by many in 1940.

"A PHENOMENON MORE THAN AN INFLUENCE"

It is not necessary to rely on the German chargé's assessment of Lewis's importance. A *Fortune* survey asking for one's favorite radio commentator in November 1939 failed to include Lewis's name as a possible response. Nor was there any mention of this broadcaster in *Radio Daily*'s popularity poll released in January 1940. A year after,

Lewis's Hooperating was a modest 3.8. As late as March 1941, he was sponsored in only twenty-three cities.[56]

The frequency with which he broadcast in Chicago and New York tells a similar story. In Washington, D.C., Lewis spoke five nights a week at 7:00 P.M. from 1938 until Pearl Harbor. For citizens in the nation's capital, he was a most important commentator. But in New York, he did not broadcast at all during most of 1941, and only sporadically before that. In Chicago, he appeared at a dizzying variety of times. In January 1940 he spoke at the unpopular hour of 11:15 P.M. on Monday, Wednesday, and Friday. In October he was off the air. By May 1941 he appeared on Tuesday, Thursday, and Friday at 6:00 P.M. In November 1941 his number of listeners must have been minuscule. True he appeared five days a week at 6:00 P.M., but on W59c, a shortwave station in part experimental. This sort of coverage in major metropolitan areas proves that Chargé Hans Thomsen sent accurate information to Berlin when he belittled Lewis's importance.[57]

Along with trying to make himself known to the President, the commentator cultivated the friendship of other administration leaders. In both 1938 and 1939, the broadcaster persuaded Harold Ickes to substitute for him during a vacation. In December 1939 he arranged for Sumner Welles to speak on an hour-long Mutual program "designed as a Christmas and New Year greeting to the American people and the American services." Ten months later he discussed with Pierrepont Moffat a British corporation that sought to make purchases in the United States.[58] After October 1939 there is no further indication of contacts with State Department officials.

He did earn the admiration of Bernard Baruch. On April 20, 1942, the financier sent Lewis a note of thanks. "You squeezed a lot of information into your broadcast and it was all so understandable," he wrote. In 1947 Baruch praised the commentator for his realism: "I must confess that I always wanted some broadcast coming from America, stating *facts,* in order to meet the lying propaganda that is continually preached from the other side."[59]

Lewis proved particularly effective in cultivating the friendship of Herbert Hoover, whom he had first met in 1929. The ex-President opposed the New Deal and, after September 1939, what he considered the prowar attitude of Franklin D. Roosevelt. Hoover felt ignored by the regular press. Beginning in 1939, he paid careful attention to what Lewis said on the air. On several occasions before Pearl Harbor he wrote Lewis seeking publicity for speeches he planned to make or urging the commentator to include specific items in his broadcasts. Lewis was eager to help.

In April 1939 Hoover told the newscaster that he would be "delighted" to discuss the "national situation" with him.[60] Nine months later Lewis devoted part of a broadcast to Hoover's attempts at providing relief for the Finnish people. The news analyst mentioned his source of information (and made sure to send a copy of his remarks to Hoover himself): "It so happens that I saw Mr. Hoover myself while I was on my way through New York on this trip. We had quite a long chat. . . . Incidentally, he told me that he has received more than a million-and-a-half dollars, in the Finnish Relief Fund, to date." Hoover expressed special satisfaction with Lewis's 1943 attack on the Four Freedoms, in particular Freedom from Fear and Freedom from Want, which the commentator considered socialistic measures. As he put it:

> Let me remind you that Joe Louis didn't become the most famous and the most powerful fighter in the world or in world history by lying in bed twenty-four hours a day and having a government of college economists in Washington serve him his meals on a tray.

He called for a fifth freedom, "freedom of individual enterprise."[61]

Lewis enjoyed great popularity among many congressmen. As one magazine commented in 1943: Constant association with politicos has given 39-year-old Fulton Lewis many of their mannerisms. He indulges in deep senatorial guffaws, interminable telephone calls; gives his autograph freely and smokes his incessant cigarets in a long black holder."[62]

In February 1939, though still looking for his first commercial sponsor, Lewis received a letter of appreciation from Representative John J. Dempsey, Democrat of New Mexico. Five months later he made himself better known. He persuaded Congress to allow the introduction of radio facilities similar to the press galleries. The commentator arranged a formal opening, even managing to get a message from the White House for the occasion. He thanked his friend John Dempsey for his untiring efforts and invited fellow broadcaster Boake Carter to say a few words at the end of the ceremony.[63]

Soon after, Mutual released a poll concerning Congress's favorite commentators. It showed that Lewis was favored by 39 percent of the legislators, as opposed to 18 percent for second-place Lowell Thomas. An impressive number of testimonials from Congressmen lend credence to the poll's findings. Senators as different as Arthur H. Vandenberg, Claude E. Pepper, and Henry Styles Bridges all agreed that they benefited greatly from Lewis's news analyses.[64]

In October 1939, during the congressional debate over revision of the Neutrality Act, Lewis came up with another way to promote his name on Capitol Hill. He purchased fifteen thousand copies of a pamphlet put out by the House Foreign Affairs Committee containing pertinent resolutions and existing legislation printed in parallel columns. He told his listeners that "Mr. [Sol] Bloom was furnishing them."[65] Representatives spent the better part of an hour arguing whether it would be possible to get the publication from Lewis for nothing or if it would be necessary to appropriate money for printing additional copies. Lewis gained valuable publicity in the process.

An even better opportunity presented itself in early 1942. Congress had voted itself a handsome pension, but there was a good deal of unfavorable public comment. Lewis jumped in with an impassioned defense of the hard-working solons:

> I've seen many a Member of Congress spend his whole life in the House or Senate, and finally go out of office a broken, penniless old man, and it's hard to understand why they shouldn't be allowed the same pension arrangement the regular civil-service employees enjoy.[66]

The obvious justness of these remarks was immediately discussed on the floor of Congress.

A few months later, the newscaster began a crusade concerning synthetic rubber, which presented an opportunity for attacking Oil Coordinator Harold Ickes as well. Many members of Congress became convinced that here was a commentator who spoke to their needs and desires. In one sense Lewis was bound to have a large following in Washington. After all, he spoke five days a week from the beginning of 1938. Only Elmer Davis broadcast with greater frequency. But Lewis's assiduous cultivation of congressmen and his willingness to defend their every action greatly increased his popularity.

Congressman Charles A. Eaton of New Jersey sent a handwritten letter in July 1942, which no doubt expressed the sentiments of others as well: "You have long been my favorite commentator because of your absolute fairness, your painstaking endeavor to get at the truth of every situation you discuss, and, above all, because of your courage in always 'hewing to the line.' "[67] There is no question that this was sincerely meant. Senator Gerald P. Nye found the broadcaster's newscasts extremely informative. Lewis, he wrote a constituent, "is one of the very few of these commentators who has been able to hold an even balance during these trying times and to deal sensibly with current events. That is why he carries such real weight when he digs into the rubber question as he has."[68]

Thanks to his friends in Congress, the news analyst's right to stay on the air became relatively secure by the middle of 1941. Isolationists expressed delight when in late April Lewis belittled stories that 40 percent of "the material that we have sent, and are now sending, to Britain under the lend-lease program has been sent to the bottom on the way across." Gerald Nye fully accepted the broadcaster's corrective and cited it in a speech on the Senate floor. The commentator's evidence consisted of "three unidentified government sources." Lewis told his listeners that he was providing this information merely "to keep the record straight."[69] Actually Lewis hoped to prove that American naval vessels were not needed to convoy merchant ships across the Atlantic. One listener told of Lewis's daily assertions that Roosevelt opposed any use of convoys.[70]

Such clever misinformation about what was happening led to rumors that the administration hoped to force Lewis off the air. Reports that Lowell Mellett, of the office of Government Reports, had tried to end Lewis's broadcasts were the subject of serious Senate inquiry in May. By September, *Time* referred to "Isolationist Fulton Lewis, Jr.," without many sponsors growing fearful. After all, he had been chosen one of the ten outstanding young men of 1939. And in 1943 a committee of judges headed by the president of Washington and Lee University even decided to give Lewis the first Alfred I. Dupont award for "aggressive, consistently excellent and accurate gathering and reporting of news."[71]

Lewis's national prominence came mostly in the period following Pearl Harbor. By July 1942 he had quite a following, particularly in Congress. During the early Cold War years he had millions of listeners.

By 1954, however, he attracted a special audience. As an official *Pulse* survey that year showed: "Fulton Lewis, Jr. has great appeal among retired people and among professional and business men. On the other hand, his audience is made up of a below-average number of so-called working class people."[72]

This survey suggests that aside from conservative, elderly business-men, few could listen nightly for twenty years to stories of government ineptitude and Communist conspiracy. Fulton Lewis, Jr. made a career out of proving that New Dealers never acted as they publicly claimed. Accordingly, certain congressmen, and persons such as Herbert Hoover, listened regularly to the commentator and approved of what he said. But Lewis's own crusades had little to do with the news. His coverage of foreign affairs consisted mostly of stories that would seem to prove American participation in European affairs unnecessary. Had Lewis considered being pro-Roosevelt salable before 1941, he might will-ingly have traded his isolationist label for that of administration spokes-man.

Lewis typified the attitudes of more than one commentator on the air before Pearl Harbor. He generally ignored what took place in the Far East. He may have sounded fierce and full of righteous indignation, but that was mostly good showmanship. News broadcasts became vehicles to advance his career—and being controversial seemed the best way to attract attention. It is thus more important to understand what use Lewis made of the news than to remember exactly what courses of action he favored.[73] Radio was a medium where skills in self-promotion mattered. Only an "inexperienced, impractical, theoretical college professor" would be silly enough to care seriously about what was said. On the other hand, Lewis's willingness to serve as publicist for Herbert Hoover and Charles Lindbergh suggests that before 1941 there were influential Americans who found his radio broadcasts a vehicle for furthering their particular points of view. They cared seriously about what Lewis said, but only because he reinforced beliefs they already held. Lewis was an isolationist—one of two on the air after 1939—but his impact was no greater than that of Boake Carter after September 1939. The importance of Lewis comes from realizing how little he influenced the average person—no matter what many congressmen thought. Only in Washing-ton, D.C., did Lewis make radio news and isolationism seem closely related.

NOTES

1. Quoted in H. N. Oliphant, "Fulton Lewis, Jr.: Man of Distinction," *Harper's* 218 (March 1949): 78.

2. Quoted in *ibid.*, p. 77.

3. Quoted in Booton Herndon [Gordon Carroll, ed.], *Praised and Damned: The Story of Fulton Lewis, Jr.* (New York, 1954), p. 5.

4. Swing to author, July 11, 1968.

5. Herndon, *Praised and Damned,* pp. 16-19.

6. Herndon, *Praised and Damned,* p. 20.

7. *Time,* March 15, 1943.

8. Herndon, *Praised and Damned,* pp. 20-22.

9. *Time,* March 15, 1943, p. 52; Herndon, *Praised and Damned,* pp. 21-24; for example, Lou Henry Hoover to Alice Huston, April 24 [1930?]; White House invitation to Mr. and Mrs. Fulton Lewis, Jr., January 15, 1931, both in Correspondence of Others, Box 15; Herbert Hoover to Mrs. Lewis, Jr., May 5, 1949, Incoming Correspondence, Box 3, all in Series I, Fulton Lewis, Jr., MSS, Manuscript Division Syracuse University, Syracuse, New York [hereafter Lewis MSS].

10. Kenneth S. Davis, *The Hero: Charles A. Lindbergh and the American Dream* (Garden City, N.Y., 1959), pp. 331-38; Richard Wilson, "Radio's Top Fault-Finder," *Look,* April 1, 1947, pp. 35-36; Herndon, *Praised and Damned,* pp. 28-31.

11. John J. McSwain to Roosevelt, May 23, 1934, carbon copy in Incoming Correspondence, Box 4, Lewis MSS.

12. Lewis to wife, n.d. [spring 1933?], Correspondence of Others, Box 15, Lewis MSS.

13. "Washington Sideshow," *Washington Herald,* December 30, 1935, copy in News Publications, Box 35, Lewis MSS. Box 35 contains a number of similar columns from 1935.

14. Lewis, "The Paradox of Reciprocal Tariff Agreements," n.d. [1934], 15; letter attached to "Cordell Hull: Errand Boy," signature torn off [Paul Palmer, editor], to Lewis, February 15, 1935, both in Manuscript Articles, Box 60, Lewis MSS.

15. *Liberty Magazine,* January 11, 1936, pp. 20-21, copy in Manuscripts, Box 64, Lewis MSS.

16. Herndon, *Praised and Damned,* pp. 31-39. Concerning Farnsworth, see Michael Sayers and Albert E. Kahn, *Sabotage!: The Secret War Against America* (New York, 1942), p. 66.

17. Herndon, *Praised and Damned,* pp. 40-42.

18. WOL broadcast, n.d. [December 1936], Broadcasts, Box 16, Lewis MSS; Kenneth Crawford and Hobart Rowen, "Voice with a Snarl," *Saturday*

Evening Post, August 30, 1947, pp. 23, 105. F.W. Marbut, *News from the Capital: The Story of Washington Reporting* (Carbondale, Ill., 1971) p. 211, states that Lewis broadcast hunting and fishing news over WCAP in Washington during 1925. Marbut interviewed Lewis in 1954, but other incorrect details he cites suggest that the broadcaster's memory was a bit vague.

19. WOL broadcast, n.d. [November, 1936]; WOL broadcast, n.d. [December, 1936], both in Broadcasts, Box 16, Lewis MSS.

20. Quoted in "Fulton Lewis Sets New Record," reprint from *Human Events,* 1962; "We Pay Our Respects to Fulton Lewis, Jr.," *Broadcast Advertising,* May 15, 193[9?], copies of both in Box 64, Lewis MSS; Herndon, *Praised and Damned,* p. 44.

21. *Variety,* November 1, 1939, p. 30; October 18, 1939, p. 27.

22. Oliphant, "Man of Distinction," p. 77.

23. Recorded MBS broadcast, November 17, 1939, tape 5404, reel 82, RSS-LC.

24. Fulton Lewis, Jr., "The Barter Theatre" (excerpt from MBS broadcast), *Scribner's Commentator* 7 (July 1940): 108. The organ music can be heard on recorded MBS broadcasts, September 23 and October 30, 1940, tapes 54 and 68, Radio Archive, Professor Marvin R. Bensman, Department of Speech and Drama, Memphis State University, Memphis, Tenn. [hereafter Radio Archive-Memphis].

25. Recorded MBS broadcast, November 7, 1941, tape 68, Radio Archive-Memphis. Mr. Michael Biel, Department of Speech, University of Missouri, Columbia, Mo., kindly let the author hear a taped copy of Fulton Lewis, Jr., covering Roosevelt's "Day of Infamy" speech, MBS broadcast, December 8, 1941. Ernest D. Rose, "How the U.S. Heard About Pearl Harbor," *Journal of Broadcasting* 5 (Fall 1961): 292-93, contains extended excerpts from Lewis's error-filled broadcast the day before.

26. Based on recorded MBS broadcast, September 17, 1946, original transcription in Lewis MSS; recorded MBS broadcast, September 23, 1940, tape 54, Radio Archive-Memphis; 33 1/3 rpm original transcription, MBS broadcast, September 17, 1946, Lewis MSS.

27. See for example recorded MBS broadcasts, September 23 and October 1940; November 7, 1941, tapes 54 and 68, Radio Archive-Memphis.

28. MBS broadcast, June 6, 1940, reprinted in *Congressional Record,* 76th Cong., 2d Session, Appendix 3736-37.

29. Lewis had favored efforts to increase national defense preparedness since the spring of 1940. See MBS broadcast May 29, 1940, reprinted in *Congressional Record,* 76th Cong., 2d Session, Appendix, 3653-54.

30. *Variety,* May 28, 1941, p. 26.

31. MBS broadcast, May 20, 1941, Broadcasts, Box 22, Lewis MSS.

32. MBS broadcast, June 24, 1941, Broadcasts, Box 22, Lewis MSS.

33. MBS broadcast, January 19, 1944, Broadcasts, Box 16, Lewis MSS.

34. MBS broadcast, January 24, 1944, Broadcasts, Box 16, Lewis MSS; MBS broadcast, April 3, 1942, "Daily Radio Digest No. 48," Box 1848, RG 44; reprinted in *Congressional Record,* 77th Cong., 2d Session, 6754-65.

35. Further discussion of Lewis's rhetoric and techniques may be found in Giraud Chester, "What Constitutes Irresponsibility on the Air?—A Case Study," *Public Opinion Quarterly* 13 (Spring 1949): 73-83; Fulton Lewis, Jr., "Critique on a Critic: An Analysis of a 'Case Study,' " *Public Opinion Quarterly* 13 (Fall 1949): 462-71; and further correspondence between the two, *Public Opinion Quarterly* 13 (Winter 1949): 733-36. See also Sidney Reisberg, "Fulton Lewis, Jr.: An Analysis of News Commentary" (Ph.D. dissertation, New York University, 1952). These studies evaluate only post-1945 broadcasts.

36. Quoted in Charles Van Devander, "Radio's Golden Voice of Reaction—III" (an eleven-part series), *New York Post,* December 7, 1949, p. 3, copy in Lewis file, Box 9, Davis MSS; MBS broadcast, original transcription, Lewis interviewing McCarthy, March 11, 1954, Lewis MSS.

37. Television videotapes, n.d. [1953-1954], discussing Harry Dexter White, Army-McCarthy Hearings, J. Robert Oppenheimer, all in Lewis MSS. See also George Racey Jordan, USAF (Ret.) with Richard L. Stokes, *From Major Jordan's Diaries* (New York, 1952).

38. Mimeographed transcript, Mike Wallace Interviews Fulton Lewis, Jr., February 1, 1958, copy in "Fulton Lewis, Jr." folder 1102(2), PPI 98, HHL.

39. On March 5, 1959, Lewis prepared a "farewell" broadcast. When he gained a sponsor "five minutes before he was to go on the air," he sent a mimeographed copy of "The Broadcast *NOT* Made" to friends.

40. Roosevelt to Lewis, August 14, 1935, Incoming Correspondence, Box 5; "Fulton Lewis, Jr. . . . Ace Commentator on National News," *The Delta of Sigma Nu,* 1940, p. 20, copy in Manuscripts, Box 64, Lewis MSS; quoted in Lewis to Laurence Richey, March 25, 1939, "Fulton Lewis, Jr." folder 1102(1), PPI 98, HHL. A slightly different version of the inscription is quoted in *Newsweek,* November 29, 1943, p. 90.

41. Presidential Press Conference 618, Franklin D. Roosevelt, White House, January 26, 1940, microfilm reel 6, Vol. XV, 101.

42. In both 1938 and 1939 Castle had agreed to "play news commentator" while Lewis took a vacation. See Lewis to Castle, August 1, 1938, Box 15, William R. Castle MSS; telegram, Lewis to Hoover, August 23, 1939, "Fulton Lewis, Jr." folder 1102(1), PPI 98—both in HHL.

43. Charles A. Lindbergh, *The Wartime Journals of Charles A. Lindbergh* (New York, 1970), p. 245. The dinner is reported in Davis, *The Hero,* pp. 386-89, (cited above, note 10) based on C. B. Allen, "The Facts About Lindbergh," *Saturday Evening Post,* December 28, 1940, p. 12, and Roger P. Butterfield, "Lindbergh," *Life,* August 11, 1941, pp. 68-69. Castle's version of

the dinner is not currently available to scholars. Mrs. William R. Castle recently claimed to recall no such meeting. Nannie Chase, secretary to Mrs. Castle, to author, October 15, 1969.

44. Lindbergh, *Wartime Journals.* September 10, 1939, p. 253. The aviator claims that on the afternoon of September 15, Roosevelt sent an emissary to offer him a cabinet post if he would not go on the air. *Ibid.,* September 15, 1939, pp. 257-58.

45. Even before the *Life* story Lewis's association with Lindbergh had led to difficulties. Lindbergh reports that in June 1940, ''[Lewis] told me that someone had started the rumor that he had taken part in writing my radio addresses and that two of his 'sponsorships' in New York City had been canceled as a result. Lewis had been forced to state over the radio that he had nothing whatever to do with writing my addresses.'' Lindbergh, *Wartime Journals,* June 14, 1940, pp. 357-58.

46. For instance, the *Chicago Tribune,* September 16, 1939, p. 1; the *New York Times,* September 16, 1939, p. 1; *Variety,* September 20, 1939, p. 34; October 29, 1941, p. 35; *Time,* September 25, 1939, p. 14. See also Lindbergh, *Wartime Journals,* September 16, 1939, p. 259.

47. Lindbergh, *Wartime Journals,* September 14, 1939, pp. 255-56; September 15, 1939, pp. 258-59.

48. Lewis, Jr., ''Has the Youth Congress Washed Itself Out?'', *Liberty Magazine,* April 6, 1940, p. 10, copy in Manuscript Articles, Box 60, Lewis MSS.

49. Macfadden, *Liberty Magazine,* April 6, 1940, p. 1.

50. Original punctuation, MBS broadcast, July 4, 1940, Broadcasts, Box 19; reprinted with slight changes in *Congressional Record,* 76th Cong., 3d Session, Appendix, 4440; Cf. MBS broadcast, July 3, 1945, Box 21, both in Lewis MSS.

51. Recorded MBS broadcast, September 23, 1940, tape 54, Radio Archive-Memphis.

52. Tauchnitz, chargé d'affaires in Cuba, to Joachim von Ribbentrop, Foreign Minister, forwarding telegram by Kurt Sell, press adviser, July 26, 1940, *Documents on German Foreign Policy 1918-1945, Series D: The War Years (1937-1945)* (Washington, D.C., 1964), 10: 297-98 [hereafter DGFP-D].

53. Alton Frye, *Nazi Germany and the American Hemisphere, 1933-1941* (New Haven, Conn., 1967), p. 143.

54. Dr. Paul K. Schmidt, director of News Service and Press Dept., Berlin, to Embassy in United States, August 6, 1940; Hans Thomsen, Chargé d'Affaires in United States to Foreign Minister, August 8 [7?], 1940, both in *DGFP-D* 10: 424, 435.

55. Copy of statement by Lewis, July 14, 1950, Lewis file, Box 9, Davis MSS.

56. *Fortune* Survey 12, November 1939, copy sent to author by Professor

Philip K. Hastings, RPORC; *Radio Daily* poll January 19, 1940, copy in Box 2, OF 228, FDRL; Harrison B. Summers, compiler, *A Thirty-Year History of Programs Carried on National Radio Networks in the United States 1926-1956* (Columbus, Ohio, 1958), p. 94; *Variety,* March 19, 1941, p. 26.

57. Based on daily radio schedules in the *New York Times, Chicago Tribune,* and the *Washington Evening Star,* 1938-41.

58. Ickes, *The Secret Diary of Harold L. Ickes,* 3 vols. (New York, 1953-1954), 3: 429; telegram, Lewis to Hoover, August 23, 1939, "Fulton Lewis, Jr." folder 1102(1), PPI 98, HHL; memo, Welles to Sheldon Thomas, Division of Current Information, Department of State, December 9, 1938, both in 111.16 Welles, Sumner/56; memorandum of conversation, Lewis with Moffat, October 3, 1939, concerning British Purchasing Agency and De Nemours Foundation, 841.24/97, both RG 59.

59. Baruch to Lewis, April 20, 1942; Baruch to Lewis, May 6, 1947, both in Incoming Correspondence, Box 1, Lewis MSS. Box 1 contains additional correspondence from Baruch to Lewis.

60. Hoover to Lewis, April 19, 1939, "Fulton Lewis, Jr." folder 1102(1), PPI 98, HHL.

61. Typed excerpt, MBS broadcast, January 31, 1940, enclosed in Lewis to Laurence Richey, February 8, 1940; printed copy, MBS broadcast, June 2, 1943, with letter, Hoover to Lewis, June 5, 1943, "Fulton Lewis, Jr." folder 1102(1), PPI 98, HHL. Folders (1), (2), and (3) contain over 100 letters between Hoover and Lewis.

62. *Time,* March 15, 1943, p. 53.

63. Dempsey to Lewis, February 13, 1939; MBS broadcast, July 24, 1939, both in Reference file, Box 83, Lewis MSS; Roosevelt to Lewis, July 24, 1939, OF 419-c, FDRL.

64. *Variety,* August 23, 1939, p. 31; advertisement in *Broadcast Advertising,* September 15, 1939, p. 30, copy in Box 6; Claude Pepper to Lewis, July 11, 1942, Box 5, all in Lewis MSS.

65. Reported on the House floor. *Congressional Record,* 76th Cong., 2nd Session, 255-57.

66. Quoted on Senate floor, February 17, 1942, *Congressional Record,* 77th Cong., 2d Session, 1327.

67. Eaton to Lewis, July 10, 1942, photostatic copy in Box 2, Lewis MSS.

68. Nye to A. W. Bergstrom, Devils Lake, N.D., June 29, 1942, copy in Box 4, Lewis MSS.

69. MBS broadcast, n.d. [c. April 25, 1941], quoted by Gerald Nye on Senate floor, *Congressional Record,* 77th Cong., 1st Session, 3382.

70. Telegram, Robert Morison to James Rowe, White House, May 5, 1941, Box 7, OF 4193, FDRL.

71. *Variety,* May 28, 1941, p. 23; *Time,* September 15, 1941, p. 58;

"Today's Young Men," *Future,* 1940, copy in Box 64; Dupont award, Box 21, both in Lewis MSS.

72. *Pulse* survey, January, 1954, WOR Office Message, February 16, 1954, Box 21, Lewis MSS.

73. For instance, in 1944 an assistant produced a newspaper column under Lewis's byline that sharply attacked Hoover. The ex-President demanded an explanation. Lewis's reply suggests the care with which he sometimes prepared his material: "The column in question was one of three written at the last minute rush before going on my vacation and turned out partially by me and partially by my assistants without, I am sorry to say, my own personal proof reading of it in final form. That, however, is no excuse and I must, of course, take full responsibility. I can only say that had I done what I should have done the paragraph would not have appeared in the form it did. It is, of course, untrue that you had 'long since ceased trying to do anything about it,' and it also is untrue that you were 'fighting' the public." Hoover to Lewis, August 1; Lewis to Hoover, August 16, 1944, both in "Fulton Lewis, Jr.", folder 1102(2), PPI 98, HHL.

7 | Edward R. Murrow: The Foreign Correspondent as Broadcaster

He seemed inordinately proud of a photograph given him by Carl Sandburg, inscribed "To Ed Murrow, reporter, historian, inquirer, actor, ponderer, seeker." Yet the same person once admitted: "Never in my life have I had a horizon that extended beyond 90 days."[1] At fifty he felt: "For my own part, I have not yet reached the age where reminiscences fascinate me. One of the advantages of reporting through a medium as fast as radio is that you don't have the time or the inclination to look back."[2] Such is not often the characteristic of the philosopher or historian.

Murrow was sometimes bitter, often purposely unreflective, in success mightily unsure of himself. He remained troubled about his occupation: "My father does not go so far as to say that there's something dishonest about a man making a living merely by talking. But he does think there's something doubtful about it."[3] Withdrawn, pretentious, eloquent, manly and virile, grasping, self-consciously antiintellectual yet alive to the fine points of protecting individual liberties, he seemed an impossible mass of contradictory tendencies. As Eric Sevareid noted, he "was a remarkable and remarkably complicated personality."[4]

He had a magnificent voice—better than virtually any other commentator who has ever worked in radio and television. Indeed, Murrow's sense of how to speak made him recognizably superior to his colleagues from almost the first time he broadcast. Unlike most radio news commentators of the 1930s, he never worked on a newspaper. In content and

179

approach to the news, too, he differed from others on the air before Pearl Harbor. As a foreign correspondent in England, he brilliantly captured the sounds and spirit of a people living with daily air raids, bombings, and the ever-present threat of invasion. His newscasts still convey what it was like to live in London after the outbreak of World War II. He employed the medium of radio to promote interventionism in a brilliantly creative fashion.

Murrow felt that he spent his most valuable years in Britain, particularly before 1941. "And you were living a life, not an apology" was the compliment he sometimes paid the English.[5] In print, this seems overly rugged—the spirit of the executive who thinks himself an outdoorsman for donning an expensive plaid wool shirt on weekends—but Murrow sometimes created this impression while trying to talk in a manly way of courage he considered admirable. No newspaper coverage equaled Murrow's ability to make events in Europe seem immediate and compelling to millions of Americans. And his talents extended beyond reporting. After 1945 he became a powerful CBS vice-president.

HE DROVE HIMSELF TERRIBLY

Egbert Roscoe Murrow was born near Polecat Creek, Guilford County, North Carolina, on April 15, 1908. His mother displayed the true Southerner's penchant for unusual names. She called Egbert's brothers Lacey Van Buren and Dewey Joshua. During the Civil War a grandfather had been one of Stonewall Jackson's staff officers. Egbert's family should have been prosperous. But the father failed as a farmer. A big, laconic man, he seemed unable to make up his mind easily. A relative remembers that Roscoe disliked Polecat Creek. He was "restless and always 'looking away, wanting to go.' "[6] But he remained in North Carolina for years.

He let his tiny, nervous wife make most of the decisions. Ethel Lamb Murrow frequently suffered from asthma. She made her sons read a Bible chapter every night. Years after, the broadcaster described his mother as so religious that she feared to say hello when answering the telephone "because one syllable of that tells the name of Satan's home. She says 'hey-yo.' "[7]

In 1913 the entire family moved to the state of Washington. Ethel

Lamb had a cousin there who made the area sound promising. At first the Murrows lived in a tent in this relative's backyard. Happy to give up farming, the father became a locomotive engineer for a logging camp near the then primitive settlement of Blanchard, seventy miles north of Seattle.

The Industrial Workers of the World were active in the area. Later the commentator occasionally spoke of a radicalism imbibed from being near such people, but it seems to have been an afterthought. Murrow enjoyed the outdoors for the rest of his life. He spent an entire year between high school and college working with his father as a logger on Beaver Lake, about one hundred miles west of Seattle. But the news analyst's enthusiasm was for the woods and the sort of person who worked in lumber camps, not radical movements.[8]

For instance, when Murrow entered Washington State College in Pullman, Washington, in 1926, he faced two years of compulsory ROTC. He liked the drilling so much that he remained in the program all four years. As a senior he became a cadet colonel and taught a course in machine guns his final semester. Although this was the extent of his military experience, he never forgot its pleasures.[9]

In 1926 Washington State College was exceptional in few respects. It did, however, have a good speech department, and offered one of the first college courses in radio broadcasting given anywhere in America. Murrow had been an excellent debater in high school. Now he found his voice continued to be an asset. He debated, became active in dramatics, and even made a reputation for himself as a local sportscaster. A loyal fraternity man and campus leader, he served as president of the student body his junior year. In 1928, tired of endless jokes about his name, he changed Egbert to Edward and shortened Roscoe to a middle initial. Thanks partly to high marks in military science and speech courses, he graduated a member of Phi Beta Kappa in 1930.[10]

He had been elected president of the National Student Federation in 1929. In June the following year, he moved to New York City. As president, he received no salary. There was a living allowance of twenty-five dollars a week. Duties consisted only of those he managed to create. For instance, Murrow sent a telegram to the Secretary of the Interior proclaiming the federation's approval of an action taken by the Secretary of State.[11] The student leader and a friend persuaded CBS to let them present a radio program promoting their organization. In September 1930 a lecture entitled "Looking Forward with Students" was heard by a small group at 3:30 in the afternoon. Two years later, "Youth in Revolt," no doubt attracted more listeners.[12]

During the summer of 1930, Murrow made his first trip to Europe. The Washington State graduate arrived fashionably attired. "I wore a straw boater and carried a cane. No one laughed at me, at least not openly," he recalled.[13] Back in New York, it proved difficult to live on twenty-five dollars a week. As a recent biographer puts it, Murrow "retired" from his presidency in 1932.[14] He became an assistant to Stephen P. Duggan, director of the Institute for International Education. Carnegie and Rockefeller funding provided most of the financial support; Murrow quickly learned about the world of foundations. His duties often seemed a bit dull. He edited a monthly magazine and prepared for publication a list of all those who had held American Field Service fellowships at French universities. He wrote a treatise entitled *Fellowship Administration.*[15]

Some tasks proved more interesting. In 1933 he helped set up the Emergency Committee in Aid of Displaced German Scholars. Afterward he described himself as "the youngster who did the donkey work."[16] Another assignment involved planning exchange programs between the United States and Europe. During the summer of 1934 a group of students studied in the Soviet Union. Despite its success, the Russians abruptly canceled a similar arrangement the following year. In 1954 Joseph McCarthy tried to prove that Murrow was a Communist because he had helped arrange a trip to Leningrad in 1935.[17]

In October 1934 the broadcaster married Janet Huntington Brewster, a graduate of Mt. Holyoke College. They had met in 1932, when both attended a National Student Federation conference in New Orleans. Later, Mrs. Murrow was not very sure why the marriage actually took place: "I think Ed was trying hard to avoid it. He was a young man who thought he had few prospects at the time."[18] This may have been true. But Murrow explained himself differently in a letter he sent his fiancée around 1933: "I'm no boy wonder, but I've driven myself terribly in the past few years to get where I am."[19]

It is hard to be certain what kind of person Murrow was during these years. At the institute he seemed a conscientious, deferential, somewhat colorless administrative assistant. He also could be found wearing clothes of the dandy. One person remembers seeing him about 1935 addressing a group of German exchange students. He was decked out in a light-beige gabardine suit with a Norfolk-style jacket, a brown shirt, and a canary yellow tie. In London, a few years later, the broadcaster decorated his den with "Navajo Indian blankets, totems, [and] tomahawks."[20] Yet a formal photograph from this period shows a rather ill-at-ease young man, sitting at a desk. He holds a brand-new, carefully sharpened pencil. An unused pad of paper is in front of him. He seems unsure what to do next.[21]

A manufactured vita that Murrow used before 1941 provides a good indication of his determination to impress others. He apparently felt too young to be working for the Institute of International Education. Accordingly, he changed his birth date to 1905. A speech major from Washington State College did not sound like much in New York. He claimed to have taken courses at the University of Washington and to have received an M.A. from Stanford. His undergraduate major became political science and international relations. One year as a logger blossomed into "two years as compassman and topographer for timber cruisers in Northwest Washington, British Columbia and Alaska." Also a favorite pastime in New York involved numerous trips to a shooting gallery in Times Square.[22] Perhaps such tendencies during the 1930s explain how Murrow later became a CBS executive.

HE NEVER WORKED ON A NEWSPAPER

Murrow's radio career began in September 1935, when he became Columbia's director of radio talks and education. Though he had no journalism experience, he was used to arranging speakers. He edited *Talks,* which reprinted network radio broadcasts of an educational sort. He also endured innumerable heated discussions with politicians seeking radio time. In November 1936 he went to Hyde Park to help facilitate the transmission of any statement Roosevelt wished to make on election night.[23] In general, his job, which permitted no broadcasting, lacked excitement.

In February 1937, CBS asked him to become its European director. César Saerchinger, who had held the position for several years, wanted to return to the United States. He felt the assignment offered no chance for advancement. In 1937 this was not an unwise judgment. One did little more than line up children's choirs or soloists to fill program time that Columbia could not sell. The pace was leisurely. The rewards consisted largely of travel abroad. Murrow accepted, even though he realized that it meant something of a step down from director of talks. Overseas events soon made his decision seem amazingly prescient.

At first, instead of broadcasting himself, Murrow hired others to do so. Occasionally, however, he offered a few remarks on the air. In July 1937 he described an encampment being held in the Netherlands for boy scouts from all over the world. During a bank holiday shortly thereafter, he conducted a man-in-the-street interview at Brighton Beach in England. On Christmas Day 1937, from London, he read a prepared translation of Haile Selassie's season's greetings.[24]

His first important news broadcast came in 1938, when the Nazis marched into Vienna. On March 14 CBS presented its first European roundup. Murrow was in Vienna; his assistant, William L. Shirer, regularly speaking from Berlin, found himself in London. Hearing commentary from several countries on one program seemed remarkable to those who tuned in. Five days later, Murrow presented an analysis of what had happened in Austria. His remarks included some effective imagery:

> I'd like to be able to forget . . . the thud of hobnailed boots and the crash of light tanks in the early hours of the morning on the Ringstrasse, and the pitiful uncertainty and bewilderment of those forced to lift the right hand and shout "Heil Hitler" for the first time. I'd like to forget the sound of the smashing glass as the Jewish shops were raided; the hoots and jeers aimed at those forced to scrub the sidewalk.[25]

Sometimes what a journalist writes is not based entirely on what he really believes. This passage came from intensely felt personal experience. Shirer reports that on the evening of this particular broadcast, he and Murrow entered a bar for a talk. They did not remain long. As the European director explained: " 'I was here last night about this time,' he said. 'A Jewish-looking fellow was standing at that bar. After a while he took an old-fashioned razor from his pocket and slashed his throat.' "[26]

Though radio's Vienna coverage appealed to network executives and some listeners, in the immediate aftermath, Murrow went back to London to arrange special events. In July 1938 he covered Howard

Hughes when the aviator landed in Paris on his round-the-world flight. In November Murrow returned briefly to the United States. In a speech before the Chicago Council on Foreign Relations he discussed familiar differences between state-controlled radio in Europe and independent networks in America. He reminded his audience that the first thing taken over by the Nazis in Vienna was a broadcasting station.[27]

MUSICIAN OF THE SPOKEN WORD

By the time that war began in September 1939, Murrow commented from London almost every day. He also helped arrange for broadcasts by others from a variety of European capitals. One of several persons speaking on a nightly fifteen-minute newscast, Murrow rarely talked for more than a couple of minutes. A description of his style makes clear just why he differed from other news analysts on the air during these years.

He began with "This is London." It quickly became his hallmark. How he said these three words explains why he was so much better than his competitors as a broadcaster. *Time* tried to depict the aural sense as "This (pause) is London."[28] But there was not really a pause. "This" was the powerful opening; "is London," was unaccented. The latter two words fell away naturally from what preceded, suggesting a perfect example of natural speech patterns. There was no affectation. Rather, in these words could be heard the sounds of a man alive to a proper sense of timing. Many have written about the nuances and shadings of which the spoken word is capable. Anyone who listened to Murrow heard a person able to manipulate these nuances properly. Murrow was actually a sensitive musician of the spoken word. He realized that the duration of sound—the distance between two words, for instance—could make a listener's imagination enlarge the meaning of what was said.

Unlike any other news commentator on the air before 1941, Murrow understood the difference between broadcasting and the printed word. He dictated his commentaries, to find phrases with special aural appeal. Sometimes he used a vivid image that required no special presentation. For instance, in June 1940 "Mr. Churchill needed only wings and an engine to take off as he talked of the air force. . . ."[29] On other occasions, the way Murrow said certain words became of critical importance.

Discussing the problem of building airfields in one country a month earlier, he explained that "most of Norway stands on edge."[30] Not only was the image good, but because he said "stands" and "edge" incisively, listeners heard pointed words creating the feeling of sharpness. A radio broadcast in a few seconds made people aware of logistical problems that a newspaperman might need pages to describe.

Murrow's sense of timing is exemplified in a description of Parliament's reaction to an address by a discredited leader on May 2, 1940: "When Mr. Chamberlain concluded his speech there was a dead, flat silence." The news analyst sensed exactly how long to wait after "dead" and "flat." When he got to "silence," the audience knew the utter failure of the Prime Minister's program because of two momentary pauses.

In the same broadcast, Murrow noted the reactions of one important participant to Mr. Chamberlain's remarks: "All during the Prime Minister's speech, Mr. Winston Churchill slumped in his seat playing with his fingers and watching the House and its reactions with great interest."[31] In print, this sentence seems of no particular interest. On the air, Murrow placed special emphasis on the word "slumped." It followed the clause "All during the Prime Minister's speech," read in a straightforward manner. Suddenly the newscaster's speech pattern collapsed. As the figure slumped, the listener was jarred with the sense of cadence interrupted. Suddenly more than Mr. Churchill's body was involved: an entire policy of a political opponent fell from official (or rigid) acceptance.

Another example further demonstrates Murrow's sense of timing. "I reported to you yesterday concerning the increase in the 'get on with the war' sentiment in this country," the foreign correspondent declared in 1939.[32] He lingered ever so slightly between the "the" and "get." Then "get on with the war" came out hurriedly. The listener heard impatience expressed with extraordinary clarity. Murrow understood that, as in music, the duration of a rest must be used to point up, not expand out of context, what precedes or follows.

The voice itself proved to be a marvelous device for broadcasting images. In 1965 James Reston called it a "voice of doom." Earlier someone described it as "apocalyptic."[33] Neither is a good description. Many announcers have a fulsomely rich vocal quality. They attempt to persuade by enveloping the listener with broad tones and false friendliness. Murrow might have developed such a commercial sound, but never did. He made no attempt to ingratiate. Instead, one heard an honest baritone, at a rather low speaking level. There was a convincing rugged truthfulness. As one popular magazine concluded, an "outsize sense of responsibility fill[ed] Murrow's work with conviction and sincerity."[34]

The news analyst enunciated clearly. In the process, pronunciation occasionally sounded a bit unnatural. For instance, "bellicose" became "bellycose." When he said "school," one could see the protruding lips. As he lingered over the final "l" of this word, he seemed to savor what he was saying. Murrow made effective use of alliteration. He subtly played with the change in sound following the initial "v" in "those vague voices."[35] Careful listeners heard the "a" and the "oi" and immediately sensed how the same initial consonant had been slightly transformed by different vowels. Murrow also spoke slowly enough to make comprehension easy.

Murrow used emotion-charged adjectives and words sparingly. For example: "He fairly spat the words at jeering Labor members on the opposite side of the house."[36] Listeners heard the explosive "p" and the short "t" in "spat." The news analyst's mouth opened wide as he said the "eer" in jeering."

In spite of his speaking ability, as late as 1938 Murrow had not developed the radio style for which he became so well known. A visit to the Maginot Line included the following dull recital of detail: "This subterranean building is really very comfortable. It is air-conditioned and has central heating; moreover, it is bomb, shell and gas proof."[37]

Murrow rarely attempted to be humorous on the air. A 1941 broadcast suggests that he was not always adept at the light touch:

> While the diplomats are busy and the soldiers wait, Britain's inventors are active. One man advocates a new style in glasses, the lens and blinders are to be made of cardboard. Naturally that prevents you seeing anything at all, but this particular gentleman insists that if they are worn consistently day and night you won't notice the blackout.[38]

And not every broadcast overflowed with original imagery. In 1939 he felt war might "spread over the world like a dark stain of death and destruction." In 1941, on the air, the newscaster chose to introduce a colleague with some flowery poetry. In flat Indiana accents, Elmer Davis quickly returned matters to a more sensible level:

> MURROW: "Who tells me true though in his tale lay death I hear him as he flattered."
> DAVIS: I can't tell you much about London for I've been here less than twenty-four hours.[39]

Those who listened regularly to Murrow's commentaries knew that he had his dull or unorganized moments. Just before leaving Britain in 1941, he found himself at the end of a broadcast without having said very much. As the newscaster admitted, "Here I am at the end of this rambling talk without yet having decided what should be said."[40] But such lapses were infrequent.

Murrow's abilities as a broadcaster are particularly evident in his nightly descriptions of London during the Battle of Britain. From the beginning of the war, however, his images had been good. In September 1939 he suggested what the outbreak of hostilities meant to Britain:

> London as usual is black tonight. One gets accustomed to it, but it can hardly be called pleasant. I don't know how you feel about the people who smoke cigarettes, but I like them, particularly at night in London. . . . For a moment tonight I thought I was back in the London of Mr. Pickwick's time. I heard a voice booming through the stark London streets. It said, "Courtland Place, all's well." It was an air raid warden; he had shouted to someone to cover their window, they had done so, and so he was telling them that no more light came through.[41]

Almost a year later Murrow more openly praised the heroism of British civilians under bombardment. "If the people who rule Britain are made of the same stuff as the little people," he declared, "the defense of Britain will be something of which men will speak with awe and admiration so long as the English language survives."[42]

On August 24, 1940, he located himself outside a shelter on Trafalgar Square. Listeners heard traffic noises and the unearthly lingering sound of an air raid siren. Murrow described a man stopping to light a cigarette in front of him. He told of a red double-decker bus coming around the corner with a few lights on top. "I'll just ooze down the steps and see if I can hear the ghosts shoed with steel shoes," he added in a rather theatrical touch.[43]

Hitler's nightly raids increased in intensity. Two weeks later Murrow described how "huge pear-shaped bursts of flame would rise up into the smoke and disappear. The world was upside down." Still optimistic, he reminded listeners that "several days of terror bombing will not cause this country to collapse." On September 13 he explained what it was like to live in a city under constant bombing attack:

> One night I stood in front of a smashed grocery store and heard a dripping inside. . . . Two cans of peaches had been drilled clean through by flying glass and the juice was dripping down onto the floor. . . . Today I went to buy a hat—my favorite shop had gone, blown to bits. . . . I went to another shop to buy flashlight batteries. I bought three. The clerk said: "You needn't buy so many. We'll have enough for the whole winter." But I said: "What if you aren't here?" There were buildings down in that street, and he replied: "Of course, we'll be here. We've been in business here for a hundred and fifty years."[44]

In a change of pace during the same broadcast, Murrow reported a comment concerning Winston Churchill's siren suit, "one of those blue woolen coverall affairs with a zipper." He added: "Someone said the Prime Minister must resemble a barrage balloon when attired in his siren suit."[45] Two nights later he discussed a fire bomb that had hit the House of Lords: "I heard a parcel of people laughing about it when one man said: 'That particular bomb wouldn't seriously have damaged the nation's war efforts.' "[46]

The intensity of the raids caused even such pro-British commentators as Raymond Gram Swing to despair of Britain's holding out for long.[47] Murrow never doubted that the Germans would fail. On September 24, 1940, he presented a thirty-minute broadcast from London "during a blackout" that brought him special acclaim. The CBS correspondent stood on a rooftop "looking out over London." Colleagues interviewed people in various parts of the city, including an air raid shelter in the crypt of St. Martin's-in-the-Field. Listeners heard bombs exploding and antiaircraft guns in action. The next day the *Christian Science Monitor* praised the spectacular broadcast. The editorial stated that "the simple words of people sheltered" in St. Martin's crypt "conveyed a message which newspapers, even with the most brilliant reporting, photography and editing, cannot deliver."[48]

Such creative broadcasting involved obvious danger. Murrow seemed to feel that risking his life improved the quality of his reporting. Worried CBS executives ordered their man to remain under cover. He insisted on speaking from rooftops, even in the midst of battle. In 1940 he wrote his brother Lacey about what drove him to keep testing himself:

> Have reached point where hands shake so much, can't even read my own writing. . . . Hasten to say that overwork and no sleep is responsible, not fright. . . . Am going to Dover again tomorrow. No particular reason for going but just can't stay away. Maybe it's because that shelling shakes me up a bit and I want to find out why.[49]

Eric Sevareid suggested that Morrow found a "certain release" in the fact that he quite literally faced death so often in London. His studio was bombed a number of times. He once explained why he had never gone into an air raid shelter: "I was afraid of myself; I feared that if I did it once I could not stop doing it."[50] Murrow seemed to believe that it was unmanly not to risk his life on a daily basis.

"MERELY A RECORDING TAPE"

After the war, the correspondent returned to Columbia as a vice-president. In fact he received a larger salary during the 1950s than the president of CBS himself. Two television programs, "See it Now" and "Person to Person," became extremely popular. Involved in many projects, the television celebrity soon needed a good deal of assistance. For years Raymond Swing and Edward Bliss wrote most of the copy for Murrow's newscasts. So much ghostwriting led one careful listener to dismiss the broadcaster as "merely a recording tape."[51]

As a CBS executive, Murrow became involved in some unpleasant situations. In 1948 he fired his friend William L. Shirer, the only news analyst on a major network to oppose the Truman Doctrine. Many people thought that the dismissal was for political reasons; Murrow himself felt that his colleague had stopped doing his best work.[52] Deeply embittered,

Shirer six years later published a fictional account based on the affair. In *Stranger Come Home,* Murrow appeared before a Senate subcommittee investigating the alleged pro-Communist sympathies of a commentator Shirer intended to be autobiographical. One senator asked:

> 'Mr. Fletcher [Murrow], the charges here are that Mr. Whitehead [Shirer] was a Communist and a Soviet agent. Having known him over many years and having worked with him closely, would you say that either accusation or both of them—were true?'
> 'Senator, I am not here to pass judgment. That, sir, if I may say so, is your task.' Bob [Murrow] replied.[53]

The same year that this book came out, Murrow openly attacked Joseph McCarthy on his "See it Now" program because of the senator's army investigation. But Murrow waited until the proper moment. He later admitted that he could have destroyed McCarthy or been destroyed himself. It was all a matter of timing.[54] Thus it appears that some uneasy ethical compromises, emphasized in Shirer's novel, have a certain truth. Murrow could have kept his colleague on the air in 1948; instead he got rid of him completely. In 1945, for no particular reason, he fired his old superior, Paul White, formerly head of Columbia's news department. In other words, Murrow as executive did not remain immune to the cut-throat tactics of the advertising and broadcasting world. But a complete tool of the industry would never have risked anything so dangerous as a program exposing McCarthy in 1954. He never would have openly condemned the commercialism of his own network's news department in a major address before the prestigious Radio and Television News Directors Association in 1958. He never would have resigned from a position that paid hundreds of thousands of dollars a year.[55]

In January 1961 Murrow became the director of the United States Information Agency. To the public, he was probably John F. Kennedy's best-known appointment. After years of intimidation, Voice of America employees expressed delight at having someone with such enormous prestige in charge of those assigned to publicizing the United States abroad. In terms of agency morale, the commentator proved a wonderful success as director. He was less able as an administrator. After lingering a couple of years, in and out of hospitals, he died at his home in Pawling, New York, on April 27, 1965.

"THIS *IS LONDON*"

Murrow knew how effective his broadcasts were before 1941. He made Americans personalize an ideological struggle against the Nazis in terms of the Battle of Britain. His depiction of English heroism provided effective imagery—or propaganda—for an administration committed to aiding Hitler's enemies. Murrow's listeners numbered in the millions, including persons close to Franklin D. Roosevelt. Felix Frankfurter understood the importance of Murrow's work. And Robert Sherwood wrote elegantly—if a bit inaccurately—of Harry Hopkin's careful attention to the commentator: "From the outbreak of war, when he had lain in the Mayo Clinic believing that he was soon to die, Hopkins had listened to Murrow's grim voice announcing, 'This—is London,' in a tone which seemed to suggest the thuds of German bombs."[56]

When Hopkins visited London in January 1941, he talked for a long time with Murrow, particularly concerning "personalities" and "public morale" in Britain. The President's personal representative returned to England in July; he again discussed the war with the news analyst. He brought back to the United States a film, *This is England,* whose commentary was written and spoken by Murrow. It played in more than two hundred movie theaters in New York within a single week.[57]

Murrow's broadcasts—which dealt only with European affairs and required the prior approval of a British censor—became increasingly outspoken between September 1939 and December 1940. He employed the device of describing changing English attitudes as to what America's role in the war should be. It took no special effort on the part of listeners to detect Murrow's complete agreement with the increasing militancy of the opinions he reported. In September 1939 he claimed that most Englishmen believed Congress would repeal the arms embargo and that "eventual American participation is not to be ruled out entirely."[58] He did not expand this remark; in daily broadcasts he concentrated on depicting British courage. In March 1940, he noted an extended attack on American ambassador Joseph P. Kennedy that Harold Nicolson had written for the *Spectator.* The commentator explained that lack of American support for England would lead to worsening relations between the two countries in coming months.[59]

The Nazi invasion of the Low Countries on May 10 resulted, the broadcaster declared, in an intensified British hatred of not just Hitler but even the average German:

> A few weeks ago German prisoners of war in this country were receiving packages of food and clothing from British civilians. German prisoners arriving in this country were greeted with silence or good-natured jests. But yesterday when twenty-two German airmen were landed at a southeast coast port, an angry crowd, including many women, shouted, "Shoot the murdering swine!"

In June he took seriously the likelihood of a Nazi invasion. He described a circular sent to "millions" of "British homes" ominously titled "If the Invader Comes."[60] Throughout the summer and early autumn he reported the Battle of Britain, continually indicating to his listeners the courage of the British and, by implication, the obligation of America to assist such a brave people.

On December 3, 1940, he explained England's need for more than all aid short of war:

> A theory advanced by certain British and American journalists in the weeks preceding the American presidential election has perished. That theory was that the United States would be greater help to Britain as a nonbelligerent than as a full-fledged ally. . . . You must expect repeated references in the press and in public statements to the British belief that a democratic nation at peace cannot render full and effective support to a nation at war.[61]

A careful listener could scarcely help realizing that if a "democratic nation" did not remain "at peace," the result might be full hostilities. And this several weeks before Roosevelt had raised publicly his plan for Lend-Lease—in theory no more than all-aid-short-of-war.

Throughout 1941 Murrow described British unhappiness with the slowness, size, and kind of American assistance being provided. When H.R. 1776 passed Congress in March, the commentator described the unenthusiastic reception in London: "There was no dancing in the streets here. . . . The gap between legislation and realization can be very wide." He stressed England's belief that America must not remain "nonbellige-rent" but become a "fighting ally."[62] For Murrow, a declaration of war

against Germany—for which "fighting ally" was a not-so-subtle substitute—could not be considered certain with the passage of Lend-Lease.
During the next months he kept trying to find new ways to express the
same thought: America must become a full belligerent.

Just before Pearl Harbor Murrow returned to the United States for a
visit. On December 2, 1941, the president of CBS held a dinner in New
York to honor the commentator's work in Britain. Over one thousand
people attended. Archibald MacLeish declared that "you burned the city
of London in our houses and we felt the flames that burned it. . . . You
destroyed the superstition of distance and of time."[63] Murrow discussed
what America's policy toward Britain should be: "The position is quite
simply that lend-lease is not enough, that unless the United States enters
this war Britain may perish or at best secure a stalemate peace—a delayed
action defeat."[64] His blunt words were broadcast all over the United
States and Great Britain.

Franklin Roosevelt sent a telegram expressing sorrow at not being able
to be present. Ordinarily this might seem but another of those polite
gestures that Presidents are constantly called upon to make. In this case
Roosevelt apparently meant what he said. Five days later he invited
Murrow to a private dinner at the White House. It turned out to be quite an
evening: the date was December 7, 1941. Roosevelt himself did not make
the meal. Finally, after midnight, Murrow talked alone with him. The
commander-in-chief asked about Churchill, Britain, and the air attacks.[65]
Roosevelt apparently believed that Murrow's broadcasts from London
had helped greatly in making Americans accept the possibility of a
declaration of war.

Aside from Hopkins, one administration supporter in particular has
recorded his impressions of the commentator's work. When John G.
Winant was appointed the American ambassador to the Court of St.
James's in 1941, Murrow wrote him that "this is indeed good news!"
Winant claimed that Murrow's broadcasts "became a kind of institution." He added that information given him by Murrow and several
others "was invaluable to me in my official position and their reporting
was an all-time credit to American journalism."[66] Since Murrow was in
Europe from 1937 to the end of November 1941, he had few chances to
become personally acquainted with other major figures in Washington.

In determining the news analyst's impact on the average citizen, one
consideration is Britain itself. The BBC asked Murrow in February 1941

to offer fortnightly interpretations of the United States to a British audience. Like Raymond Gram Swing and Elmer Davis, he offered listeners hope that more United States aid would soon be forthcoming. A *Variety* reviewer complained only that the correspondent should be used in this role more often.[67]

Many Englishmen heard the broadcasts sent nightly to America. In December 1940 a member of the Ministry of Economic Warfare questioned Murrow concerning the morale of the German people. Notes from the conversation were sent to the Foreign Office. In the preface to *Reflections on the Revolution of Our Time,* written in the months following Pearl Harbor, Harold J. Laski summed up the feelings of many in Britain. He dedicated his book to the CBS commentator and went on to say:

> Our country owes an immense debt to Mr. E. R. Murrow. Day and night since before the war began he has done everything that courage and integrity can do to make events in this country a living reality to his fellow citizens of the United States. I am only one of the many Englishmen who have found in his faith and truth in our people a new power to endure and hope.[68]

In the United States, Murrow's "courage and integrity" did not go unnoticed. Listeners quickly learned that the CBS European roundup included something not to be found on other radio news programs. In September 1940, when the news analyst made his first broadcast from a rooftop in London, his remarks were already being carried as news dispatches by New York's *PM*. The paper's headline read: "Murrow Ducks Bombs in London" after this particular commentary. In April 1941 a number of broadcasts appeared in book form.[69] *This is London* included a collection of Murrow's most effective descriptions of Britain over a period of eighteen months. It sold surprisingly well.

The average American could hear a report from London nearly every day unless weather conditions made reception impossible. Murrow offered a special Sunday broadcast in which he attempted to provide longer discussions of British affairs. His September 1940 air raid broadcast is an example of this. So too, was a March 1941 attempt to sum up what England should expect for the rest of the spring. But in general, the foreign correspondent spoke once, and sometimes twice, six or seven days a week. After September 1939—Murrow broadcast only rarely before then—he appeared on "The World Today." The network's principal overseas news program, it was carried by virtually every CBS affiliate. This meant that Murrow's comments could be heard all over the United States. The hour was good: 6:45 P.M. in New York and Washington; 5:45 P.M. in Chicago. The program came on in the early evening on the west coast. The time remained the same six days a week for nearly two years. Listeners learned to depend on news at this hour. Occasionally the news analyst also broadcast in the morning. Columbia's "News of Europe" appeared at 8:00 A.M. on the east coast; an hour earlier in the Midwest. In sum, only Elmer Davis was heard over so many stations with such frequency.[70]

Edward R. Murrow offered unique broadcasts before 1941. More than any other newscaster, he successfully depicted what England was experiencing. Nightly, listeners heard that wonderful voice begin "This is London." What followed made clear the urgent need for additional American assistance. Speaking from Britain, Murrow spent his time depicting what it was like to live in a country under German attack. Intertwined with the description was prescription as well: Murrow's belief in England's cause led him by December 1940, in radio broadcasts, to urge a declaration of war against Hitler. Even so strong a friend of the British as Raymond Gram Swing did not go this far on the air before 1941. When Murrow used a phrase such as "fighting ally" in March 1941, only the obtuse failed to get the meaning.

Murrow's partisanship should not obscure the brilliance of his description of London under attack. Not only did these broadcasts find tremendous public acceptance, but as examples of aural imagery they remain a model for radio journalism that has yet to be surpassed. Murrow's fame was greater—his salary even more so—in the period after 1945, but it is not surprising that he felt his greatest usefulness came in the months before Pearl Harbor. Roosevelt had a spokesman no isolationist could match; Murrow, for possibly the only time in his life, had a cause to believe in.

NOTES

1. CBS publicity release, April 30, 1953, quoted in Ben Gross, "Looking and Listening," *New York Daily News,* June 21, 1953, both in Edward R. Murrow folder, CBS Library.

2. Murrow, "We Take You Back," CBS publicity release, March 14, 1958, Murrow folder, CBS Library.

3. Quoted in CBS publicity release, November 30, 1953, Murrow folder, CBS Library.

4. Eric Sevareid to author, September 22, 1969.

5. Final broadcast in England, BBC, February 24, 1946; "we have lived a life, not an apology" appears in CBS broadcast, March 9, 1941, both in "Edward R. Murrow: A Reporter Remembers, Vol. I The War Years," 33 1/3 rpm commercial recording, Columbia 02L-332 [hereafter "A Reporter Remembers"].

6. Alexander Kendrick, *Prime Time* (Boston, 1969), pp. 77, 72-76; this book includes many excellent photographs of the commentator. Murrow, "Television and Politics," *The British Association Granada Lectures* (London, 1959), p. 47, copy in CBS Library.

7. Howard K. Smith *et al.,* "Friends of Edward R. Murrow," ABC television transcript, May 2, 1965, p. 5 (remarks by Smith), Murrow folder, CBS Library; Kendrick, *Prime Time,* p. 79.

8. Kendrick, *Prime Time,* pp. 81-83, 92, 97; CBS publicity release, April 30, 1953, Murrow folder, CBS Library.

9. CBS publicity release, April 30, 1953, Murrow folder, CBS Library.

10. Kendrick, *Prime Time,* pp. 100-105; Chester S. Williams, "Memories of Your Father" [to Casey Murrow], typed copy, June, 1965, p. 6; CBS publicity release, November 30, 1953, both in Murrow folder, CBS Library.

11. Murrow, president, National Student Federation of America, Pullman, Washington, to Dr. Ray Lyman Wilbur, Secretary of Interior, March 27, 1930, 500 A 15 A 3/807, RG 59.

12. Kendrick, *Prime Time,* p. 112; CBS Talent File (new), Murrow, CBS Program Information.

13. BBC broadcast, February 24, 1946, "A Reporter Remembers."

14. Kendrick, *Prime Time,* p. 116.

15. CBS publicity release, August 27, 1937, Murrow folder, CBS Library; Murrow, comp., *American Field Service Fellowships for French Universities Including Record of Former Fellows* (New York, 1933), and *Fellowship Administration* (New York, 1933).

16. CBS publicity release, November 30, 1953, Murrow folder, CBS Library; see also, Murrow to Laurence Duggan, October 14, 1933, 800.42711/56, RG 59.

17. Kendrick, *Prime Time,* pp. 62-66.

18. CBS publicity release, November 30, 1953; quoted in Irwin Ross, "Women Behind the Men—Mrs. Ed Murrow," *New York Post,* March 20, 1957, both in Murrow folder, CBS Library.

19. Quoted in Kendrick, *Prime Time,* p. 124.

20. Professor Hans W. Gatzke, interview with author, March 10, 1970, New Haven, Conn.; Robert J. Landry, "Edward R. Murrow," *Scribner's Magazine* 104 (December 1938): 52.

21. Photograph in Landry, "Edward R. Murrow," p. 7.

22. CBS publicity release, August 27, 1937, Murrow folder, CBS Library; Landry, "Murrow," p. 9; Kendrick, *Prime Time,* p. 135.

23. Harry C. Butcher to Marvin McIntyre, October 30, 1936, "CBS 1936," Box 1, OF 256, FDRL. For a typical example of Murrow's duties, see correspondence between Murrow and Stimson, October 15, Box 335; November 5 and 6, Box 336; November 12, 1935, Box 337, all in Stimson MSS.

24. Murrow, "We Take You Back," Murrow folder, CBS Library; CBS Black Book, "Radio Programs 1937," CBS Program Information.

25. CBS broadcast, March 19, 1938, Box 155, Kaltenborn MSS. A number of commentaries from 1938 to 1941 can be found in Murrow, *In Search of Light: Broadcasts of Edward R. Murrow 1938-1961,* ed. Edward Bliss, Jr. (New York, 1967), pp. 3-48.

26. William L. Shirer, *Berlin Diary: The Journal of a Foreign Correspondent, 1934-1941* (New York, 1941), p. 109.

27. "News and Public Affairs—Radio (News Events)" folder, CBS Program Information; cf. A. A. Schechter, *I Live on Air* (New York, 1941), p. 154; Murrow, "Propaganda on the Air," November 4, 1938, folder 150, The Chicago Council on Foreign Relations MSS, Manuscript Division, Circle Campus of the University of Illinois, Chicago, Illinois.

28. "This is Murrow," cover story, *Time,* September 30, 1957, p. 48; see opening of CBS broadcast, May 8, 1940, "A Reporter Remembers"; opening of CBS broadcast, April 22, 1940, reel 1246, Phonoarchive. For a long, not very satisfactory analysis of the commentator's style after 1945, see Thomas Russell Woolley, Jr., "A Rhetorical Study: The Radio Speaking of Edward R. Murrow" (Ph.D. dissertation, Northwestern University, 1957). See also the superb discussion of Murrow in William Stott, *Documentary Expression and Thirties America* (New York, 1973) pp. 84-91.

29. CBS broadcast, June 4, 1940, "A Reporter Remembers"; Smith, "Friends of Murrow," p. 13 (remarks by Smith).

30. CBS broadcast, April 22, 1940, reel 1246, Phonoarchive.

31. CBS broadcast, May 2, 1940, reel 1258, Phonoarchive.

32. CBS broadcast, September 11, 1939, reel 995, Phonoarchive.

33. James Reston, "Washington: Farewell to Brother Ed," *New York Times,* April 28, 1965, p. 14; *Time,* September 30, 1957, p. 48.

34. *Time,* September 30, 1957, p. 49.

35. CBS broadcast, August 31, September 4, 1939, and April 9, 1940, all in "A Reporter Remembers."

36. CBS broadcast, May 8, 1940, "A Reporter Remembers."

37. Murrow, "The Maginot Line," *Talks* 3 (July 1938): 9.

38. CBS broadcast, October 21, 1939, in Murrow, *This is London* (New York, 1941), pp. 36-37.

39. CBS broadcast, September 1, 1939, in Murrow, *This is London,* p. 13; CBS broadcast, April 29, 1941, reel 1767, Phonoarchive.

40. CBS broadcast, November 9, 1941, reel 1973, Phonoarchive.

41. CBS broadcast, September 4, 1939, Murrow, *This is London,* p. 20.

42. CBS broadcast, August 18, 1940; *ibid.,* p. 146.

43. CBS broadcast, August 24, 1940, "A Reporter Remembers."

44. CBS broadcast, September 8, 9, 13, 1940, Murrow, *This is London,* p. 159.

45. *Ibid.,* p. 173.

46. CBS broadcast, September 15, 1940, *ibid.,* p. 175.

47. See Culbert, "Tantalus' Dilemma," (Ph.D. dissertation, Northwestern University, 1970), pp. 594-95.

48. CBS broadcast, September 24, 1940, Murrow, "London After Dark," *Talks* 5 (October 1940): 2-10; editorial, *Christian Science Monitor,* September 25, 1940, reprinted in *ibid.,* p. 2. This broadcast, in recorded form, can be found in "A Reporter Remembers."

49. Murrow to Lacey Murrow, c. September, 1940, quoted in Kendrick, *Prime Time,* p. 203.

50. Quoted in Sevareid, *Not So Wild a Dream* (New York, 1946), pp. 170, 19; see also cable from Murrow, quoted in Paul W. White, "Radio Covers the War," *Talks* 5 (October 1940): 11-12.

51. Frank W. Buxton, emeritus editor, *Boston Herald,* quoted in Felix Frankfurter to Elmer Davis, June 6, 1952; see also Frankfurter to Davis, June 11, 1952, both in Box 51, Frankfurter MSS.

52. Shirer did not respond to a letter sent to him by this author in 1969 asking for his version of the firing. Apparently Murrow got rid of his colleague partly because of the prevailing Cold War consensus. But Shirer, even in 1940, sounded pompous on the air; his delivery left much to be desired.

53. Shirer, *Stranger Come Home* (Boston, 1954), p. 319. Shirer insisted that his account was strictly fictional, but few have believed him. See also Kendrick, *Prime Time,* pp. 295-97, for details concerning Shirer's dismissal.

54. Smith, "Friends of Murrow," p. 12 (remarks by William Downs).

55. Murrow speech before Association of Radio and Television News Directors, Chicago, Illinois, October 15, 1958, copy in Murrow folder, CBS Library.

56. Robert E. Sherwood, *Roosevelt and Hopkins* (New York, 1948), p. 236. Not until about March 1940 did Murrow arrive at the final form of his celebrated

opening, *"This* is London." Radiogram, Murrow to Frankfurter; note, Frankfurter to Missy Le Hand, April 14, and 15, 1941, Max Freedman, *Roosevelt and Frankfurter* (Boston, 1967), p. 595.

57. Kendrick, *Prime Time,* p. 234.

58. CBS broadcast, September 7, 1939, reel 1004, Phonoarchive.

59. CBS broadcast, March 10, 1940, reel 1192, Phonoarchive.

60. CBS broadcast, May 23, June 19, 1940, Murrow, *This is London,* pp. 106-107. See also CBS broadcast, June 17, 1940, in Max Wylie, ed., *Best Broadcasts of 1939-40* (New York, 1941), pp. 338-39.

61. CBS broadcast, December 3, 1940, Murrow, *This is London,* pp. 216-17.

62. CBS broadcast, March 9, 1941, *ibid.,* pp. 235-36.

63. Archibald MacLeish, William S. Paley, and Murrow, *In Honor of a Man and an Idea . . .: Three Talks on Freedom* (New York, 1941), pp. 7-8, copy in CBS Library; Kendrick, *Prime Time,* p. 238.

64. Murrow speech, in MacLeish et al., *In Honor of a Man,* p. 23.

65. Telegram, Roosevelt to Paley, December 2, 1941, note, PPF 7854, FDRL; CBS publicity release, April 27, 1956, Murrow folder, CBS Library; list of President's Appointments, December 7, 1941, *Personal Letters,* 2: 1252.

66. Murrow to Winant, February 7, 1941, quoted in Bernard Bellush, *He Walked Alone: A Biography of John Gilbert Winant* (The Hague, 1968), p. 160; John G. Winant, *Letter from Grosvenor Square* (Boston, 1947), p. 165. Leonore Silvian, "This . . . is Murrow," *Look,* March 15, 1952, p. 58, quotes Winant as saying that Murrow was "doing the greatest job of all" as "ambassador and interpreter of American ideas and opinions in England."

67. *Variety,* February 26, 1941, p. 26.

68. Typed notes of conversation, M. Zvegintzov with Murrow, December 28, 1940, in Memorandum, Gladwyn Jebb, Minister of Economic Warfare, to Foreign Office, January 8, 1941, C494/19/18, FO (New York, 1943), p. viii. The preface is dated November 27, 1942; see also Kendrick, *Prime Time,* p. 62.

69. Kendrick, *Prime Time,* p. 208; *Variety,* April 9, 1941, p. 29.

70. CBS broadcast, September 24, 1940 and March 9, 1941, both in "A Reporter Remembers"; based on daily radio schedules in the *New York Times,* the *Chicago Tribune,* and the *Washington Evening Star,* 1938-1941. Since Murrow was but one of several foreign correspondents on the same program, polls and industry rating services did not ask about his popularity.

Six Commentators
and Their Medium

In television news departments there is a widespread feeling that the late 1930s represented a "golden age" for radio news commentary.[1] Then, so the legend goes, brilliant independent analysis of the news proved radio the equal of even the most distinguished newspaper. A close reading of the broadcasts of six prominent commentators on the air before Pearl Harbor suggests that the soothing effects of a remembered past have obscured what was actually said. But the legend, like most legends, has some basis in fact. Murrow, Davis, and Swing displayed a brilliance and creativity rarely seen on television today.

This book does more than simply demonstrate the deficiencies of past journalism. In retrospect, with primary and secondary sources available, it is easy to point out—rather smugly—that in days gone by, public information left much to be desired. Not many students of foreign policy would gain startling insight into the major crises of the late thirties from listening to the analyses of any of the commentators who have been discussed. But the specialist is expected to know more than the journalist trying to offer perspective in the heat of the moment. Each broadcaster described major news stories from all over the world as frequently as seven times a week. All made mistakes; all sounded superficial on occasion. Some were uninformed most of the time even if they made up in self-confidence what they lacked in preparation.

By any objective standard, the commentaries of all six newscasters contain serious shortcomings. Perhaps most noticeable is the lack of attention given to news about the Far East. Davis, Lewis, and Carter barely mentioned even major changes in the Japanese cabinet during 1940-41. With the exception of Swing, information about China consisted of occasional ritualistic pronouncements as to whether or not Chiang Kai-shek was a democratic leader. Again with the exception of Swing, those who depended on radio news would not have known that the Chinese Communist party even existed—which indicates how little the civil war in China was understood.

Even critics like Carter and Lewis, who so vigorously opposed American involvement in the rest of the world, at the same time praised administration attempts at restricting the export of raw materials to Japan. No commentator questioned whether an embargo might make the Japanese consider war with America the alternative to national dishonor; none asked whether a policy of increasing firmness might be unwise. Carter insisted that the United States must not "'meddle'" in the Orient but failed to explain what the word might mean in practice. After late 1939, Lewis opposed American involvement overseas yet disliked Japan enough to applaud a "get-tough" policy toward that country. Kaltenborn, Swing, and Davis were delighted when Roosevelt abrogated the Japanese trade treaty in January 1940 and froze all Japanese assets in America eighteen months later. They termed such actions nonprovocative or long overdue.

All six news analysts readily linked Tokyo's aggression with that of Berlin and Rome. After the Tripartite Pact was made public on September 26, 1940, even Carter and Lewis considered Japan and Germany one and the same. As Kaltenborn put it on November 3, "Japan has now joined Germany and Italy to conquer the world."[2] After dividing the world into good and bad nations, the commentators gave little thought to distinguishing between what German and Japanese aggression hoped to accomplish and what chance either had of clearly threatening American security. Radio's benign neglect of the Far East did not help bring about the attack on Pearl Harbor, but it is important to note that no commentator urged a peaceful settlement for the Far East or tried to explain the limits of America's commitment toward the Chinese people.

Radio's impact on foreign policy-making is the way it contributed to maintaining or changing the climate of opinion in the United States. This process, so difficult to be precise about, cannot be measured more accurately by reference to public opinion polls even though they reveal a general trend from isolationism to interventionism after 1939. In these early years of the scientific poll, respondents gave self-contradictory answers in the area of foreign policy. On August 20, 1939, the American Institute of Public Opinion (AIPO), headed by George H. Gallup, released this question: "If there is another general European war, do you believe the United States can stay out?" Sixty-two percent said "yes"; 38 percent answered "no." Ten days later a second question was made public: "Do you think the United States will be drawn into the war?" Sixty percent of those who had an opinion said "yes;" 14 percent had no opinion. Nor is this an isolated example.[3] The most convincing way to gauge the impact of radio news is to look at how widely and how often individual commentators were heard as well to assess their general attitudes toward foreign policy issues. When such attitudes were repeated in daily broadcasts for months on end, it is reasonable to assume that listeners learned to identify a particular commentator's beliefs.

Before the Munich crisis of September 1938, radio commentators attracted, for the most part, little attention. Swing broadcast over one station in New York City once a week; Davis substituted on radio at most a few times a year; Murrow was in Europe, but with the exception of several excellent broadcasts from Vienna after Germany's annexation of Austria in March 1938, was not heard regularly. Lewis was without a commercial sponsor and thus subject to cancellation at the whim of any local affiliate; Kaltenborn also lacked a sponsor and a regular time.

Boake Carter was a major and notorious exception. Between 1935 and 1938 he had a sponsor, broadcast over CBS at a good hour, and had a regular following of millions of persons. At a time when radio news was in its infancy Carter made violent opposition to Roosevelt a commercially acceptable commodity. He represented an extreme form of isolationism; his foreign policy prescriptions so worried the administration that they forced him off the air. Carter was radio's greatest contribution to American isolationism. He deserves at least as much credit as the *Chicago Tribune* or William Randolph Hearst's chain. Carter said what most people wanted to hear: don't get involved. The message was simple, and events in the rest of the world suggested to many that America had more than enough to do at home.

The Munich crises of September 1938 changed radio's role. Indeed round-the-clock coverage of this crisis did irreparable damage to isolationism; this time you could hear international diplomacy being practiced. Foreign affairs attracted continuing popular interest because Munich was not the end but the beginning of final European disintegration. There is another reason why European affairs received such complete and careful coverage from September 1938 on: all of the commentators (aside from Lewis) had lived in Europe for a considerable amount of time. They found the specifics of European events fascinating; they conveyed this feeling to listeners with evident enthusiasm. Once war began in September 1939, news analysts described Hitler's invasions, stated what America's response to the Nazis should be, and urged greater defense preparedness along with less labor unrest. Radio news dominated the public's understanding of what was going on in the rest of the world.

The change produced some unique features. The serious news commentator developed commercial possibilities. Radio now offered news and analysis at the same time. Before Munich, Carter stridently advocated isolationism; after Munich, Swing, Davis, Murrow, and Kaltenborn all gained tremendous followings; just as important, they all gained commercial sponsors and a large number of station affiliates. From a medium where one isolationist dominated news commentary, radio emerged as a major source of interventionism.

Carter and Lewis, speaking over the weakest of the three national networks, formed radio's ineffectual opposition after September 1939. The two were remarkably similar in political beliefs, vocal mannerisms, and preparation of broadcasts. Both learned early that being controversial attracted listeners, and that attacking the New Deal made them newsworthy. Many broadcasts of both men are excellent examples of what Daniel Boorstin has termed pseudo-events, news which of itself has no value, but gains artificial importance from the medium's need to present something every day.[4] Why should anyone remember a case involving an American sailor named Lawrence Simpson? Who cares about Lewis's attacks on Rubber Coordinator Harold Ickes? What scholarly account makes much of such events? Both Carter and Lewis traveled around the country. On the air they told where they had been. Often they used a news broadcast as a vehicle for personal reminiscence. They went on crusades so listeners would tune in to find out what happened. The crusades were pseudo-events; they consisted of what physicists term "noise"—random and persistent disturbances that obscure what is actually taking place. The actions of Carter and Lewis make it easier to understand the difficulties of decision-making in a democracy.

Both men abused the right of the journalist to criticize those in office. The exposés were based on misinformation. Tremendous self-assurance convinced the ignorant that what was said must be true. Carter and Lewis stirred up trouble; they did not offer constructive opposition. They lacked the powers of reflection needed to come up with carefully considered alternate courses of action.

Kaltenborn is harder to assess. His commentaries contained little analysis. He had a good mind, but prepared his newscasts carelessly. Using the same evidence, he often contradicted himself. He presented a great deal of unsupported opinion. But he also pioneered radio news commentary in the 1920s. He broadcast from Spain in 1936 in the midst of battle. His facility with languages enabled him to discuss European affairs in ways most of his colleagues could not.

Kaltenborn's most important contribution came during September 1938. His daily broadcasts captured the public's imagination. After 102 broadcasts in 18 days, radio replaced the newspaper as the major source for foreign news. From that time on, and particularly after September 1939, most people in America listened to the news before reading about it. Kaltenborn's contribution to interventionism is regional after 1940; his commercial sponsor marketed in the Midwest and South, and in these two areas Kaltenborn spoke with particular effectiveness. His stilted delivery was passé even in 1940, but his public reputation ensured his commercial success through 1945.

The commentaries of Elmer Davis and Raymond Gram Swing lend themselves more easily to historical treatment. Neither understood the difference between the spoken and printed word; reading their broadcasts was the same as hearing them. Both had terrible voices; both provided scholarly explanations, though Swing's formal education ended after one year of college. Davis lavished great care on finding some way to slip in a humorous remark about the day's news. He loved to ridicule talk of conspiracy—a favorite claim of the President's opposition. After May 1940 Davis used his first-rate mind and wit in urging full and unquestioning support for every proposal of Roosevelt's toward greater intervention in Europe and the Far East. He believed that Germany would conquer Europe as a prelude to invading the United States. Accordingly the problem of stopping Hitler became not that of what policies to follow— whatever Roosevelt did gained his support—but making listeners understand that Germany represented a clear and present danger both to Western civilization and to American security. By 1941 Davis spoke more often and over a greater number of stations in America than any other commentator. He remains the only news analyst that radio or television has produced who understood the subtleties of sarcasm and humor as explanatory devices.

Not Swing. He took his job with the utmost seriousness. On the air he sounded terribly earnest; a rather dull newscast occasionally resulted. His commentaries would never have appealed to the average citizen during normal times. Indeed, the fact that Swing found millions of listeners in America before 1941 suggests how grave the international situation seemed to most people. Swing made himself an unofficial spokesman for the Department of State. He justified American policy to British listeners fortnightly over the BBC. He was the only commentator whose remarks were rebroadcast by shortwave to Latin America and most of the rest of the world. Swing produced the most thorough analyses of anyone on the air before Pearl Harbor; he also explained the correctness of every move toward greater overseas involvement made by Roosevelt.

Both Swing and Davis stopped serving as independent critics—the journalist's supposed function—after the spring of 1940. They, along with Kaltenborn and Murrow, came to believe in one course of action so fervently that they lost the capacity for objectivity; they ceased offering even constructive criticism of administration foreign policy. At the time they thought they restrained themselves in their remarks; today it is clear that the implication of what they said could only be full-scale intervention. Stopping Hitler had become, they felt, a sacred obligation of the American people. They became tools of the administration. They did not worry about whether massive amounts of aid for Britain might lead to a declaration of war against Germany. After May 1940 full hostilities, to them, became a necessary risk the United States had to take. These four commentators felt that the news they were reporting demanded such conclusions; the isolationists never had much foreign news that supported their belief that America had no business worrying about the rest of the world.

Edward R. Murrow occupied a unique position in news broadcasting before Pearl Harbor. A foreign correspondent, his job did not differ much from that of such persons as Eric Sevareid, Max Jordan, and William L. Shirer. But Murrow's broadcasts from London in 1940-1941 to this day have retained their effectiveness thanks to his ability to employ the medium of radio to enlarge the meaning of words. It is likely that Murrow's broadcasts, not the only brilliant radio news coverage by any means on the air before Pearl Harbor, will nevertheless continue to be regarded as the best of the lot, and with reason: he was unique, and anyone who listens to commercial recordings of his broadcasts from those years is likely to agree even if the listener is unable to explain precisely what makes them so good. Speaking from London, Murrow made Americans think of the Battle of Britain as a prelude to the bombing of New York or Washington. Nobody else conveyed urgency so successfully. On September 23, 1940, Fulton Lewis, Jr. offered a dull recital of detail to prove that Nazi bombing raids had hardly damaged London. He summarized at length his interview with a recently returned American military observer. Even his method made ineffective use of radio as a medium. The next night Murrow stood on a rooftop in London. As air raid sirens sounded, listeners heard bombs dropping on unknown points. Those who tuned in suddenly felt personally the unpredictable terror of bombing raids. The sense of waiting helplessly is something television can never depict as well; radio's ability to make the listener feel he had actually stood by Murrow on that rooftop is what Marshall McLuhan was getting at in his phrase about the medium as the message. In a different way William Stott makes the same point when he singles out Murrow's broadcasts as superb examples of the social documentary: they "increase our knowledge of public facts, but sharpen it with feeling. . . . They sensitize our intellect or educate our emotions about actual life."[5]

Not every listener was so taken with Murrow's broadcasts in 1940, nor was every broadcast brilliant. But because of their ability to make the listener a direct participant, Murrow's broadcasts were especially effective in creating a favorable climate of opinion toward Britain. By December 1940 he called for a declaration of war against Germany; his statement, made three months later, that America must become Britain's "fighting ally" left few listeners confused about what Murrow stood for. After the war in Europe began, Murrow came to admire deeply English bravery. Hearing even one of his broadcasts during the Battle of Britain convinced listeners that England stood ready to sacrifice all to prevent German victory. Murrow made abstractions like patriotism and national honor seem real.

Radio news came to serve as an integrating force in America by helping create a national foreign policy consensus. As one student of popular culture has stated:

> The mass culture is left to find its own taste level which while generally
> lowering the "high culture" level for many, also tends to heighten the
> "low culture" level for others. The net result is a general tendency
> toward a "cultural consensus" or a type of mass popular culture whose
> major function is to help maintain an equilibrium in society.[6]

This is what radio did by making America's moral commitment to fight fascism seem the only sensible thing to do.

In two respects all six news analysts were alike. First, each was a pioneer; each developed a reputation in a field where there were no accepted rules about how to do the job. Each had an opportunity for experiment denied to those who came later. Second, each developed a large following by promoting personal idiosyncrasies. All had voices that made them instantly recognizable. All loved the publicity and prestige that came from being a commentator, no matter how often they claimed otherwise. The style of these men is as important in understanding their impact as what they said. Listeners associated a certain spirit with each man. For Davis it was the twit; for Swing, a sense of religious experience; for Kaltenborn, the opinionated blast; for Lewis and Carter, special inside information; for Murrow, the bravery of the British people. In short, style explains how each of the six contributed to a changing climate of opinion; style made the medium the "massage." As the *Chicago Tribune* noted, after September 1938, "inflamed by commercial radio commentators," Americans began sensing an urgency in events taking place overseas.[7] The medium originally designed for entertainment had developed a new function. For news about the rest of the world, the age of the electronic media had begun. Before Pearl Harbor, radio supported demands for an interventionist foreign policy in every possible way; how different from the mass media's position on American foreign policy during a more recent time.

Radio made the news personal and immediate in a way television has never been able to equal. Bertold Brecht once wrote of radio in this way:

> You little box, held to me when escaping
> So that your valves should not break,
> Carried from house to ship from ship to train,
> So that my enemies might go on talking to me
> Near my bed, to my pain

The last thing at night, the first thing in the morning,
Of their victories and of my cares,
Promise me not to go silent all of a sudden.

Nobody would write such a poem about television.

NOTES

1. For a particularly good example, see Michael J. Arlen, "The Eyes and Ears of the World," *New Yorker,* January 6, 1975, pp. 52-56.

2. NBC broadcast, November 3, 1940, Kaltenborn MSS.

3. For example, Dorothy Borg, *The United States and the Far Eastern Crisis of 1933-1938: From the Manchurian Incident Through the Initial Stage of the Undeclared Sino-Japanese War* (Cambridge, Mass., 1964), footnote 38, p. 625; the AIPO questions from Hadley Cantril and Mildred Strunk, *Public Opinion 1935-1946* (Princeton, N.J., 1951), p. 966.

4. Daniel J. Boorstin, *The Image: A Guide to Pseudo-Events in America* (New York, 1964), pp. 7-76.

5. Stott, *Documentary Expression and Thirties America* (New York, 1973), p. 18.

6. Garth S. Jowett, "Popular Culture and Concept of Consensus," *Popular Culture Methods,* n.d. [Spring 1973], p. 21; see also Warren Breed, "Mass Communication and Socio-Cultural Integration," *Social Forces* 37 (December 1958): 109-16, and John G. Cawelti, "The Concept of Formula in the Study of Popular Literature," *Journal of Popular Culture* (Winter 1969), pp. 383-90.

7. Quoted in Walter Johnson, *The Battle Against Isolation* (Chicago, 1944), p. 2.

Bibliography

BIBLIOGRAPHICAL NOTE

This bibliography is divided into three sections. Part I lists, in alphabetical order without additional comment, primary and secondary material of a general nature cited in the text. Part II selectively surveys sources for radio as an industry and the development of news broadcasting in the 1930s. A special attempt has been made to describe carefully materials not easily accessible. Part III consists of six sections, one for each commentator. Primary sources are noted, with particular emphasis on the location of broadcasts, in recorded and written form. The more important interpretive articles and books concerning each news analyst are also evaluated.

PART I: PRINTED WORKS—GENERAL

PRIMARY

Blum, John Morton. *From the Morgenthau Diaries: Years of Urgency, 1938-1941*. Boston: Houghton Mifflin, 1965.

Cantril, Hadley, and Strunk, Mildred. *Public Opinion 1935-1946*. Princeton, N.J.: Princeton University Press, 1951.

Congressional Record. 74th to 77th Congress (1935-1942).

Dodd, William E., Jr., and Dodd, Martha, eds. *Ambassador Dodd's Diary, 1933-1938*. New York: Harcourt, Brace, 1941.

Frankfurter, Felix. *Felix Frankfurter Reminiscences* (recorded in talks with Harlan Phillips). New York: Reynal, 1960.

Freedman, Max, annotator. *Roosevelt and Frankfurter: Their Correspondence, 1928-1945*. Boston: Little, Brown, 1967.

Hooker, Nancy Harvison, ed. *The Moffat Papers: Selections from the Diplomatic Journals of Jay Pierrepont Moffat 1919-1943.* Cambridge, Mass.: Harvard University Press, 1956.

Hull, Cordell. *The Memoirs of Cordell Hull.* 2 vols. New York: Macmillan, 1948.

Ickes, Harold. *America's House of Lords: An Inquiry into the Freedom of the Press.* New York: Harcourt, Brace, 1939.

———*The Secret Diary of Harold L. Ickes.* 3 vols. New York: Simon & Schuster, 1953-54.

Langer, William L., and Gleason, S. Everett. *The Challenge to Isolation, 1937-1940.* New York: Harper & Brothers, 1952.

———*The Undeclared War, 1940-41.* New York: Harper & Brothers, 1953.

Roosevelt, Elliott, and Lash, Joseph P., eds. *F.D.R.: His Personal Letters, 1928-1945.* 2 vols. New York: Duell, Sloan and Pearce, 1950.

Rosenman, Samuel I. *The Public Papers and Addresses of Franklin D. Roosevelt.* 13 vols. New York: Random House, et al., 1938-1950.

———*Working with Roosevelt.* New York: Harper & Brothers, 1952.

Sherwood, Robert E. *Roosevelt and Hopkins: An Intimate History.* New York: Harper & Brothers, 1948.

U.S. Department of State. *Documents on German Foreign Policy 1918-1945, Series D: The War Years (1937-1945).* Vols. 10, 13. Washington, D.C., 1957, 1964.

———*Foreign Relations of the United States: Diplomatic Papers, 1936-1941.* Washington, D.C., 1953-1963.

SECONDARY

Benson, Lee. "An Approach to the Scientific Study of Past Public Opinion," *Public Opinion Quarterly* 31 (Winter 1967): 522-67.

Berelson, Bernard, and Janowitz, Morris. *Public Opinion and Communication.* 2d ed. New York: Free Press, 1965.

Borg, Dorothy. *The United States and the Far Eastern Crisis of 1933-1938: From the Manchurian Incident Through the Initial Stage of the Undeclared Sino-Japanese War.* Cambridge, Mass.: Harvard University Press, 1964.

Borg, Dorothy, and Okamoto, Shumpei, eds. *Pearl Harbor as History: Japanese-American Relations, 1931-1941.* New York: Columbia University Press, 1973.

Boorstin, Daniel J. *The Image: A Guide to Pseudo-Events in America.* New York: Harper Colophon, 1964.

Breed, Warren. "Mass Communication and Socio-Cultural Integration," *Social Forces* 37 (December 1958): 109-16.

Burns, James MacGregor. *Roosevelt: The Soldier of Freedom.* New York: Harcourt, Brace, Jovanovich, 1970.

Cantril, Hadley, with the assistance of Gaudet, Hazel, and Herzog, Herta. *The Invasion from Mars: A Study in the Psychology of Panic.* Princeton, N.J.: Princeton University Press, 1940.

Cawelti, John G. "The Concept of Formula in the Study of Popular Literature," *Journal of Popular Culture,* Winter 1969, pp. 383-90.

Chadwin, Mark Lincoln. *The Hawks of World War II.* Chapel Hill, N.C.: University of North Carolina Press, 1968.

Cohen, Bernard C. *The Press and Foreign Policy.* Princeton, N.J.: Princeton University Press Paperback, 1965.

————"The Relationship Between Public Opinion and Foreign Policy Maker," pp. 65-80, in Melvin Small, ed. *Public Opinion and Historians: Interdisciplinary Perspectives.* Detroit: Wayne State University Press, 1970.

————*The Public's Impact on Foreign Policy.* Boston: Little, Brown, 1973.

Cole, Wayne S. *America First: The Battle Against Intervention 1940-1941.* Madison, Wis.: University of Wisconsin Press, 1953.

————*Senator Gerald P. Nye and American Foreign Relations.* Minneapolis: University of Minnesota Press, 1962.

Compton, James V. *The Swastika and the Eagle: Hitler, the United States, and the Origins of World War II.* Boston: Houghton Mifflin, 1967.

Dallek, Robert. *Democrat and Diplomat: The Life of William E. Dodd.* New York: Oxford University Press, 1968.

Fielding, Raymond. *The American Newsreel, 1911-1967.* Norman, Okla.: University of Oklahoma Press, 1972.

Flynn, George Q. *American Catholics & the Roosevelt Presidency 1932-1936.* Lexington, Ky.: University of Kentucky Press, 1968.

Friedländer, Saul. *Prelude to Downfall: Hitler and the United States, 1939-41.* Trans. by Aline B. and Alexander Werth. New York: Knopf, 1967.

Frye, Alton. *Nazi Germany and the American Hemisphere, 1933-1941.* New Haven: Yale University Press, 1967.

Goodman, Walter. *The Committee: The Extraordinary Career of the House Committee on Un-American Activities.* New York: Farrar, Straus and Giroux, 1968.

Gunther, John. *Taken at the Flood: The Story of Albert D. Lasker.* New York: Harper & Brothers, 1960.

Hohenberg, John. *Foreign Correspondence: The Great Reporters and Their Times.* New York: Columbia University Press, 1964.

Johnson, Walter. *The Battle Against Isolation.* Chicago: University of Chicago Press, 1944.

Jowett, Garth S. "Popular Culture and the Concept of Consensus." *Popular Culture Methods,* n.d. [Spring 1973], pp. 19-22.

214   *News for Everyman*

Key, V. O. *Public Opinion and American Democracy.* New York: Knopf, 1961.
Kimball, Warren F. *Most Unsordid Act: Lend-Lease, 1939-1941.* Baltimore: Johns Hopkins Press, 1969.
Koch, Howard. *The Panic Broadcast.* Boston: Little, Brown, 1970.
Landecker, Manfred. *The President and Public Opinion: Leadership in Foreign Affairs.* Washington, D.C.: Public Affairs Press, 1968.
Marbut, F. W. *News from the Capital: The Story of Washington Reporting.* Carbondale, Ill.: Southern Illinois University Press, 1971.
May, Ernest R. "An American Tradition in Foreign Policy: The Role of Public Opinion," pp. 101-23, in William H. Nelson, ed. *Theory and Practice in American Politics.* Chicago: University of Chicago Press, 1964.
Reston, James B. "The Press, the President, and Foreign Policy," *Foreign Affairs* 44 (July 1966): 553-73.
Russett, Bruce. *No Clear and Present Danger: A Skeptical View of the United State's Entry into World War II.* New York: Harper Torchbook, 1972.
Tsou, Tang. "The American Political Tradition and the American Image of Chinese Communism," *Political Science Quarterly* 76 (December 1962): 570-600.
————*America's Failure in China, 1941-1950.* Chicago: University of Chicago Press, 1963.
Valaik, J. David. "Catholics, Neutrality and the Spanish Embargo, 1937-1939," *Journal of American History* 54 (June 1967): 73-85.
Wirth, Louis. "Consensus and Mass Communication," *American Sociological Review* 13 (February 1948): 1-15.

PART II: RADIO AND THE DEVELOPMENT OF NEWS BROADCASTING

Though not always readily accessible, vast quantities of material concerning radio and thousands of broadcasts, in recorded and written form, have survived. Professor Lawrence W. Lichty, Department of Speech, University of Wisconsin, Madison, a few years ago prepared a helpful mimeographed guide to the location of broadcasts, which he will send upon request. The Broadcast Pioneers Library has moved from New York to Washington, D.C. The resulting disorganization means that its published list of holdings, prepared in 1969, is of little use. The library contains all sorts of information about radio in the 1930s and has an extremely knowledgeable director. The Television Information Office, in New York City, has nothing useful for the period before 1945. Columbia University's Oral History Project has over two thousand pages concerning the history of radio in a section entitled "Broadcast Pioneers' History Project." The reminiscences of a number of commentators are in the same place. For those interested in the technical development of radio to 1925, the Clark Collection of Radioana, now in the Smithsonian Institution, Washington, D.C., is a major source. Clark's material fills hundreds of boxes, but is organized according to a complicated Navy filing system used in World War I. The Lee De Forest and Stanford Hooper Papers, both in the Manuscript Division of the Library of Congress, include material relating to the Navy's use of radio, technical matters, and the organization of the Radio Corporation of America. The Eric Sevareid Papers, in the same place, contain correspondence describing news broadcasting in the late 1930s. For the business aspects of radio's development, RCA's David Sarnoff Library, Princeton, New Jersey, is very complete. Boxes 437-448 in the Secretary of Commerce's Official File, Herbert Hoover Library, help make clear Hoover's role in the regulation of radio, particularly his radio conferences of the 1920s. The PPI and Post-Presidential Subject Files contain material about many aspects of radio after 1932.

The headquarters for NBC and CBS in New York City have enormous amounts of information concerning the history of radio and the development of news broadcasting, haphazardly located in numerous offices. Also, written permission, not always given, is necessary before using the resources of either network. CBS seems to have saved almost no programs or recordings before 1941. Its library on 57th Street however, includes bound volumes of frequently hard-to-find publications such as *Radio Daily.* In the same place are copies of many pamphlets that the network published during the 1930s. Columbia's Program Information Department, on 52d Street, is invaluable to the student of radio. Index cards in a variety of filing systems give the full title of a program, its exact date, the number of stations over which it was heard, and changes in sponsor, for virtually everything heard on CBS before 1941. An IBM system simplifies locating information for broadcasts after 1945. The office also has a number of file drawers with documents pertaining to programming before 1941. Each year a Black Book was prepared, with a typed list of all programs broadcast, arranged in a number of useful categories.

NBC's equivalent of Program Information is Program Analysis. Like everything but the network warehouse, it is located in Rockefeller Center. File cards give complete information for all programs on the air before 1941. Some of this office's mimeographed publications from the 1930s are located in the NBC Program Reference Library. For those interested in foreign news broadcasts, compilations such as one listing every news program that originated overseas from 1924 to 1936 could prove extremely useful. The Program Reference Library has stored numerous pamphlets published by NBC before 1945 in several unmarked file drawers. In the same place are bound volumes of mimeographed lectures presented to NBC employees between 1939 and 1941. These cover virtually every aspect of the company's operations, frequently with considerable candor. Central Records includes a great deal of material that researchers generally cannot see. (It depends on each individual's persuasiveness.) But anyone who gets into NBC can use the microfilm collection in Central Records, which includes every broadcast from 1927 on for which a copy was submitted in advance. The warehouse, on 56th Street, houses thousands of recorded broadcasts; Central Records has a complete index. Taped copies of these transcriptions may not be made, and an employee must be present while anything is being played. The NBC Research Department has a number of file drawers with information relating to the 1930s. In sum, NBC has massive amounts of material, but no centralized place for keeping it nor any sort of proper organization. The enormous NBC collection at the State Historical Society of Wisconsin, Madison, proved of little use. Its thousands of recordings and printed materials mostly concern the period after 1945.

There is no place where MBS material can be easily obtained. The WOR Recording Service, 1440 Broadway, New York, New York, has some Mutual broadcasts from before 1941 of which they will sell copies. For most MBS material it is necessary to go through the pages of *Variety*, the holdings of such places as the Broadcast Pioneers Library, or the papers of individual commentators.

The FCC Radio Division, RG 173, National Archives, has quantities of information to 1932, organized according to individual station call letters. After that date, FCC records, also arranged by station, are found at the National Records Center, Suitland, Maryland. Once materials are ordered from Suitland, they must be used at the FCC Reading Room, 1919 "M" Street, N.W., in Washington. The FCC dockets apparently include only documents pertaining to license renewals.

The Roosevelt, Hoover, Truman and Eisenhower libraries all have quite a number of folders concerning radio. Information may be filed according to network, or by the name of the program or individual. At each library a knowledgeable staff will gladly help locate materials for researchers. For the period 1941-1945, the holdings of the Office of Government Reports (RG 44) and the Office of War Information (RG 208), both at Suitland, Maryland, are helpful. Numerous news broadcasts, starting in January 1942, are quoted verbatim in daily summaries, found mostly in RG 44. A major source of complete broadcasts for 1936 and early 1937 is the Federal Trade Commission (RG 122), National Archives. Though confusingly arranged—in some instances by station, in others by network—there are transcripts for almost every national program on the air at the time. The Recorded Sound Section of the Music Division, Library of Congress, has thousands of broadcasts from the early 1930s through 1945. The James A. Farley Collection, for instance, has recordings of numerous public figures with whom the Postmaster spoke. The enormous Office of War Information collection of recordings is currently being catalogued. The staff will be happy to explain what is available.

Twenty-five hundred private collectors in the United States and Canada have recorded broadcasts—the problem is locating them. A good place to begin is Dennis William Walker III, "A Representative Catalog of Old Radio Programs Held by Private Collectors" (Master's thesis, Memphis State University, 1972), a computerized list of the contents of 104 of the largest collections. J. David Goldin, Bronx, New York, has thousands of broadcasts, from the 1920s on, for sale. A list, not updated since 1969, with an exact description of each item he has, can be found in the Broadcast Pioneers Library. Radio Yesteryear, Croton-on-Hudson, New York, also has a catalog of broadcasts for sale. The following periodicals have extensive sections of classified advertisements where collectors offer broadcasts for sale or exchange: *Hello Again,* North Haven, Connecticut; *Reminiscing Time,* Atlanta, Georgia; and *Radio Dial,* Cloquet, Minnesota. A good source for further information about recorded broadcasts in private hands is Mr. Les Waffen, Audiovisual Archives Division, National Archives.

A number of institutions have begun collections of radio recordings, based in many cases on gifts from local network affiliates. Northwestern University's Radio Archive Project contains more than twenty thousand items, partly catalogued, mostly from the years before Pearl Harbor. Professor Marvin R. Bensman, Department of Speech and Drama, Memphis State University, has prepared an unalphabetized list of several hundred broadcasts in his Radio Archive, which he will send on request. Finally, a major source of newscasts for the war years, with a convenient published guide to the exact contents of each broadcast, is Washington (State) University. Phonoarchive, *History in Sound: A Descriptive Listing of the KIRO-CBS Collection of Broadcasts of the World War II Years and After, in the Phonoarchive of the University of Washington* (Seattle: University of Washington Press, 1963). Mr. Daniel Godfrey, curator of the Milo Ryan Phonoarchive, will tape broadcasts ordered from the catalog at minimal cost. A brilliant introduction to the meaning of radio news in America during the 1930s is William Stott, *Documentary Expression and Thirties America* (New York: Oxford, 1973), in particular pp. 5-17, 75-91.

There is no monograph concerning the history of radio or news broadcasting that is clearly superior to the records of participants published in the 1930s and 1940s. Accordingly the following printed sources have been arranged in a single alphabetical list. Two complete issues of the *Annals of the American Academy of Political and Social Science,* both edited by Herman S. Hettinger, include a number of articles on various aspects of radio. See "Radio: The Fifth Estate," 177 (January 1935): 1-223; and "New Horizons in Radio," 213 (January 1941): 1-215. Gleason L. Archer, *History of Radio to 1926* (New York: American Historical Society, 1938) and *Big Business and Radio* (New York: American Historical Society, 1939), are long, turgid accounts, basically official company histories of RCA and NBC. Merlin H. Aylesworth, NBC's first president, published a four-part series in *Collier's,* beginning on April 17, 1948, which provides many amusing and revealing anecdotes about the network's early years.

A fine study of an early station that reveals much about broadcasting in the 1920s is William Peck Banning, *Commercial Broadcasting Pioneer: The WEAF Experiment, 1922-1926* (Cambridge, Mass.: Harvard University Press, 1946). Erik Barnouw, *A Tower in Babel, The Golden Web,* and *The Image Empire,* the three volumes of his *A History of Broadcasting in the United States* (New York: Oxford University Press, 1966-1970), include many entertaining anecdotes. A good history of broadcasting in Great Britain is Asa Briggs, *The Birth of Broadcasting, The Golden Age of Wireless,* and *The War of Words,* the three volumes of his *The History of Broadcasting in the United Kingdom* (London: Oxford University Press, 1961-1970). The best of many articles concerning the relations between the press and radio in the early 1930s is Giraud Chester, "The Press-Radio War: 1933-1935," *Public Opinion Quarterly* 13 (Summer 1949): 252-64. Elmer Davis, "Broadcasting the Outbreak of War," *Harper's* 179 (November 1939): 579-88, is an excellent account of news broadcasting as World War II began. A dry but thorough treatment of its subject is the second edition of Walter B. Emery, *Broadcasting and Government: Responsibilities and Regulations* (East Lansing, Mich.: Michigan State University Press, 1971). The editors of *Fortune* published several substantial articles concerning various facets of radio in the 1930s. See, in particular, "The Radio Industry," 17 (May 1938). The second edition of Sydney W. Head, *Broadcasting in America* (Boston: Houghton Mifflin, 1971), pp. 103-84, contains a fine introduction to the history of radio in a relatively small number of pages. L. S. Howeth, *History of Communications-Electronics in the United States Navy* (Washington, D.C.: Government Printing Office, 1963), describes the Navy's role in the development of radio during World War I. Glenn A. Johnson, "Secretary of Commerce Herbert C. Hoover: The First Regulator of American Broadcasting, 1921-1928" (Ph.D. dissertation, University of Iowa, 1970), based on a thorough search of the Hoover Library holdings, explains Hoover's role in the development of radio. Max Jordan, *Beyond All Fronts: A Bystander's Notes on This Thirty Years War* (Milwaukee: Bruce Publishing Company, 1944), stresses the patriotism of its author, the German director of NBC's European operations accused by some of being pro-Nazi. A classic account of the social and intellectual limitations of those in the radio business is E. J. Kahn, Jr., "At Home with the Paleys," in E. B. and Katherine S. White, eds., *A Subtreasury of American Humor* (New York: Coward-Mc Cann, 1941), pp. 624-7. Alexander Kendrick, *Prime Time: The Life of Edward R. Murrow* (Boston: Little, Brown, 1969) contains some helpful information about radio before 1941, though the emphasis is on a later period. A detailed history of a major station is Lawrence W. Lichty, " 'The Nation's Station': A History of Radio Station WLW" (Ph.D. dissertation, Ohio State University, 1964). An important collection of material, much not found elsewhere, is in Lawrence W. Lichty and Malachi C. Topping, eds., *American Broadcasting: A Sourcebook on the History of Radio and Television* (New York:

Hastings House, 1975). The increasing influence of radio in America between 1925 and 1935 may be gauged by comparing Robert S. and Helen Merrell Lynd, *Middletown: A Study in Contemporary American Culture* (New York: Harcourt, Brace, 1929), with their *Middletown in Transition: A Study in Cultural Conflicts* (New York: Harcourt, Brace, 1937). A useful study of a major figure in radio is Eugene Lyons, *David Sarnoff: A Biography* (New York: Harper & Row, 1966). There is plenty of detail in the 1,354 pages of William McKinley Randle, "History of Radio Broadcasting and its Social and Economic Effect on the Entertainment Industry, 1920-1930" (Ph.D. dissertation, Western Reserve University, 1966). César Saerchinger, *Hello America!: Radio Adventures in Europe* (Boston: Houghton Mifflin, 1938), is a valuable account by CBS's head of European operations. A. A. Schechter with Edward Anthony, *I Live on Air* (New York: Stokes, 1941), is unsuccessfully frothy. But along with Paul White, *News on the Air* (New York: Harcourt, Brace, 1947), it tells much about what a news director did at NBC and CBS before 1939. Eric Sevareid, *Not So Wild a Dream* (New York: Knopf, 1946), is an unusual, sometimes rather emotional, account of a young broadcaster working in Europe and Washington between 1939 and 1941. William L. Shirer, *Berlin Diary: The Journal of a Foreign Correspondent 1934-1941* (New York: Knopf, 1941), contains many details about overseas broadcasting before Pearl Harbor. Some helpful information, particularly about propaganda, can be found in Robert West, Ph.D., *The Rape of Radio* (New York: Rodin, 1941).

An early study of radio's ability to influence listeners is Hadley Cantril and Gordon W. Allport, *The Psychology of Radio* (New York: Harper & Brothers, 1935). A valuable listing of sponsored programs that received ratings is Cooperative Analysis of Broadcasting, *Ten Years of Network Program Analysis* (New York: CAB, 1939). There is a copy in the NBC Program Reference Library. Matthew N. Chappell and C. E. Hooper, *Radio Audience Measurement* (New York: Stephen Daye, 1944), describes how a Hooperating works. Additional information about rating techniques may be found in numerous CBS and NBC pamphlets, located in the CBS library and NBC Program Reference Library file drawers, respectively. Paul Lazarsfeld prepared several major studies of radio's influence on American life. See his *Radio and the Printed Page: An Introduction to the Study of Radio and its Role in the Communication of Ideas* (New York: Duell, Sloan and Pearce, 1940); Lazarsfeld and Frank N. Stanton, eds., *Radio Research, 1941* (New York: Duell, Sloan and Pearce, 1941); Lazarsfeld and Stanton, eds., *Radio Research: 1942-1943* (New York: Duell, Sloan and Pearce, 1944); Lazarsfeld and Harry Field, *The People Look at Radio* (Chapel Hill, N.C.: University of North Carolina Press, 1946); Lazarsfeld and Patricia L. Kendall, *Radio Listening in America: The People Look at Radio—Again* (New York: Prentice-Hall, 1948); and Lazarsfeld and Stanton, eds., *Communications Research, 1948-49* (New York: Harper & Brothers, 1949).

Harrison B. Summers, compiler, *A Thirty-Year History of Programs Carried on National Radio Networks in the United States, 1926-1956* (Columbus, Ohio: Ohio State University, January, 1958), gives Hooperatings and some CAB ratings for programs found in the daily radio listings of the *New York Times* during the month of January each year.

Finally, several publications are important sources of information for almost any aspect of radio. *Variety* and *Broadcasting* are not indexed, but the time-consuming process of going through each weekly issue results in quantities of useful material. *Variety* reviewed many programs, avoiding, as a matter of policy, the polite whitewash. The *New York Times* has complete daily program listings, as does almost every newspaper, but before 1941 its radio page was pallid compared to the opinionated comments of *Variety* or, for that matter, *Radio Daily*. Also, three scholarly journals occasionally publish articles concerning the history of broadcasting: *The Journal of Broadcasting, Journalism Quarterly*, and the *Columbia Journalism Review*. Christopher H. Sterling, editor of *The Journal of Broadcasting*, is currently writing (with John M. Kitross) a one-volume history of broadcasting. Sterling published a helpful five-part bibliographical essay concerning books about broadcasting in the *Educational Broadcasting Review*, 5, 6 (April 1971-February 1972). He also edits a monthly *Mass Media Booknotes*, full of information about radio sources.

PART III: SIX COMMENTATORS

BOAKE CARTER

There are no Carter Papers. However, folders 339(1) and (2), PPI 24, at the Hoover Library contain over one hundred letters between Carter and Hoover, 1937-1944. And OF 2103, the only file established for an individual commentator at the Roosevelt Library, also includes a large amount of correspondence, some from the newscaster himself. There are several important letters concerning Carter in the Cordell Hull and Wilbur J. Carr Papers, both in the Library of Congress. The Moffat Diary contains several extended references to the news analyst, as does Ickes's *Secret Diary*. Roosevelt referred to Carter in several letters, available in his *Personal Letters*. The State Department Files (RG 59) have detailed reports of official investigations concerning the broadcaster, as does the *Congressional Record*.

The commentaries themselves are in several places. From September 1933 to May 1935, program cards under "Carter" in the (old) Talent File, CBS Program Information, list briefly the contents of every newscast. The Federal Trade Commission Files (RG 122), National Archives, include almost one hundred complete transcripts, mostly for 1936, but with a few examples from 1937. A number of additional commentaries are reprinted in the *Congressional Record.* One 1938 broadcast is located in folder 339(1), PPI 24, Hoover Library. Beginning in January 1942 there are extended quotations from Carter's broadcasts in the records of the Office of Government Reports (RG 44), Suitland, Maryland. Recordings of Carter's programs can be found in two locations. The James A. Farley Collection, Recorded Sound Section, Library of Congress, has one 1936 interview. The NBC warehouse in New York contains five complete transcriptions; three for 1936, two for 1938.

Carter's ideas appear in his daily syndicated newspaper column, which began on March 1, 1937. The *Boston Daily Globe,* on microfilm in the Newspaper Room at the Library of Congress, took every column before 1941. Carter also published seven books. Though based on actual broadcasts, they avoid certain subjects and sometimes use more temperate language than what was said on the air. See *Black Shirt, Black Skin* (Harrisburg, Penn.: Telegraph Press, 1935); *"Johnny Q. Public" Speaks!* (New York: Dodge, 1936); *I Talk as I Like* (New York: Dodge, 1937); *This is Life* (New York: Dodge, 1937); *Made in U.S.A.* (New York: Dodge, 1938); with Thomas H. Healy, *Why Meddle in the Orient?* (New York: Dodge, 1938); and *Why Meddle in Europe?* (New York: McBride, 1939).

Valuable autobiographical information appears in Richard Sheridan Ames [Boake Carter], "News on the Air," *Saturday Evening Post,* January 23, 1937, 23 ff. A. J. Liebling, "Boake Carter," *Scribner's Commentator* 104 (August 1938): 7-11 ff., is excellent. Stanley High, "Not-So-Free Air," *Saturday Evening Post,* February 11, 1939, pp. 8-9 ff., discusses rumors about administration attempts to force Carter off the air. Edward L. Bernays, *Biography of an Idea: Memoirs of Public Relations Counsel Edward L. Bernays* (New York: Simon & Schuster, 1965), pp. 571-80, describes his promotional schemes for Philco and Carter in 1935 and 1936. Bernays also sent this author detailed letters concerning his relations with Carter, January 7, 14, 26, 1974. The legal aspects of the Simpson case are carefully evaluated in Thomas Herman Etzold, "Fair Play: American Principles and Practice in Relations with Germany, 1933-1939" (Ph.D. dissertation, Yale University, 1970). Additional information on the commentator is found in scattered places, such as *Variety, Time, Newsweek, Current Biography,* and the *New York Times,* 1933-1944. There is some further detail in the Correspondence of the Foreign Office, in the Public Record Office in London. Dust jackets on a couple of Carter's books list facts about his career not available elsewhere. These jackets are part of the as yet uncatalogued Hunt L. Unger collection of Franklin D. Roosevelt material, Northwestern University Library, Evanston, Illinois. The Audiovisual Archives Division of the National Archives has newsreels showing Carter covering the trial of Bruno Hauptmann in 1935, but only in negative form.

Concerning the end of Carter's life, see David Horowitz, *Thirty-three Candles*

(New York: World Union Press, 1949); and Stewart Robb and Linda Folkard, *The Strange Death of Boake Carter and Other Matters* (New York: Plymouth Press, 1946), an obscure pamphlet apparently available only at the New York Public Library. The chief result of the newscaster's religious interest is Moses Guibbory, *The Bible in the Hands of Its Creators: Biblical Facts as They Are,* Vol. I (New York: The Society of the Bible in the Hands of Its Creators, 1943), a copy of which is in the Library of Congress.

A variety of sources are helpful in gauging the size of Carter's listening audience. Since the hour, network, and time of his broadcasts changed many times after 1939, and since he was heard in some cities during some months but not others, it is necessary to consult daily newspaper radio listings for details. Newspapers used were the *New York Times,* the *Washington Evening Star* and the *Chicago Tribune. Variety* reviewed Carter's programs and occasionally discussed his popularity. CAB, *Ten Years of Network Program Analysis,* is of some use. Summers, *A Thirty-Year History of Programs Carried on National Radio Networks in the United States, 1926-1956,* is very helpful, even listing many Hooperatings for Carter. The Broadcast Pioneers Library has some 1936 CAB ratings for him. CBS Program Information's Talent File and yearly Black Books give exact details for Carter's station coverage, and the hour at which he broadcast, 1932 to August 1938. *Variety's* yearly *Radio Directory,* published from 1939 to 1941, offers summaries of various popularity polls concerning the commentator. Cantril and Strunk, *Public Opinion 1935-1946,* contains poll questions asking for one's favorite radio commentator. The Roper Public Opinion Center, Williamstown, Mass., has enormous quantities of poll data, some about Carter's popularity, but in difficult-to-use form.

H. V. KALTENBORN

The Kaltenborn Papers, State Historical Society of Wisconsin, have enormous amounts of information about the commentator. Business correspondence (especially valuable since no other news analyst seems to have saved such material) and over fifteen thousand fan letters are included, along with a virtually complete file of broadcasts, in rough drafts, beginning in 1936. A few programs from the late 1920s have also survived. The collection includes numerous recordings, mostly for the late 1930s and 1940s. The NBC warehouse has a number of Kaltenborn transcriptions. An Iconographic division at Madison contains hundreds of photographs of the newscaster. A thirty-two-page introduction to the Wisconsin holdings, "The H. V. Kaltenborn Collection" (Madison, 1961) has been published by the Mass Communications History Center of The State Historical Society of Wisconsin. The Kaltenborn Papers at the New York Public Library contain about one hundred fan letters from the spring of 1940.

Everything the commentator said on the air between September 10 and September 30, 1938, is reprinted verbatim in CBS, *Crisis: September 1938,* mimeographed, 10 vols. (New York: CBS, November 1938). A number of other broadcasts were reprinted in *Talks* and *The Commentator,* beginning in 1936. Neither publication is indexed in *Reader's Guide,* but both are available in many libraries. Kaltenborn published three books containing excerpts from his commentaries. See *We Look at the World* (New York: Henckle, 1930); *Kaltenborn Edits the News* (New York: Modern Age Books, 1937); and *I Broadcast the Crisis* (New York: Random House, 1938). The news analyst's autobiography, *Fifty Fabulous Years, 1900-1950: A Personal Review* (New York: Putnam's Sons, 1950), reveals little of the man. His "Reminiscences," part of Columbia University's Oral History Project, have a few interesting things to say about radio in the 1920s, but in general are disappointing. The Olga V. Kaltenborn Oral History Interveiw in the Hoover Library is very thin. Folders 981(1), (2), and (3), PPI 84, Hoover Library, contain over 150 letters between Kaltenborn and Hoover, mostly after 1944. The State Department Files (RG 59) contain a number of communications from Kaltenborn, who is also mentioned in Ickes's *Secret Diary.* The Stimson Papers and Diary include several references to Kaltenborn. There is a little information about the commentator in the Roosevelt Library. The *Congressional Record* for 1940 contains some acrid discussion of the broadcaster. The late Leo Burnett, of the Leo Burnett Company, the agency that handled Kaltenborn for Pure Oil after April 1939, provided the author with important information concerning why and how Kaltenborn was chosen by the oil company.

No journalist has yet done a successful piece on Kaltenborn as a person, though the newscaster's Munich broadcasts are the subject of Frederick Lewis Allen's entire twelfth chapter in *Since Yesterday: The Nineteen-Thirties in America* (New York: Harper & Brothers, 1940). There is a vast amount of biographical information, and some interpretation, in three massive dissertations about the commentator. The first, Giraud Chester's "The Radio Commentaries of H. V. Kaltenborn: A Case Study in Persuasion" (Ph.D. dissertation, University of Wisconsin, 1947), is the best. Chester formed an intense dislike for his subject. Indeed, Kaltenborn attempted to remove some of Chester's notes, now part of the Kaltenborn Papers at Madison. David Gillis Clark, "The Dean of Commentators: A Biography of H. V. Kaltenborn" (Ph.D. dissertation, University of Wisconsin, 1965), is a long corrective to Chester's occasional excesses. Two important sections of Clark's dissertation have appeared in print. See "H. V. Kaltenborn's First Year on the Air," *Journalism Quarterly* 42 (Summer 1965): 373-81, and "H. V. Kaltenborn and his Sponsors: Controversial Broadcasting and the Sponsor's Role," *Journal of Broadcasting* 12 (Fall 1968): 309-21. Earl Sidney Grow, Jr., "A Dialogue on American International Involvement, 1939-41: The Correspondence of H. V. Kaltenborn, His Sponsors, and His Public"

(Ph.D. dissertation, University of Wisconsin, 1964), is of limited usefulness but is helpful in determining which of Kaltenborn's newscasts apparently received the most mail.

Concerning the size of the broadcaster's radio audience, see those items discussed at the end of the section on Boake Carter in Part III. Until April 1940, detailed information concerning Kaltenborn is available in the Talent Files and Black Books of CBS Program Information. After that date, see NBC's Program Analysis.

RAYMOND GRAM SWING

Ample material concerning Swing's career as a commentator has survived. Virtually all of his newscasts, typed and in chronological order, are in his Papers at the Library of Congress. In published form, some may be found in his *How War Came* (New York: Norton, 1939) and *Preview of History* (Garden City, N.Y.: Doubleday, Doran, 1943). The Recorded Sound Section of the Library of Congress contains hundreds of Swing's commentaries, transferred to tape. Aside from a single 1938 newscast, these begin with 1941. The Swing Papers also contain many published articles, in particular the valuable columns written for the *London Sunday Express* in 1941. Except for a quantity of letters from Evans F. Carlson beginning shortly after Pearl Harbor, and some correspondence with Albert Einstein in 1947 and 1949, there are practically no additional letters. This lack is partially offset by the commentator's first-rate memoirs, *"Good Evening!": A Professional Memoir* (New York: Harcourt, Brace & World, 1964). Shortly before his death in 1968, Swing corresponded with the author and granted an extended interview.

The broadcaster's opinions and activities are discussed in correspondence either about or from Swing in such places as folder 1825, PPI 185, Hoover Library, the Felix Frankfurter Papers, Cordell Hull Papers, Fred I. Kent Papers, State Department Files (RG 59), Henry L. Stimson Papers, and Pierrepont Moffat's Diary at Houghton Library. The Harry Hopkins Papers at Hyde Park have little concerning his close friendship with the commentator. The Roosevelt Library, however, does have some letters and telegrams concerning Swing. Sherwood's *Roosevelt and Hopkins,* Ickes's *Secret Diary,* and Rosenman's *Working with Roosevelt* document the news analyst's importance to the administration before 1941. The General Correspondence Files of the Foreign Office, in the Public Record Office in London, contain valuable material concerning Swing's importance to the Foreign Office. The old precis jacket system still functioned in 1941, so it is possible to see exactly what specific members of the American Department thought about Swing. A complex double filing system, however, makes getting at this material slow work. Also helpful is John G.

Winant, *Letter from Grosvenor Square: An Account of a Stewardship* (Boston: Houghton Mifflin, 1947).

Swing's *Forerunners of American Fascism* (New York: Julian Messner, 1935) brings together in book form a series of perceptive articles he wrote for the *Nation* concerning American demagogues. He frequently contributed to such journals as *Foreign Affairs* and the *Nation* during the 1930s. In addition, the *New York Times* covered in detail his speeches and activities. He also contributed an introduction to John R. Tunis, *Democracy and Sport* (New York: Barnes, 1941).

Richard O. Boyer, "The Voice," the *New Yorker,* November 14 and 21, 1942, pp. 24-31, 24-35, is a revealing though malicious study of the commentator's personality and career. Jack Alexander and F. I. Odell, "Radio's Best Bedside Manner," *Saturday Evening Post,* December 14, 1940, pp. 15-16 ff., is a helpful if somewhat pedestrian attempt to explain Swing's personality. Robert Rutherford Smith, "The Wartime Radio News Commentaries of Raymond Swing, 1939-1945" (Ph.D. dissertation, Ohio State University, 1963), based in part on several interviews with the news analyst, concludes that Swing's analyses were usually as informative as the *New York Times* but makes little attempt to discuss their impact.

Swing's number of listeners can be determined in part by consulting those sources listed at the end of the section on Boake Carter in Part III. For 1935, there is information in the Talent File and Black Book at CBS Program Information.

ELMER DAVIS

The Davis Papers at the Library of Congress include valuable correspondence and other material concerning his early years. There are, however, no broadcasts before 1941, and virtually none until 1945. Happily, the Milo Ryan Phonoarchive at the University of Washington possesses transcriptions of almost all of Davis's five-minute broadcasts between 1939 and 1941. These can be transferred to blank reels of tape sent to the researcher for a small charge. The Davis Papers at the New York Public Library have a couple of fifteen-minute broadcasts from April 1940 and the only surviving Davis fan letters, along with his entertaining replies. The Hornbeck Papers at the Hoover Institution include about thirty-five letters between the two men, 1937-1944. The Felix Frankfurter Papers have about fifteen letters, 1942-1953. The State Department Files (RG 59) contain nothing about or from Davis. Sherwood's *Roosevelt and Hopkins* and Roosevelt's *Personal Letters* include information about the commentator's importance.

Roger Burlingame, *Don't Let Them Scare You: The Life and Times of Elmer Davis* (Philadelphia: Lippincott, 1961), is weak on the years just before Pearl Harbor, but quite good on Davis to 1914. The Burlingame Papers at Syracuse

University have numerous kinds of documentary evidence not included in the biography. Mark Lincoln Chadwin, *The Hawks of World War II,* briefly discusses Davis's activities as a member of the Century Dinner Group before Pearl Harbor. Some amusing anecdotes concerning the newscaster appear in Richard Lauterbach, "Elmer Davis and the News," *Liberty Magazine,* October 23, 1943, pp. 12-13 ff., a copy of which is in the Davis Papers at the Library of Congress. Philip Chalfant Ensley, "The Political and Social Thought of Elmer Davis" (Ph.D. dissertation, Ohio State University, 1965), is a conscientious catalog of the commentator's published works. It is based on virtually no broadcasts before 1941.

Davis was a prolific and excellent writer. Of his many books, see in particular *Giant Killer: A Novel* (New York: Press of the Readers Club, 1943), originally published in 1928, and *But We Were Born Free* (Indianapolis, Ind.: Bobbs-Merrill, 1954). Elmer Davis, *Elmer Davis,* ed. Robert L. Davis (Indianapolis, Ind.: Bobbs-Merrill, 1964), is a fine selection of Davis's best writings but includes almost no broadcasts. The news analyst was an editor of the *Saturday Review of Literature* in 1940 and 1941. He also contributed numerous articles to *Harper's.* His "Broadcasting the Outbreak of War," which appeared in the latter magazine in 1939, is especially informative, but almost everything he wrote for the *Saturday Review* and *Harper's* is well done.

To estimate the number of Davis's listeners, see the items at the end of the Boake Carter section in Part III. The Talent Files and Black Books as CBS Program Information are also important sources.

FULTON LEWIS, JR.

The Lewis Papers at Syracuse University include large amounts of material, mostly after 1945. There are virtually no broadcasts for the pre-Pearl Harbor period save a series of 1941 testimonials concerning American industry done under the auspices of the National Association of Manufacturers. Beginning in January 1942 the Office of Government Reports (RG 44) has many daily excerpts from the news analyst's broadcasts. *Scribner's Commentator* reprinted several newscasts in 1940-1941; the *Congressional Record* contains copies of many more. The Lewis Papers also have quite a few recorded broadcasts, beginning in 1944, and a number of the commentator's television videotapes made in the 1950s. The Radio Archive, Department of Speech & Drama, Memphis State University, contains four Lewis broadcasts from 1940-1941. Mr. Joseph P. Hehn, Allentown, Pa., a private collector, has six of the commentator's broadcasts for 1940. Mr. Michael Biel, Department of Speech, University of Missouri, Columbia, has a taped copy of Lewis's coverage of Roosevelt's December 8, 1941, speech. There is one 1939 transcription in the Recorded Sound Section of the Library of Congress. J. David Goldin has another broadcast from the same year on tape. Not many other pre-1941 Lewis broadcasts, in written or recorded form, seem to have survived. A good bit of biographical information, too, is based on sources for the postwar period. At Syracuse there is correspondence from Congressmen and prominent individuals. The Davis Papers at the Library of Congress have a Lewis file relating mainly to the early 1950s. There are also letters from the newscaster in the State Department Files (RG 59) and a few references in the Roosevelt Library. Of much greater value are folders 1102 (1), (2), and (3), PPI 98, Hoover Library, which contain over a hundred letters between Lewis and Hoover, mostly after 1942 but with a number of pre-1941 communications.

Booton Herndon [Gordon Carroll, ed.], *Praised and Damned: The Story of Fulton Lewis, Jr.* (New York: Duell, Sloan and Pearce, 1954), is a brief, heavily varnished account. Kenneth G. Crawford and Hobart Rowen, "Voice with a Snarl," *Saturday Evening Post,* August 30, 1947, pp. 23 ff., is a generally favorable portrait. The same cannot be said for H. N. Oliphant's "Fulton Lewis, Jr.: Man of Distinction," *Harper's* 198 (March 1949): 76-84. Charles Van Devander, "Radio's Golden Voice of Reaction," an eleven-part series that appeared in the *New York Post* in December 1949, is as hostile as the title indicates. Copies are located in the Lewis file in the Davis papers. Richard Wilson, "Radio's Top Fault-Finder," *Look,* April 1, 1947, pp. 32 ff., is much more friendly. Giraud Chester, "What Constitutes Irresponsibility on the Air?— A Case Study," *Public Opinion Quarterly* 13 (Spring 1949): 73-83, is a harsh indictment of the commentator's misuse of factual evidence. There is an angry rejoinder from Lewis in the next issue and further correspondence between the two in the Winter number of *Public Opinion Quarterly.* Sidney Reisberg, "Fulton Lewis, Jr.: An Analysis of News Commentary" (Ph.D. dissertation, New York University, 1952), is an attack on Lewis's broadcast techniques, based on newscasts from the winter of 1948-1949.

The commentator's 1939 meeting with Lindbergh at the home of William Castle is described in Charles A. Lindbergh, *The Wartime Journals of Charles A. Lindbergh* (New York: Harcourt, Brace, Jovanovich, 1970); see also Kenneth S. Davis, *The Hero: Charles A. Lindbergh and the American Dream* (Garden City, N.Y.: Doubleday, 1959). The Castle Papers, Hoover Library, have only one 1938 letter from Lewis and no references to the dinner. The Castle Diaries, now in Houghton Library, Harvard University, Cambridge, Mass., are closed to researchers until fifteen years after Mrs. Castle's death. *Documents on German Foreign Policy, Series D.*, Vol. X, prints the telegrams concerning Lewis's suggestion to Nazi officials at Havana in July 1940. They are evaluated in Alton Frye, *Nazi Germany and the American Hemisphere, 1933-1941*, whose conclusions differ from those of this author. The broadcaster's exposé of John Semer Farnsworth, convicted of selling naval secrets to the Japanese in 1936, is discussed in Michael Sayers and Albert E. Kahn, *Sabotage!: The Secret War*

Against America (New York: Harper & Brothers, 1942). Lewis's support of one who claimed that Harry Hopkins gave uranium to the Soviet Union during World War II is recounted at length in George Racey Jordan, USAF (Ret.), with Richard L. Stokes, *From Major Jordan's Diaries* (New York: Harcourt, Brace, 1952). Athan G. Theoharis, *The Yalta Myths: An Issue in U.S. Politics 1945-1955* (Columbia, Mo.: University of Missouri Press, 1970), includes Lewis as an "extremist" in the Republican party but cites no specific Lewis broadcasts or columns.

The size of the commentator's audience can in part be estimated by referring to the sources mentioned at the end of the section on Boake Carter on Part III. Also, the Lewis Papers have a number of special audience surveys, mostly for the period after 1945.

EDWARD R. MURROW

The Edward R. Murrow Papers, Edward R. Murrow Center of Public Diplomacy, Fletcher School, Tufts University, Medford, Mass., contain little material before 1945 since Murrow's London files were completely destroyed in three bombing attacks. A rough "Guide to Edward R. Murrow Files," prepared with volunteer student help, describes the contents of the collection and is available on request. Considerable biographical information, some in the form of surprisingly useful press releases, is located in two large folders of Murrow material in the CBS library. Almost all of the commentator's broadcasts before 1941 are available from the Milo Ryan Phonoarchive at the University of Washington. Also, extended excerpts from many of his best programs were published in Murrow's *This is London* (New York: Simon & Schuster, 1941). Columbia 02L-332, "Edward R. Murrow: A Reporter Remembers, Vol. I, The War Years," contains two 33 1/3 rpm records of broadcasts before 1945, mostly before 1941. A second volume includes postwar broadcasts. CBS, "Vienna: March, 1938" (New York: CBS, 1938), has selections from the news analyst's Vienna broadcasts. CBS, *Crisis—September 1938*, does the same for the period a few months later. Many of the best broadcasts, though few before 1941, are reprinted in Edward R. Murrow, *In Search of Light: The Broadcasts of Edward R. Murrow 1938-1961*, ed. Edward Bliss, Jr. (New York: Knopf, 1967).

One 1938 speech before the Chicago Council on Foreign Relations can be found in the Chicago Council on Foreign Relations Papers, Manuscript Division-,Chicago Circle Campus of the University of Illinois, Chicago, Illinois. Some Murrow correspondence is located in the State Department Files (RG 59) and the Stimson Papers. There are also a few items in the Roosevelt Library at Hyde Park. A couple of letters from Murrow are in the Davis, Sevareid, and Kaltenborn Papers. Sherwood's *Roosevelt and Hopkins*, Freedman's *Roosevelt and Frankfurter*, and Roosevelt's *Personal Letters* provide evidence for the newscaster's importance before 1941. William Shirer's *Berlin Diary* includes quite a lot of information concerning Murrow before 1941. Shirer's bitter and just barely fictional *Stranger Come Home* (Boston: Little, Brown, 1954) describes the postwar actions of his former colleague. Harold J. Laski felicitously dedicated his *Reflections on the Revolution of Our Time* (New York: Viking, 1943) to Murrow and describes his contribution to English morale. On the same topic see John Winant, *Letter from Grosvenor Square,* and Bernard Bellush, *He Walked Alone: A Biography of John Gilbert Winant* (The Hague: Mouton, 1968). Concerning the commentator's early years in New York, see a typed account of limited value, Chester S. Williams, "Memories of Your Father," in the CBS Library. Finally, of general interest is the broadcaster's speech to the Association of Radio and Television News Directors, presented in Chicago on October 15, 1958, copies of which are available in many places.

Alexander Kendrick, *Prime Time: The Life of Edward R. Murrow,* provides less information about the news analyst than its more than five hundred pages would suggest. Aside from some excellent photographs, there is more on the oft-noted shortcomings of television news than on Murrow the man. Robert J. Landry, "Edward R. Murrow," *Scribner's Magazine* 104 (December 1938): 7-11 ff., is thin but is the only biographical sketch published before 1945. Leonore Silvian, "This . . . is Murrow," *Look,* March 15, 1952, pp. 56 ff., is a solid piece. So is Isabella Taves, "Edward R. Murrow," *McCall's* 81 (February and March 1954): 24-96, 53-105. *Time*'s cover story on Murrow, September 30, 1957, pp. 48-54, includes a couple of photographs of Murrow as a small child. Charles Wertenbaker, "The World on His Back," *New Yorker,* December 26, 1953, pp. 28-45, is not as effective as are many of that magazine's profiles. Thomas Russell Woolley, Jr., "A Rhetorical Study: The Radio Speaking of Edward R. Murrow" (Ph.D. dissertation, Northwestern University, 1957), is a long, not very satisfactory analysis of Murrow's style, based almost entirely on broadcasts after 1941. For a short, brilliant discussion, see William Stott, *Documentary Expression and Thirties America,* pp. 75-91.

The size of Murrow's listening audience can be gauged in part by referring to the items at the end of the Boake Carter section in Part III. However, he almost never appeared under his own name but as a member of CBS's "European Roundup." Both headings should be checked in the Talent File and Black Books at CBS Program Information.

Index

ABOUT THE AUTHOR

David Holbrook Culbert is assistant professor of history at Louisiana State University. He received his B.A. from Oberlin College and his Ph.D. from Yale University. Professor Culbert has published articles in numerous journals and is currently writing a book about the U.S. Army's use of film in World War II.